When someone starts a church in his home and sees it grow to the largest church in the area, he clearly has a missionary emphasis! But David Horner carefully distinguishes this domestic concern from the passion to see Christ honored worldwide and to see this vision shaping a church's life. Passion for worldwide mission is currently weak in most U.S. churches, and this book is a wake-up call to congregations, particularly to their pastors. It is superbly researched, eminently practical, very challenging, and the fruit of a lifetime's passion—exemplified in his own church.

—Rev. Dr. Michael Green, Oxford University
British Theologian, Anglican Priest, Christian Apologist

In reading this book several words immediately come to mind: hard-hitting, sobering, honest, challenging, and helpful. *When Missions Shapes the Mission* is written by a Great Commission pastor who has built a Great Commission church. His goal is to assist you in doing the same. He has succeeded.

—Daniel L. Akin, President
Southeastern Baptist Theological Seminary
Wake Forest, North Carolina

What an important book!! This is a sobering analysis of the weak Great Commission involvement of most evangelical churches with practical steps to change this. The characteristics of a mission focused church are detailed, showing how these can be implemented. Best practices of churches are reviewed with an undergirding focus on the Spirit's empowerment by our people learning to walk by the Spirit. Let us learn from and apply the principles of this book!

—Frank Barker, Pastor Emeritus
Briarwood Presbyterian Church, Birmingham, Alabama

More and more pastors are discovering that church growth and spiritual vitality of church membership come from aligning a congregation with God's mission. David Horner is at the forefront of this group as he has led Providence Baptist Church in Raleigh, North Carolina, to become strategically involved with mission strategies around the world. This book will be a blessing and encouragement to those seeking to discover a practical balance for their local church to fulfill ministry and outreach in the community while focusing on the global dimension of the Great Commission.

—Jerry Rankin
Former president of the International Mission Board

As someone whose basic life and ministry experience has been to the needy areas of Africa, I have forever been amazed by the capacity of American churches and missions pastors to take the world on their hearts, into their financial generosity, and into their practical involvement. Among the very top in these has to be Providence Baptist Church in Raleigh and its pastor, David Horner. Here now, in this landmark volume, is revealed their secret.

Horner's book, which should be required reading in all western churches, gives the theological and spiritual why, the practical how, and the personal who for bringing missions to center stage in every church in North America and Europe. It's hard for me to picture a better and more compelling challenge on the importance of being mission minded than what we have here. Pick up this volume. Read. And experience the bomb under your seat.

—Michael Cassidy, African Enterprise
Pietermaritzburg, South Africa

In *When Missions Shapes the Mission*, David Horner paints a clear picture of the need for missions around the globe. He challenges us to follow Christ's mandate to go and teach all nations. And not only does he write about it, he leads his church to do it. A great reminder and encouragement for us all.

—Bryant Wright, Senior Pastor
Johnson Ferry Baptist Church, Marietta, Georgia
President, Southern Baptist Convention

In recent years many western churches appear to have departed from the traditional church "model" of gathering for worship, discipleship, and fellowship, and then scattering for mission. Instead of going to the people, many churches sit and wait for the people to come to them. Frequently this has led to a deterioration of worship and discipleship as well as a diminishing of mission. David Horner seeks in his thoughtful book to call local churches to a serious evaluation of their concept of mission and their commitment to it.

—Stuart Briscoe, minister
Large Elmbrook Church, Brookfield, Wisconsin

David Horner not only makes a disheartening and appealing analysis of current USA church mission practices, illustrated by the reality of his own denomination, the Southern Baptist Convention; but then he contrasts it with where the church should be and spices it with current examples of how to get there after an extensive and informative survey of churches.

While missions in the North American experience has been agency-centric, David appeals to a solid biblical basis to move it back to where it belongs—on the lap of the local church. He even argues that only when this happens can the church really find its true North. Further, the key is really the pastor!

When Missions Shapes the Mission is a delightful reading that should move pastors and those interested in impact and increased effectiveness in missions to adjust methodology. In so doing, maybe they will even recover their own joy in a rediscovered realization of what church is really all about.

—Carlos Calderon, Vice President Partners International—
International Ministries.

I don't know how to describe this book other than to say that David Horner has nailed the "95 theses" of the Great Commission to the door of the evangelical church. He is serious about missions being the priority of the church. He takes no prisoners. Prepare to be challenged. His zeal is matched only by the carefulness of his research and soundness of his advice.

—J. D. Greear, lead pastor of The Summit Church
Durham, North Carolina

David Horner has issued a very insightful, totally biblical call to reach the world for Christ. Will we be shaped by culture or by Christ, by temporal concerns or eternal ones? How much do we have to hate people in order not to tell them about Christ? Read this book and allow the Holy Spirit to stir your heart to reach the nations for Christ in a thoughtful, prayerful way.

—Cliffe Knechtle, Grace Community Church
New Canaan, Connecticut

It seems as though we are living in a day of kingdom expansion. With that being said, my good friend, David Horner, has honored us by writing *When Missions Shapes the Mission*. I am always thrilled when I pick up a book that in the early pages I begin to hear the heart of the presenter, recognizing that there are obstacles in front of all of our opportunities, but how we can overcome them and become focused on expanding His kingdom. This book will help you to get there. Read it, and pass it on!

—Johnny Hunt, senior pastor, First Baptist Church,
Woodstock, Georgia

A challenging biblical, systematic and practical approach to missions and mission! Once this book is published, I believe that no theology students, pastors, missionary agencies, or missionaries could ignore it. Dr. Horner's book confronts us with the ultimate question and requires a response. Does missions glorify God or man?

—Paul Negrut, President, Emanuel University
of Oradea, Romania

WHEN MISSIONS SHAPES THE MISSION

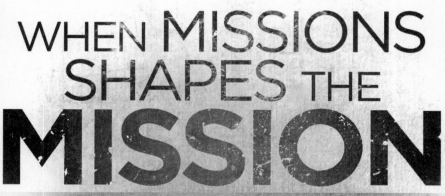

YOU AND YOUR CHURCH CAN REACH THE WORLD

DAVID**HORNER**

PUBLISHING GROUP

Nashville, Tennessee

978-1-4336-7137-1

Published by B&H Publishing Group
Nashville, Tennessee

Dewey Decimal Classification: 266.023
Subject Heading: FOREIGN MISSIONS \ CHURCH \
MISSION SUPPORT

1 2 3 4 5 6 7 8 • 15 14 13 12 11

CONTENTS

Section Four: Closing Considerations

Appendixes

ACKNOWLEDGMENTS

My wife, Cathy, who has encouraged and prayed for me throughout this project and endured much to make it possible for me to take the time needed to write.

To the elders and staff of Providence Baptist Church who share my desire to make the glory of Christ known among the nations and have permitted me to invest in this project and prayed for me as I did.

Mike Williams, Nick Roark, Sue Blau, Lynn Swanson, George Tissiere, Madalyn Gaito, and Lindsey Parker from Providence Baptist Church in Raleigh, North Carolina, for their invaluable research and survey work on the best practices of missions-minded churches; Mike in particular contributed a massive amount of time and effort in assimilating and analyzing the survey to make the results accessible in a convenient form.

Al Jackson for his insights and suggestions regarding the structure and direction of this book as well as the ministry model he has provided for decades through his tenure as pastor of Lakeview Baptist Church in Auburn, Alabama; and for Ed Stetzer from LifeWay Research who sat in on the early meetings and made helpful suggestions regarding the content and structure of this book.

Brad Waggoner and Tom Walters from B&H Publishing Group for their determination to get this book into the hands of pastors and Christian leaders as an effort on their part to expand the reach of churches and expand their vision to make missions an essential part of their mission.

Carolyn Smith for her gracious generosity in offering a place for much of the writing to be done, far from the distractions of the office and in an environment of comfort, beauty, and quietness. The same can be said of Neil and Carol Miller, and Steve and Sandy Munshower for making it possible for me to spend time writing in their homes, graciously made available through their kindness.

A special word of thanks also is due to David Platt, senior pastor of The Church at Brook Hills in Birmingham, Alabama. With all his pressing responsibilities, he still took the time to write a foreword for this book. After hearing the extraordinary challenge he presented at the Southern Baptist Pastors Conference in Orlando, Florida, in June of 2010, I knew then that if he were willing to provide a brief summary of that message in the form of a foreword, it would serve as a great starting point for all that follows here.

FOREWORD

by David Platt

I am obligated both to Greeks and barbarians,
both to the wise and the foolish. So I am eager
to preach the good news to you also who are in Rome.
For I am not ashamed of the gospel, because it is
God's power for salvation to everyone who believes, first
to the Jew, and also to the Greek. For in it God's righ-
teousness is revealed from faith to faith, just as
it is written: The righteous will live by faith.
ROMANS 1:14–17

Why would Paul say he was *obligated* to preach the gospel? He was writing this letter on the way to Rome, but his sights were set on Spain. His ambition was to take the gospel to people who had never heard, and he was compelled to give his life toward that end. I believe Paul's sense of obligation to preach the gospel, particularly to the unreached, was grounded in four rock-solid realities. And I believe these realities create an obligation for you and me to go to the unreached among the nations, as well.

First, Paul knew that people who had never heard the gospel had only enough knowledge of God to damn them to hell. God has made His character known in creation, and all men and women everywhere have seen God's revelation of Himself. Yet all men have rejected God. They have rebelled against Him, and as a result, they stand condemned before Him. Apart from hearing the good news, they have no eternal hope. Feel the weight of this reality: At this moment millions of people in thousands of unreached people groups have a knowledge of God that is only sufficient to damn them to hell. For this reason we are obligated to preach the gospel to the nations.

Second, Paul knew that the grace of God is powerful enough to save people everywhere for heaven. The just and gracious Creator of the universe has looked upon hopelessly sinful men and women in their rebellion, and He has sent His Son, God in the flesh, to bear His wrath against sin on the cross and to show His power over sin in the resurrection, so that everyone who believes in Him will be reconciled to God forever. This is the greatest news in the world! But in the words of a famous preacher, "The gospel is only good news if it gets there on time." No people group on this planet is beyond God's power to save. We know that people everywhere will believe the gospel when they hear the gospel. For this reason we are obligated to preach the gospel to the nations.

Third, Paul knew that God's plan warrants the sacrifice of His people. Paul was a servant, a slave, set apart and sent out with the gospel into the world. Mission was not a calling for him; it was a command around which his life revolved. The only reason he had breath was to testify to the gospel among the nations. And the same is true for us. The proclamation of the gospel to the ends of the earth is not a calling for us to consider; this is a command for us to obey. We breathe for mission. For this reason, we are obligated to preach the gospel to the nations.

Finally, Paul knew that the Son of God deserves the praise of all peoples. Paul knew that the King he served warrants worship from every nation, tribe, and tongue, and he gave himself with all-consuming dedication to making the glory of Christ known. We serve the same King, and our King is still worthy of the same worship. We want the name of Christ to be heard and hailed among all the peoples of the earth. For this reason we are obligated to preach the gospel to the nations.

In light of this holy obligation, we do not have time to waste. We do not have time to play artificial games in contemporary culture or wage artificial wars in comfortable churches. We have been compelled by a God-centered passion, and we have been created for a global purpose. Every Christian and every church has been called to participate on the front lines of this mission. Together we sacrifice our lives and our churches in death-defying obedience to His commands, confident that one day soon we will gather with a ransomed people from every nation, tribe, and tongue; and we will declare His praises for all of eternity.

I thank God for David Horner—for his life and for his leadership, for the church he leads and for their commitment to missions. I pray that the Lord will inspire, teach, educate, and motivate us all through this book toward the end that we as Christians and we in our churches might lock arms together in radical abandonment to spreading the gospel of God and declaring the glory of God to the ends of the earth.

INTRODUCTION

Why are more churches not engaged in a more practical and substantial way in taking the gospel to the nations? With alarming consistency local churches around the world give little more than a token acknowledgement for missions so clearly defined and mandated in the Scriptures. That seems to be particularly true of nations traditionally and historically connected with a Christian heritage. The United States has millions who profess faith in Christ but rarely demonstrate even the slightest interest in making Him known to the ends of the earth as He commanded.

This is hardly a new problem. Back in the 1780s, William Carey, a simple cobbler who developed a passion for Christ, began to preach as a guest and member of a Baptist church in the small English village of Barton. In his studies of the Scriptures and through reading about the explorations going on in the world at that time, Carey's love for Christ translated into a longing to reach the nations with the gospel. Often referred to as the father of modern missions, Carey wrote a little book entitled *An Enquiry into the Obligations of Christians, to Use Means for the Conversion of the*

Heathens. In the opening paragraph he explains his concern for the state of missions in the church of his day.

> Our Lord Jesus Christ, a little before his departure, commissioned his apostles to *Go*, and *teach all nations*; or, as another evangelist expresses it, *Go into all the world, and preach the gospel to every creature.* This commission was as extensive as possible, and laid them under obligation to disperse themselves into every country of the habitable globe, and preach to all the inhabitants, without exception, or limitation. They accordingly went forth in obedience to the command, and the power of God evidently wrought with them. Many attempts of the same kind have been made since their day, and which have been attended with various success; but the work has not been taken up, or prosecuted of late years (except by a few individuals) with that zeal and perseverance with which the primitive Christians went about it. It seems as if many thought the commission was sufficiently put in execution by what the apostles and others have done; that we have enough to do to attend to the salvation of our own countrymen; and that, if God intends the salvation of the heathen, he will some way or other bring them to the gospel, or the gospel to them. It is thus that multitudes sit at their ease, and give themselves no concern about the far greater part of their fellow-sinners, who to this day, are lost in ignorance and idolatry.[1]

The more things change, the more they remain the same. Time has passed, and the possibilities of reaching the nations have increased many times over what they were in Carey's day, but the problems with people remain the same. Christians who profess to love Christ and live for Him still have no prevailing interest in taking Him seriously regarding His commission to reach all nations with the gospel. Either there is no true conviction that lost people are lost, or too much theoretical conviction that God will reach them in ways other than the ways He commanded in His Word. In either case, a biblical understanding of the last instructions and commands of Christ leave little room for misunderstanding our responsibility: preach the gospel to everyone everywhere!

A current trend among younger evangelical leaders, one which serves as a badge of relevant thinking and marks them as particularly insightful, is the use of a series of words to describe the purpose and direction of the church. By using the words *mission*, *missions*, and *missional* correctly, a leader can raise his credibility among his peers and set himself apart as one who possesses an advanced level of understanding and expertise on matters related to church vision and emphasis. That is especially true of the word *missional* because it has in recent years come to function as an adjective to describe any church with an intentional kingdom-focused ministry.[2]

For the purposes of this book, *missions* is the primary word and the main subject. A church can be missional and yet miss the breadth of the command of Christ to take the gospel to the nations. It can narrow its "mission"[3] to local ministries, to its own congregational life, or various combinations of emphasis which may or may not include the threefold range of missions Jesus outlined in Acts 1:8—Jerusalem, Judea and Samaria, and the uttermost parts of the earth. Missions is not really biblical missions until it strategically and comprehensively embraces a plan to reach all those areas with the message of salvation through Jesus Christ. As we shall see in the progression of the sections and chapters of this book, how we define missions makes a major difference in how we approach it and what it does in shaping the mission of our churches. When missions shapes the mission of the church, the significance of what we are called to do transforms what could be routine and mundane into what should be profound and meaningful. Lighting the fire of missions under a congregation sets them in motion and ignites their passions in a way that is hard to extinguish once it gets started.

However, the church does not exist for missions. The church exists to glorify God, to worship Him and delight in Him. Missions is a necessary part of the mission of the church because His glory needs to be made known before He will be rightly worshipped. John Piper explains it this way:

> Missions exists because worship doesn't. . . . Worship, therefore, is the fuel and goal of missions. It's the goal of missions because in missions we simply aim to bring the nations into the white-hot enjoyment of God's glory. The goal of missions is the gladness of the peoples in the greatness of God. . . . Missions begins and ends in worship.[4]

Missions, properly defined, is making God's glory known in all the earth so that in and through Jesus Christ all will be glad and sing for joy in His presence.

Missions Defined

We need to distinguish between *missions* from a biblical perspective and the way the word has come to be used as a catchall expression to elevate, validate, or justify nearly anything people have introduced as a worthy cause for their church, denomination, or agency to embrace. If the word becomes so broadly defined that it can mean taking the gospel to a tribal people with no previous exposure to the gospel, or it can mean supporting the annuity program of the denomination, then I would venture to say that we need a new word—or that we should be careful not to allow it to be diluted by piling more onto it than it was ever intended to carry!

The word *missions* comes from the Latin word *missio*, which means "to send." A brief survey of several books about missions indicates that the prevailing understanding given to the word is *sending people* and *spreading the gospel*. Peter Wagner says that missions is "the composite of the efforts that Christians make to spread the gospel of Christ throughout the world."[5] Using the word *mission* as his reference point, John Stott offers his perspective by saying, it is "properly a comprehensive word, embracing everything which God sends His people into the world to do. It therefore includes evangelism and social responsibility, since both are authentic expressions of the love which longs to serve man in his need."[6]

After the Lausanne Congress on World Evangelization in 1974, Stott and many others wrestled with the shifting tides trying to redefine *missions* in terms that marginalized the gospel and emphasized social action. Those discussions had been going on for years, but the opportunity for clarity at Lausanne gave evangelicals the chance to affirm both the Great Commandment (love God, love one another) and the Great Commission (make disciples of all nations) as important aspects of missions. Missions therefore could not be practiced properly in a one-dimensional way—leaving out the gospel of Jesus Christ or neglecting the variety of needs of those we are called to love. To that task, the church is sent on its way as bearers of the good news that God's love through Christ transforms whoever trusts in Him.

By identifying the aim of missions, we move even closer to a working definition of it. At the Ecumenical Missionary Conference in New York City in 1900, more than seven hundred missionaries and thousands of others assembled to address the challenge of missions at the beginning of the twentieth century. Robert E. Speer, secretary of the Board of Missions of the Presbyterian Church in the USA at the time, summarized the matter by saying, "You can adopt other phraseology, if you please. You can say the aim of missions is the evangelization of the world, or to preach the gospel to the world. . . . To make perfectly clear what the aim of missions is, I paraphrase them in these words—the aim of foreign missions is to make Jesus Christ known to the world."[7]

The central idea of missions as *sending* is commended by Walter Kaiser Jr. in *Mission in the Old Testament*.[8] Using *mission* as a synonym for our word *missions*, he wrote, "Mission points to a central action: the act of being *sent* with a commission to carry out the will of a superior. It is God who commissions and God who sends. . . . It is our hope that the formative theology of Genesis 12:3 may once again be seen for what it is and has always been in the discussion of mission: *a divine program to glorify himself by bringing salvation to all on planet earth.*"[9]

So again, the central idea in each of these descriptions of the missions enterprise is sending God's people to announce hope and forgiveness through the gospel of Jesus Christ and demonstrating His love in practical ways in the lives of those we are sent to reach for His name's sake.

The word *missions* carries many threads of meaning, not all of them consistent with the biblical concept with which this book is concerned. Therefore, the reader needs to understand what I mean when I use the term. So taking the best current and historic uses of the word, the original intent of the word in the Scriptures, when I speak of missions and the calling of God and commission of Christ to take the hope of the gospel to everyone everywhere, I define the word as follows:

> Missions is God's plan for reaching all nations with the good news of Jesus Christ by sending His people to tell them about and show them the gracious, redeeming love of a glorious God.

From a biblical perspective this definition is fully supported by the Great Commission as recorded in Matthew 28:19–20; Mark 16:15; Luke 24:47–48. It lines up with the sending nature of God as described and prescribed by Christ in John 17:18 and John 20:2. Paul captures the heart of it when his enthusiasm for seeing Jews and Gentiles alike saved from their sins prompted him to write a stirring tribute to missions and missionaries in Romans 10:14–15:

> How can they call on Him in whom they have not believed? And how can they believe without hearing about Him? And how can they hear without a preacher? And how can they preach unless they are sent? As it is written: How welcome are the feet of those who announce the gospel of good things!

Confusion about what missions is can hardly be blamed for the failure of churches and their members to send their own to proclaim the gospel to the nations. Granted, for some it serves as an excuse to limit their efforts to their own backyards to operate with a loose definition of the word, but the fact remains that the breadth of Scripture addresses the issue so thoroughly that disputes over the definition of one word can never account for the neglect of God's command to reach out to the nations with the gospel.

Through the pages of this book, I hope you will find your own commitment to missions challenged and examined. Rallying the troops to the battle cry of Christ to go and make disciples is one of the highest honors any church, pastor, or leader can enjoy. By taking a look at the current state of missions in churches in the United States, then reviewing where we should be and ending with a practical series of suggestions about how to get there, I hope to offer a helpful tool to pastors and churches who already know in their hearts that something is missing in the role missions plays in their ministry.

Frankly, most of you pick up a book like this because you already have a predisposition to learn more and a desire to do better. If that is your situation, I pray that God will stir something up in you to lead the way and go further than you have before. Or if you have not yet started, I pray that you will be convinced and convicted by the Scriptures and the witness of the Holy Spirit to take the first steps to being a part of a church where missions shapes the mission. Whether you are a beginner at this and feel somewhat sheepish that you are just coming to realize how pivotal missions is to God's plan for the church or you have been at this for years and are just looking for fresh ideas and a series of suggestions of "best practices" from other strong missions churches to invigorate your own approach, this book is intended to be a useful tool in your hands to spur you on to be a missions-focused congregation led by a missions-minded pastor looking to honor a missions-hearted Savior.

---

1. William Carey, *An Enquiry into the Obligations of Christians, to Use Means for the Conversion of the Heathens* (Leicester: Printed and sold by ANNE IRELAND, et. al., 1792), 7–8.

2. According to Tim Keller, *missional* means that a church is "adapting and reformulating absolutely everything it does in worship, discipleship, community, and service—so as to be engaged with the non-Christian society around it." Tim Keller, "The Missional Church," June 2001, http://www.redeemer2.com/resources/papers/missional.pdf, accessed August 26, 2010.

In that context, *missional* addresses the overall emphasis of a church ministry as it approaches its surrounding culture with a strategy shaped by missiological thinking within a biblical framework. Missional thinking serves the evangelistic intent of the church well so that its engagement with the non-Christian society surrounding it results in an encounter with the gospel of Jesus Christ.

3. *Mission* often refers to purpose. Many businesses and other organizations have what they call a mission statement that sets forth their purpose, their reason for existence. On page 5, the use of *mission* (singular) instead of *missions* (plural) by evangelicals usually needs clarification so that there is a distinction from the idea of mission as purpose and the same word, *mission*, to define an act of God sending out witnesses to the nations. The word *missions* does not suffer from that confusion and need for constant clarification and definition.

4. John Piper, *Let the Nations Be Glad* (Grand Rapids, MI: Baker Books, 1993), 11.

5. C. Peter Wagner, *On the Crest of the Wave* (Ventura, CA: Regal Books, 1983), 70.

6. John R. W. Stott, *Christian Mission in the Modern World* (Downers Grove, IL: InterVarsity Press, 1975), 35.

7. Robert E. Speer, *Ecumenical Missionary Conference, New York, 1900, Vol. 1* (New York: American Tract Society, 1900), 76.

8. Following the lead of Stott and others, Kaiser also uses the singular word *mission*, explaining that the plural *missions* was the operative word until the 1950s when the concept of *missio Dei* (mission of God) was identified as a single, unifying mission God had implemented prior to any human involvement in fulfilling His mission. But a shift by academics and missiologists never convinced most churches and members who stayed with the word *missions*.

9. Walter C. Kaiser Jr., *Mission in the Old Testament* (Grand Rapids, MI: Baker Books, 2000), 11, 13.

SECTION ONE
WHERE WE ARE

CHAPTER 1 **THE PLACE OF MISSIONS IN TODAY'S CHURCHES**

I f we hope to make a real difference in how missions shapes the mission of each local congregation, we have to begin with an honest assessment of where we find ourselves now. Knowing where we are going not only needs the context of where we once were but also where we stand presently regarding the call of Christ to make disciples of the nations.

The missions mandate of Christ in the Great Commission has neither been rescinded nor fulfilled. What then has happened among His people that we are witnessing a serious neglect of that mandate in how we conduct our lives together in congregations where He is gladly proclaimed to be the Lord? Rare is the occasion when I run into anyone who thinks the churches of our land are doing a commendable work in taking the gospel to the nations. Nearly all evangelicals love the *idea* of missions. Something about it is so noble and shows off the best we have to offer—that is, if we ever get around to doing anything about the idea so that it moves from theory to practice!

As a high school student, I had the privilege of going on my first mission trip. Some might question the hardship factor because we went to Jamaica! Still, my first exposure to international missions took place at the age of seventeen, and I was profoundly changed. The trip was not sponsored by a church but by a nondenominational group of students affiliated with a ministry which started in a local YMCA.

Before that trip, nearly everything I knew about missions had been thirdhand at best. The church in which I grew up supported missions financially, but I was not familiar with any hands-on involvement by anyone in our congregation. We did sing missions songs a few times a year—mainly around the time we recognized the children's ministries that had a missions emphasis. Nothing but favorable thoughts remain as I think back on those early occasions of exposure to missions, but it all seemed remote from anything that had to do with our church experience. I do remember a couple of occasions when a "real, live missionary" couple visited, showed their slides and snake skins and told their stories of life overseas. Everyone loved it, but their time with us seemed more like an interesting novelty than a model to follow.

Each Christmas a missions offering was collected as the church tried to reach its giving goal (and yes, a thermometer at the front of the sanctuary tracked progress each week in December so we all could see where we stood). But other than that, as a child I did not know much about the priority of missions in the life of our church. Perhaps I was too young to notice, or maybe it was treated as a special interest group for those inclined to care about such things. Either way, I do not ever remember any appeal made, or emphasis given, to challenge the congregation to step up in any personal way to fulfill the Great Commission.

Sadly, my experience and my limited memories reflect a reality that continues in the life of an embarrassing majority of churches all over the country. Missions is a priority in theory but not in a practical way that makes any difference in what actually happens in the life and ministry of local churches. Statistical data on what is taking place in churches regarding their call to missions reveals a sad tale of neglect for an agenda that was deeply etched on the heart of Jesus Christ.

A Case Study from One Denomination

A cursory look at the statistical data from several denominations suggests that the problem of missions neglect exists across the board. To be fair, it would not be prudent to make broad statements about the neglect of missions in local churches from a wide range of denominations without starting closer to home with my own denomination. Rather than make general statements about those problems of neglect, a specific look at one denomination's efforts may illustrate where we are as a nation of churches.

As we think about the existing state of missions in today's churches, the following case study comes from my own background. The congregation I serve is a Southern Baptist church, a denomination known historically for its commitment and dedication to missions. From its founding in 1845, the initial stated purpose was to support the proclamation of the gospel.[1] Two mission boards were established in order to pursue that end—the Foreign Mission Board (now the International Mission Board) and the Domestic Mission Board (later the Home Mission Board and now the North American Mission Board). The first appointment of foreign missionaries took place in 1846; and over the 164 years since, the Foreign, or International, Mission Board has had the honor of appointing a total of more than twenty thousand missionaries.

Over 28 percent of that number, 5,656 are currently serving as full-time international missionaries somewhere in the world beyond the borders of the United States. More than forty-three hundred of that number are career missionaries joined by more than twelve hundred additional workers who are on overseas assignments of two years or more. That number of full-time missionaries offers some encouragement to those of us who want to be a part of a movement among churches to participate in the work of the Great Commission, to make disciples of all nations.

However, if we are honest, as years of denominational life went by, like most Christian organizations, bureaucratic growth resulted in a diminishing focus and diluted emphasis on the priority of missions. As scores of other ministries have crowded the agenda and cut into the pool of resources available for that essential focus, missions received less and less support from both the individual congregations and Southern Baptists as a denomination.

In my first year as a pastor, I quickly discovered that my passion for missions was matched by fervent appeals from speakers at conventions, in publications from denominational agencies, and in state and national periodicals—all calling for loyal giving to support missions. At first I was glad for such an unabashed advocacy of our call to fulfill the Great Commission together.

What I soon came to realize is that not everyone meant the same thing when they talked about missions. The giving plan of Southern Baptists through which funds are gathered to support the work of missions is the Cooperative Program. Imagine my confusion when I first realized that in the minds of many of my Southern Baptist colleagues the words *missions* and *Cooperative Program* were synonyms. This became clear to me in a personal and painful way when a statewide denominational publication stated categorically in one of its articles that, according to their records, our church gave *nothing* to missions. The truth was that our congregation was heavily involved in missions giving but had made the decision a few years before to bypass the Cooperative Program as its chosen means of supporting missions and ministries outside our local congregation. At that time the Cooperative Program budget was allocating over 30 percent to colleges, universities, and seminaries and less than 17 percent to international missions. Because we redirected our missions giving outside the denominational plan, the editor of the publication felt completely justified in making the judgment that we gave *nothing* to missions.

So, considering that context, I believe we face a disconnect in what people understand about the definition and priority of missions. The lines have been blurred between denominational ministry and global missions. As a congregation and as a pastor, our decision to find more direct and effective ways to support missions brought many consequences as far as denominational life is concerned. The message being conveyed to churches like ours was that we should just send our money in and leave the decisions to the judgment of those in denominational leadership who were better qualified to manage the funds than those at the local church level. During those days, many Southern Baptist congregations simply made other arrangements to get a better return on their missions dollars than they could by following the course the denomination had chosen. Perhaps that trend can be reversed but not without a major overhaul of the purpose, vision, values, and priorities of both the churches and the denomination.

Denominational Bureaucracy and Spending Priorities

Although the Southern Baptist mission boards might be doing great work, the sobering reality is that for all of our public statements and affirmations in support of missions, the biblical call to support missions is still suffering from systemic neglect. By forcing all missions efforts through the bottleneck of denominational agencies, the systems we have put in place to find people and fund the effort have created a comfortable distance from the front lines of missionary action. For all the times we get goose bumps and lumps in our throats when we hear amazing stories of God's grace at work overseas through the evangelistic efforts of our missionaries—and for all the bragging rights associated with how much is given to missions from the churches and individuals who stand for Christ in our nation—the record shows that we actually have little practical interest in meaningful engagement in reaching the world beyond our own church walls with the gospel of Jesus Christ.

If we just look at certain categories of the data we have about how much money and how many missionaries are invested in international missions, we could easily draw the wrong conclusions about how well we are doing. By giving and sending more than many other groups, by comparison SBC churches feel a certain pride in the breadth of their effort. In addition, many of those same churches are expanding their impact far beyond their denominational efforts. They are entering partnerships with many nondenominational missions agencies like TEAM, Wycliffe Bible Translators, Africa Inland Mission, SIM (Serving in Mission), African Leadership, Overseas Missionary Fellowship, Operation Mobilization, and a host of others. Still, the truth we must face as followers of Jesus Christ is that the composite picture of all that we know does not provide a positive view of where we stand now or where we are heading.

Each church faces the challenge of assessing its response to missions in light of what we have seen consistently in the reports and annual statistics from various denominations. The information available from nondenominational churches suggests the same trends. Although this is not a book on missions statistics, in this case study we find a troubling trend that is just an example of how one denomination is managing its commitment to missions. After all, Southern Baptists as a denomination have a reputation for being strongly evangelistic and leading the way in global missions. A brief review of how they are doing should challenge all of us to ask if the data provided by their own agencies might not be representative of a missions-support problem facing churches all over our country.

So what do we know according to the latest records providing data from the Southern Baptist Convention? Well, the annual report from the year ending December 31, 2007, offers some encouraging news.[2] Nearly forty-five thousand churches across the United States are affiliated as Southern Baptists with a combined membership exceeding sixteen million. Total gifts reported by the churches have averaged 4.5–5.0 percent increase per year since the year 2000; $8.7 billion in undesignated gifts were received during the year 2006–2007. Of that amount, approximately $500 million per year since the year 2000 has been given through the Cooperative Program. Each state with its own denominational organization, or convention, then allocates a portion of that money to fund ministries within its own state and a portion to be sent to the national organization to support ministries on a broader scale than would be possible by individual state conventions. The philosophy behind this approach is that we can do together cooperatively what no one could do in isolation from the rest.

So if you tally up all the data from that many churches cooperating together for the common causes of the gospel, the numbers in the previous paragraph look impressive! However, rather than leading to the conclusion that this denomination is really committed to sacrificial generosity to fund missions, how do these statistics stand up under more careful scrutiny? Let's break them down to see a little more clearly what kind of priority Southern Baptists give to the commission of Christ to make disciples of all nations.

1. Membership. Although records report that there are sixteen million members of Southern Baptist churches, worship attendance hovers at just over six million people per Sunday, nearly ten million fewer than the number of members! If a business tried to operate with over 60 percent of its workforce failing to show up, that would seem to indicate that the work would need to be scaled way back or that something was wrong with how it identified who its workforce really is. But the question has to be asked, where in the world are ten million people every week?

With an average attendance each week of approximately six million people and with 5,656 missionaries appointed by the International Mission Board, we can presently account for less than .09 percent of regular attenders in Southern Baptist churches who have responded to God's calling to vocational missions overseas. If we used the stated membership number of sixteen million instead of using the attendance number (obviously more accurate than the membership number), the percentage of missionaries to members plummets to .03 percent! If we applied .09 percent to the membership number of sixteen million instead of the attendance number of six million, we would then have to find a way to fund an additional ten thousand missionaries! As it stands now, Southern Baptists cannot even find ten million of their members, much less hope to send *any* percentage of them overseas for the proclamation of the gospel! But a more immediate concern is that current giving levels do not even support the number of missionaries already qualified, committed, and waiting to go![3]

2. Local Church Stewardship. Of the $8.7 billion received in undesignated funds received by Southern Baptist churches in 2007, only about 6 percent of that amount is passed along through the Cooperative Program for the intended purpose of supporting denominational work, or *missions* in the vernacular of some within the denomination. Many of the churches, like ours, have found other avenues for achieving their missions purposes than the routine denominational giving plans. The pursuit of good stewardship has led many to find different avenues with a higher likelihood that the funds given will make it to missions endeavors more in line with traditional definitions of what constitutes missions than most denominations use.

Like many denominations, Southern Baptists are now asking how to generate more giving from local congregations so that adequate funding can be received to pay for the *smorgasbord* of ministries that have been added over the years. But if a new congregation with no history of denominational connectedness or a young pastor with no denominational loyalty asks sound management questions, it is bound to come to their attention that a passion for missions may not be served best by the current formulas for distributing the dollars entrusted to the denomination's agenda. Across the land, churches are looking for better ways to leverage their missions giving. Southern Baptists as a denomination are facing austere times financially if they do not adjust the priorities of the denomination to match the biblical heartbeat of the churches looking to make the greatest possible impact for the kingdom.

3. Cooperative Program (the SBC giving plan). Although more than $500 million was given through the spending plan of the denomination, the average amount making it out of each state to the national organization was only about 36.55 percent. Some states do much better than others, with some keeping 50 percent in the state and sending 50 percent to the national work; but others, like my own state, North Carolina, keep 65 percent in the state and send only 35 percent on to the national budget. Although the Cooperative Program is promoted broadly as the *missions* giving arm of the denomination, missions is so widely defined that nearly any form of legitimate ministry fits the bill. So across the denomination, an average of 63.45 percent stays in the state where the "missions gifts" are collected and invested in ministry close to home and a much smaller portion makes it to the "uttermost parts of the earth" and "all nations."

None of these observations are intended to suggest that there is not a need for local ministry. Of course there is! But when state conventions spend nearly as much on colleges and universities as they do in contributions to the International Mission Board,[4] it is past time to make some serious adjustments to the priority and definition we give to missions. Hearing proponents of the current allocations argue that Christian higher education should be acknowledged as missions just as much as the work of the International Mission Board or the North American Mission Board strains our common sense! When can we just tell the truth about the way things are and have been for many decades now? That is, that missions has been redefined to be an all-inclusive term for denominational ministry and has been stripped of its historic and biblical meaning.

4. Traditional Understandings of Missions. Of the money that eventually makes it outside the states to the national organization of the Southern Baptists, 50 percent of it goes to the International Mission Board (IMB), and another 22–23 percent goes to the North American Mission Board. With that information in hand, we find that out of every dollar donated through the Cooperative Program, *less than 20 cents (19.06 percent)* or *28 cents (19.06 + 8.6 percent if you include domestic missions)* makes it to what most people typically mean when they think of missions—international and domestic efforts to take the gospel to the nations. But the more difficult part to explain is why churches and a denomination with such a missions heritage give no more than they do in support of the work of missions, which without argument holds such a high place in the purposes of Christ.

Of the $8.7 billion given through local churches, only about 1.15 percent actually makes it to international missions using the current formula adopted by Southern Baptists—*barely over a penny of every dollar given!* Granted, this data does not have access to where churches are investing their missions dollars outside denominational channels, but for Southern Baptists to speak so boldly about their commitment to missions with so little to show for it in their giving through the systems set up for the distribution of their gifts in support of the Great Commission—well, the reality falls far short of the implied priority that missions shapes our mission as a denomination.

5. The Great Commission Resurgence Findings. In the summer of 2009, the Southern Baptist Convention commissioned a task force to study the issues behind the current dilemma impacting missions giving. As a part of that study (which resulted in a thirty-two page report), yet another wrinkle has come to light. Although it is well documented and understood what the percentages are for Cooperative Program spending allocations and priorities, it has not been as obvious that there is still another way that even more monies are channeled back to the local state conventions. Through a formula adopted by the denominational entities and the state conventions, many of the monies provided for the work of the North American Missions Board are actually returned to and used by the state conventions. Dr. Ronnie Floyd, chairman of the Great Commission Resurgence Task Force, explained how this works.

> In 2007–2008, our state conventions kept within their respective states an average of 63.45% of the dollars that churches gave through the Cooperative Program. The remaining percentage of 35.55% of the dollars that churches gave through the Cooperative Program went to the SBC Cooperative Program Allocation Budget. The SBC allocation formula for all funds received nationally allocates 22.79% to

the North American Mission Board. Follow me closely: While our state conventions keep an average of 63.45% of the dollars within their respective states, the North American Mission Board then sends back to the state conventions an additional $50.6 million due to these cooperative agreements and budgets. This process complicates the work at times, resulting in a lack of productivity and accountability.[5]

The task force did not calculate the impact of that formula on the overall impact on the percentage that stays in the states, but it is easy to see that the problem of localized spending is greater than it first appeared. The conclusion is simple: too much money intended for missions remains right at home instead of leaving the state and making it to the nations.

6. Missionaries and Sending Churches. One last bit of information related to statistics is that there are reported to be sixteen million members of Southern Baptist churches, as we already noted. But the IMB has only 5,656 full-time missionaries currently "on the field" from among all those people! Furthermore, even if each one of those 5,656 missionaries came from different churches, that would mean that with 44,848 churches affiliated with Southern Baptists, over 88 percent of those churches have no one serving as a missionary through the IMB. Giving them the benefit of the doubt and wishing them the best, perhaps another five thousand missionaries are serving with other agencies besides the denomination's agency. That still means that around 80 percent have sent no one. Compounding the problem is the fact that multiple missionaries have come from the same churches—obviously that is the case for husbands and wives! In other cases, churches that have made it their passion to pursue the Great Commission with people and money have sent many more than one family. The reality is that there are far fewer than 5,656 churches out of 44,848 who have sent any of their own to serve Christ in international missions.

7. Other Considerations. Two other important considerations need to be pointed out before moving on. First, in recent years there has been a shift in giving patterns among many churches, especially among new church plants and those led by younger pastors with no historic loyalties to the "traditional ways" to invest in missions beyond the scope of denominational initiatives. In an effort to get the most for their missions dollars, they are looking for solid, biblical, Christ-honoring, gospel-preaching missions entities that will provide a way to reach the nations with less overhead than the denomination. With the average church giving no more than about 6 percent through denominational channels, we have to assume they are ignoring the call of missions, or giving more generously elsewhere. Truthfully, it is probably a combination of both. For example, in 2007, the year from which these statistics have been taken, while $539 million was given through the Cooperative Program, those same churches reported "total mission expenditures" of $1.32 billion, nearly $700 million more. While $8.7 billion was given undesignated, total gifts reached over $10.8 billion.[6]

The Cooperative Program funding for international missions accounts for only a little over 43 percent of the monies given for the work of the International Mission Board. While $102 million came through the Cooperative Program, gifts for international missions outside the giving plan were over $134 million, or 13.5 percent more than the Cooperative Program contribution for that year. Those gifts came almost entirely through the Lottie Moon Christmas Offering, a major giving emphasis promoted each year to supplement regularly budgeted funds for international missions.

The impact of spending and sending priorities like these is sending shock waves through many denominations. As is the case with the Southern Baptists, a new generation of churches and leaders are looking for ways to leverage their influence for Christ more efficiently and effectively than their traditional routes would take them. Appeals to give more faithfully and loyally through denominational networks, which have fallen prey to rampant bureaucracy, are falling on sympathetic ears because many of us sadly lament the loss of a missions-giving strategy that was once great. But sympathy will not carry the day. The same ears that are listening to emotional appeals for denominational loyalty are also listening to hear a fresh new word. What might the Lord have to say to those now coming into leadership—in the churches and in denominational leadership? Efforts are under way to reverse the trends and recapture the vision of cooperative efforts to engage thousands of churches in aggressive, sacrificial commitments to take the gospel to the nations as well as the neighborhoods.

So Where Does the Missions Focus Stand?

Making a definitive statement about where the churches of today stand regarding missions from one case study of one denomination is obviously impossible. Yet a general conclusion can be drawn about the kinds of things we should note if we hope to issue a call for all evangelical churches to upgrade the level of their commitment to missions.

The bulk of this chapter has dealt with the mundane matters of nickels and noses—how much money and how many people are finding their way to the fields where millions wait for the hope of the gospel of Jesus Christ. Those are merely statistical indicators of where we actually stand, but I hope they are helpful as we assess the real place and priority missions has in our churches rather than what we hope would be the case. Wishful thinking about where we hope we are will not help. What we want and need is an accurate assessment of reality regarding missions. With the information we have in hand, here are some conclusions I have reached about where we are.

1. Without a biblical, functional definition of *missions*, we will continue to confuse local ministry with global missions and justify nearly any investment made in Jesus' name as missions spending.[7] Otherwise the cost of printing the bulletin for Sunday and the cost of translating and printing the Bible for the Daasanach people in northern Kenya or in the Nafaanra language for a people group in Ghana can all be lumped into the budget as missions. Yes, both are ministry, but we never really think of the administrative costs of local churches as missions in the same way we think of Bible translation work in Africa. But can we say that the salary of

a custodian at the denominational headquarters in our states is missions but not apply that same standard to the same work done in our local churches? By most definitions, neither qualifies as missions, but both are valued as ministry. So as long as churches are satisfied with definitions of *missions* that are so broad they include anything done for the sake of Christ, people will assume that they have fulfilled their missions responsibilities simply by sending their money to the "home office," wherever that is for their church polity and organization.

In the chapters that follow, it is our prayer that we can lay out a biblical understanding of what missions is, what Jesus called us to do, where and how He wants us to do it, and what response we should make to give missions its proper place of emphasis in letting missions play a significant role in shaping the mission of the church.

2. The biblical concept of stewardship has been violated by the churches charged with the responsibility and privilege of teaching and modeling faithful giving and prudent management of all that God has entrusted to us. Until churches grasp the importance of leading the way in giving, how can they ever expect their people to practice generosity? Tracking denominational giving from churches seldom tells the whole story of where they are investing in the work of the kingdom beyond their own congregation. As one who has been publicly ridiculed and falsely accused of leading a church to give nothing to missions, I know this as well as anyone. So the starting point for anyone reading this book is not out there somewhere but for pastors and church leaders to take a look at your own budgets. Are you modeling biblical stewardship by giving away at least a tithe of the income the Lord brings your way through the contributions of your congregation? If local churches hoard the provisions of the Lord to spend on themselves, so will the people in those churches. An assessment of the purpose statement and ministry principles and priorities as they are written and taught should result in and be reflected by a commitment to put our people and our dollars where they will accomplish the most in what God has called us to be and do.

3. New wine will not mix well with old wineskins, just as Jesus taught us. Churches and denominations, pastors and church leaders, need to recognize that what once had value has been diluted by the proliferation of add-on programs and ways to invest money and people. What once united our hearts in common passions and dreams under the umbrella of missions has been spread among so many competing agendas that churches have a difficult time distinguishing between good things and best things. If we want a greater buy-in from the upcoming generation and a stronger commitment to a dream big enough that only God can make it come true, we cannot keep pushing old agendas and tired structures if we hope to entice visionary young leaders and thoughtful older leaders to get on board. Some massive revisions and restructuring are staring down at the powers that be. Only by facing the inevitable white waters of change will we be ready to engage the hearts and hands and funds of those who have decided that they will no longer settle for the status quo. Missions is too big a calling to be relegated to a sidebar of a local church or denomination. But missions must gain and maintain the best we have to give. New wineskins designed to carry the fresh new wine of the gospel will have to be embraced, not reluctantly but wholeheartedly, if we hope to be a part of this mighty move of God to reach the nations with the hope of Christ.

The place held by missions in the church today is marked by controversy and confusion and competition. But we also find an invigorating desire to rediscover the essence, power, and authority of God's people engaged in world evangelization and global missions. Few, if any, groups are calling for a moratorium on missions anymore, such as was fashionable in mainline Protestant denominations in the late 1960s and throughout the 1970s.[8] Instead, members of Evangelical congregations across the nation are seeing the world come into their living rooms via satellite broadcasts and onto their computer screens via broadband signals becoming ever more aware of how desperately people are suffering apart from Christ. At the same time, they are reading their Bibles, listening to preachers and teachers, and hearing stories of phenomenal responsiveness to the gospel all over the world making them thoroughly familiar with the power of the gospel and the need to proclaim it far and wide. People with a love for Christ and a fire in their hearts for His glory to be made known in all the earth cannot be satisfied to sit back, write an occasional check, and count that as their only contribution to the work of the gospel. Changes in travel and communications now make it possible for us to do what has never been done before in the history of missions.

So the place of missions in the church today must take a more prominent role as a mobile, affluent, savvy people who are committed, consecrated and conscientious refuse to accept a "business as usual" approach in reaching the world with the treasure that is the gospel. We cannot make a plan to get where we know we need to be until we know where we are. As we have noted in this chapter, where we are leaves a lot of room to grow!

---

1. From the Constitution of the Southern Baptist Convention, approved May 8, 1845, that intent is clear: "Article II. Purpose: It is the purpose of the Convention to provide a general organization for Baptists in the United States and its territories for the promotion of Christian missions at home and abroad and any other objects such as Christian education, benevolent enterprises, and social services which it may deem proper and advisable for the furtherance of the Kingdom of God."

2. *Annual of the 2008 Southern Baptist Convention*, 109–11, Distributed by Executive Committee, Southern Baptist Convention, Morris H. Chapman, president and chief executive officer, 901 Commerce Street, Nashville, TN 37203.

3. Beginning in mid-2009 and continuing throughout 2010, due to the giving deficits created by stewardship problems in the churches and the impact of present budget allocations within the denomination that directs funds elsewhere, the annual appointment of missionaries (career and terms of three years or less) by the International Missions Board dropped by about four hundred people. Giving levels at that time represented only enough funds to sustain a missionary workforce of approximately five thousand, a reduction of over six hundred from previous years. With less money available, the emphasis has been on sending career missionaries and the reductions

have largely impacted short-term assignments. The overall impact has been that many candidates sensing a calling to missions have had to apply for appointment to other agencies, postpone their deployment, or in some cases abandon the pursuit of international missions.

4. To illustrate this point, in the budget for the Baptist State Convention of North Carolina, Christian higher education receives 15.21 percent of each dollar given and the International Mission Board receives 16.75 percent (half of the 33.5 percent that makes it out of the state to the national work of the Southern Baptist Convention). Do they actually mean to say that according to their priorities, international missions is worth only 1.5 percent more than the work of Baptist colleges in the state?

5. Dr. Ronnie Floyd, *Progress Report of the Great Commission Task Force of the Southern Baptist Convention*, February 22, 2010, 20–21.

6. Designated and undesignated gifts together made up this amount so that over $2 billion more was given than recorded in the undesignated gift category. How much of that money was given to special missions projects, annual Christmas and Easter offerings of the denomination, building projects, foundations, and endowments is not specified in the report.

7. Cf. Introduction, 4–6, for a reminder of how we have defined *missions*.

8. David Stoll, *Is Latin America Turning Protestant?* (Berkeley and Los Angeles: University of California Press, 1990), 72–74. The National Council of Churches determined that shifts in their theological positions and redefinitions of missions indicated that it was time for missionaries to come home. As a result of what was called a "moratorium on missions," missionaries affiliated with those churches returned home so that between 1969 and 1979 their number dropped from 8,279 to 4,817, a drop of almost 42 percent.

CHAPTER 2 RECOGNIZING THE HURDLES

When a movement as off course as a "moratorium for missions" gets started, evangelicals rise up from every corner and cry out in indignation. But is it not possible that the seeds of such destruction to the missions calling of Christ lie embedded in the soil of each of our churches? Given the sobering case study of the previous chapter, we have to admit that the missions efforts with which we are most familiar would hardly be considered vibrant and dynamic. What are the factors contributing to the wholesale neglect of the missions mandate in an overwhelming majority of churches that otherwise consider themselves to be consecrated followers of Christ, willing to follow and obey whatever instructions and commands He might give?

The present state of missions may be viewed favorably by those who compare it to what it once was in the days prior to the modern missions movements that largely began in the eighteenth century. But if we compare the meager attention it receives to other facets of the life and work of the churches of our land, the disproportional emphasis on things that we say matter less and the neglect of what we say matters greatly strikes a chord of concern in our hearts and minds. Certainly we need to identify the hurdles we face and how to remove them or get over them smoothly so that we regain our stride in running to the ends of the earth with the hope of Jesus Christ.

Hurdle 1: Pastors—Uninspired, Uninvolved, Uninformed

Honesty must begin somewhere! As a pastor for over thirty years, I try to resist and deflect criticisms whenever I can, but the truth always gets through. Some kernel of truth usually resides in the words of even the most critical spirit. But if we want to grow and mature, and if we want to lead and make a difference in effecting biblical, Christ-centered change, we have to consider the inconvenient truths about ourselves as pastors. Like it or not, the preponderance of evidence leads me to conclude that the missions direction of our churches rises or falls through the leadership of the pastor. Some have even described pastors as the cork in the pipeline, the bottleneck that constricts the flow of the church in a scriptural direction regarding missions. Most of the time, pastors talk about the way their churches are holding them back, thwarting their leadership, restricting their vision. But I cannot remember ever hearing of an Evangelical congregation complaining that their pastors are getting too biblical about missions. Now I have heard budgets debated and argued over when the ministry direction was unclear and the priorities of the church undeclared. But when there has been a consistent move to fulfill the Great Commission in the life of the church, and missions has been recognized as a key to congregational health so that God's name is most glorified, even the usual detractors fall silent in the face of strategic, comprehensive missions strategies in the local church.

So why do so few churches have such strategies? Why do they fail to give missions the place of distinction it deserves in the focus and shape of the ministry of the church? With few exceptions the stumbling block most of the time turns out to be the pastor. In *Key to the Missionary Problem*, written as a response to the addresses delivered at a major missions conference in New York City in April 1900,[1] Andrew Murray offers this quote from one of the speakers,

Dr. George Frederick Pentecost, pastor of Bethany Presbyterian Church, Philadelphia:

> To the pastor belongs the privilege and the responsibility of solving the foreign missionary problem. Until the pastors of our churches wake up to the truth of this proposition, and the foreign work becomes a passion in their own hearts and consciences, our Boards may do what they can, by way of devising forward movements or organizing new methods for raising money from the churches, yet the chariot wheels of missions will drive heavily.
>
> Every pastor holds his office under Christ's commission, and can only fulfill it when, as a missionary bishop, he counts the whole world his fold. The pastor of the smallest church has the power to make his influence felt around the world. No pastor is worthy of his office who does not put himself into sympathy with the magnificent breadth of the great commission, and draw inspiration and zeal from its worldwide sweep.
>
> The pastor is not only the instructor, but the leader of his congregation. He must not only care for their souls, but direct their activities. If there are churches that do not give and do not pray for foreign missions, it is because they have pastors who are falling short of the command of Christ. I feel almost warranted in saying that, as no congregation can long resist the enthusiastic pastor, so, on the other hand, a congregation can hardly rise above cold indifference or lack of conviction regarding missions on the part of the pastor.[2]

When these words were first preached, and then published, in 1900, how must they have been heard by the pastors whose lives were so thoroughly invested in the work of their local congregations? They were no different from pastors today. Some no doubt were offended by such strong words and became defensive. Others fell under conviction and determined to confess their failures and shortcomings and take a more prominent role in leading their churches to be shaped by the gospel and diligent in taking on missions with a fervor unlike any they had known before. Surely they were busy doing so much that had to be done locally. How could they afford to let up for a moment on the work that consumed their lives in serving the people of their own congregations? How could the priority of missions move to the place it held in the heart and commands of Jesus Christ? Murray addressed those questions with a simple, profound, convicting answer:

> The first step in returning to God for true service and new blessing is always confession. The leaders of the Church's mission work, who ought to know the tremendous needs of the world, who understand the meaning and urgency of our Lord's command, who feel the utterly inadequate provision the Church is making for His work—on them rests the solemn duty of lifting up their voices and making God's people know their sin. It is possible that we are all so occupied with our special fields of labor, and the thought of how much is being done, that the extent and guilt of what is not being done is comparatively lost sight of.[3]

The inconvenient truth pierces our hearts when we ask God to show us what He sees. Conviction by pastors will precede any significant restoration of missions emphasis in our churches. When I read such comments by preachers of the past, my first reaction is to explain how different our day is from theirs—and that is true. Today is a radically different era. But the fact remains that as an individual I am not substantially different from them, nor is the calling I have from God's Word different from theirs. If the neglect of missions in their day fell on the shoulders of the pastor's "cold indifference," then it is likely true today.

This is not intended to bury the pastor with guilt for yet another task unattended, another job unfinished. No, it is a call to the freedom of seeing and responding to what God points out to be true because if these assertions are true, then Christ says simply, "You will know the truth, and the truth will set you free" (John 8:32). Every pastor I know gets bone tired from the constant press and weight of the ministry, but what a glorious relief to know that when we are immersed fully in the stream of His revealed will, times of refreshing wash over us and give us joy even when we are exhausted! Stepping up and out into leadership in missions can change the culture of a congregation from expecting the mundane to seeing the miraculous.

Leading your congregation to embrace missions requires pastors to be player-coaches. We cannot sit on the sidelines and send in players without getting in the game ourselves. If our interest in missions is merely academic and remote, that is how it will come across to those we shepherd, and that is the level of interest they will demonstrate. Let them see your heart on fire for the glory of God and then cry out with earnestness, "Let the nations be glad!" because you yourself are glad, and watch the contagious fever of your zeal ignite the people to action!

As much as pastors would like to dodge this uncomfortable reality, the people they serve take their cue from how they treat the Great Commission. If the trend among churches to marginalize and neglect missions is to be reversed, it will start with pastors who wake up to the power of the gospel everywhere it is proclaimed. Watching the church come alive and focused beyond the walls of the local congregation provides mutual delight for pastor and member alike. Pastors, that move might begin with some passionate members of your church who love missions, but it cannot become a part of the mainstream of the life of the congregation until you take the lead. If you do not, you will continue to be an obstacle to what God wants to do through the missions effort of the congregation you serve.

Hurdle 2: Missing Role Models

If pastors have missed the boat on missions, and it appears that they have, then we should at least try to understand why. After all, since most evangelical pastors affirm a living faith in Jesus Christ and a desire to live for Him which stands in stark contrast to their lack of initiative in their pursuit of missions in the churches they serve. What happened to create that situation?

One answer among many is that there are too few role models for pastors to follow. So much of what pastors do is more caught than taught. Therefore, if they have not seen their mentors and teachers—their heroes in the faith—practicing a life engaged in missions, they are less likely to conclude that they are missing a key element in the fulfillment of their pastoral calling.

Just think of what we have already observed in the case study among a missions-minded denomination like Southern Baptists. In a generous stretch giving the benefit of the doubt to many churches, only 10–12 percent of those churches have sent missionaries out from their congregation. That means that nearly 90 percent of the models to which pastors are exposed have not demonstrated a functional commitment to missions. In the absence of such models, what else would pastors assume but that their ministry is normal if they only occasionally tip their hat to the mandate Christ has given for missions.

If we back up one more step in the process, where are our pastors being trained? Until recently, they have been trained in seminaries and Bible colleges with elective courses available about missions, but seldom have they been a part of the core curriculum. Although there are some notable exceptions,[4] most of seminary life and instruction trains pastors in the craft of biblical scholarship and pastoral ministry in the local church. Missions tracks can be selected as an alternative to the normal years of formal ministry preparation in some schools, but those who choose that direction are, without question, stepping outside the mainstream. So if each successive generation of pastors comes from churches without much exposure to missions, go to seminaries with little priority given to missions and then move out into local churches with no history of involvement in missions, what is the likelihood that they will conclude that they need to step up their own commitment? Like everyone else, pastors need role models to show them the way, mentors to help them shape the character of their understanding of missions, and positive examples of church ministries to follow which give missions their proper place in the priority order God has ordained for His people.

Anyone can read the Bible and see that God's heart for the nations holds a prominent place in Scripture. What is needed is a new generation of churches and pastors and professors to model a contagious commitment to missions that inflames the passions and informs the priorities of every pastor willing to look, listen, and learn. In a land filled with churches in survival mode and pastors struggling to manage the demands and expectations of congregations with no interest in what happens beyond the walls of their own church families, the failure in missions awareness and action makes sense. The extra effort of bucking the trends and leading a reluctant people in a selfless direction often suffers a crippling blow as pastors limp along trying to do something important, something successful, something significant within their own churches. An appeal to extend their reach to the ends of the earth can be so daunting and so distant from all they have ever seen or known that they virtually ignore what their mentors and models have neglected. I long for the day the trend is reversed in such a dramatic way that churches and pastors not involved in the practical priority of missions will be the exception and that pastors and their congregations will see role models of missions passion no matter where they look—in the seminaries as they train, among their peers as they serve local churches, through their heroes of the faith whose influence makes a profound impact on their perspectives and priorities in ministry, and from the churches themselves as they lift their eyes and see the fields that are white for harvest extending far beyond the walls of their local ministry. Limited role models do have an adverse effect on the vision pastors embrace for their ministry focus, but it does not take much effort to take a closer look at what God is blessing around you and realize that His heart always opens wide to those who trust Him enough to go and make disciples of all nations.

Hurdle 3: Verbal Commitments but Practical Disobedience

Christians in the United States know far more than they are willing to do. They say they believe with their words, but their practices prove otherwise. As someone observed, you *do* what you believe—everything else is just talk!

Perhaps I should state an assumption at this point. If you have not noticed, this book is directed to Christian leaders and pastors, who already have a commitment to a biblical model for ministry. It is assumed that you believe in the authority of Scripture and consider yourself a servant of Jesus Christ living for the glory of His name and the good of His people. Therefore, no one should be surprised that little here will be new information. The fact that you are reading this book makes a statement of your interest in finding God's best and giving yourself to it.

But the problem with people in the churches in the United States is that they have far more access to information and biblical instruction than ever finds its way into practice. We all know that we are not given the option of being hearers only but are expected to be doers of what God's Word says. Nowhere is that any more evident than in evangelism in general and missions in particular. We know the language, quote the verses, and sing the songs. This is familiar territory for most of us who have grown up in and around the church. So why such a disconnect between what we know and what we do? Becoming conversant with the issues does not necessarily result in better responsiveness to missions engagement.

Evangelical Christians have become proficient at speaking the language of missions and ministry. The problem is that there are two major areas in which our lip service about missions does not match our life sacrifices to make missions a true priority of our service to Christ. We have failed to connect belief with practice, which in fact is not belief at all, because we do what we believe—again everything else is just talk! The two problems arise in how few churches are *willing to send* their own people and how little churches are *willing to give* to support the work of missions financially.

Patterns in Giving. For years as a pastor, I have gone through the mental exercise of multiplying the number of potential givers times the average household income in our area and then figuring out what would happen if everyone who could tithe did tithe. The meager support for missions reflects the woeful and embarrassing lack of generosity among American Christians in general. Church budgets and missions agency budgets constantly scrimp and scrounge around trying to figure out how to stretch the dollars available to them so that they can do a lot for a little.

What difference would it make in the overall missions enterprise if those who profess to be followers of Christ would begin to demonstrate biblical stewardship at the most basic level of giving? In other words, millions of people all over America claim to know and follow Jesus Christ as disciples. Without going into the evidence for the biblical teaching of tithing here, for the sake of argument, let us agree for a moment that 10 percent of what every believer earns belongs to the Lord (which is what most would actually agree is what the Bible teaches).

A study published in 2008 calculated what that would generate in funds available for ministry and missions. In *Passing the Plate: Why American Christians Don't Give Away More Money*, Christian Smith, Michael O. Emerson, and Patricia Snell analyzed the average annual income of Christians in the United States who were committed enough to their faith to attend church services at least twice a month and calculated that in the year 2005, that group earned in excess of two trillion dollars. Based on that extraordinary number and comparing it to the amount already contributed to charitable causes annually by that same group, research showed that a tithe of after-tax income would result in an *additional* $46 billion per year in giving![5]

So what difference would that $46 billion in additional funds mean in supporting the work of the kingdom in fulfilling the calling of Christ? The impact would be so overwhelming that it almost defies imagination. That vast amount of wealth, however, is not just the product of an overly active imagination but passes through the hands of those who profess faith in Christ and a desire to live for Him in a manner that is consistent with His Word. Sadly, those resources are missing in action as far as the work of the kingdom of God is concerned because they have been redirected or withheld according to the whims of those to whom such abundance has been entrusted. When God promises that He will provide in abundance for all that we need and that He is able to make all grace abound for every good work, many who claim to believe all His promises quietly doubt that He is capable of resourcing His work with extravagant means. Consequently, Christian ministries in general and churches in specific languish with insufficient funds to accomplish their mission, and missions suffers especially when the followers of Christ assume that funds are in limited supply and must be rationed out sparingly.

Statistics declare otherwise. God has given all we need. We, however, have largely chosen a different course in how His generous provisions are allocated—personally as well as congregationally and denominationally. Be amazed at this truth: *the resources are in the hands of the people of God to do whatever He calls us to set our hands to do!* How much ministry is never tried and how many initiatives are never birthed because we have learned not to dream big because the financial realities are so daunting. What difference would it make in our thinking to consider what could happen tomorrow—today even—if American Christians would choose to trust God to be faithful to His promises and to do their part by simply obeying the biblical instruction to take 10 percent of what they are given and set it apart to give to the Lord?

> What really matters is grasping the *absolutely immense scope and scale of the possible goods that ordinary American Christians could accomplish in the world every year if they simply began to give away 10 percent of their after-tax income.* The possibilities are staggering.[6]

Why do we just assume that this is a foolish waste of time to think that basic obedience is possible among those who profess to love Jesus Christ and say that they want to live for Him? Prayer, uncompromising biblical instruction, contagious models of generosity, and the presence and power of the Holy Spirit can lead us into a new era of abundant giving. But will we dare to accept that challenge and embrace our calling to lead the way? Like many other patterns we want to see established in the lives of our congregations, giving patterns are directly influenced by the culture of generosity in which they find themselves.

In the meantime, why not dream big? Why not allow our eyes to look to what could be and then call on the Lord to supply what it will take to unleash the amazing floods of wealth He has already placed in the hands of His children? By squandering $46 billion on themselves each year, Christians in the United States reduce the resources available for missions in ways we cannot justify and will never be able to explain. Even as we try to convince ourselves that we did not do more for missions because we could not see how we could afford it, we will know that we took what God intended for His purposes and spent it on our own!

People Not Going. As we saw in the first chapter, the limited number of people willing to pull up stakes and go where God sends them communicates a confusing message. The evidence offered by such a small percentage of people going may lead us to think that either God expects only a few people to do an enormous task in reaching the world or, more likely, that He is calling many more people who are not listening and responding in the affirmative.

Hurdle 4: Divided Hearts and Loyalties

Although some factors contributing to the neglect of the missions mandate of Christ arise from circumstances beyond our control, by far the biggest issues stem from within our own hearts. Information, role models, misunderstanding the biblical mandate, resources—all play a part; but the problem for most has nothing to do with any of that. They have those all around them but still have chosen not to engage in missions. The problem, bottom line? The lordship of Jesus Christ!

Until we are ready to follow wherever He leads and do whatever He asks, we will suffer the consequences of a divided heart—saying one thing and doing another. Servants of Christ do not debate His commands, question His calling, or negotiate favorable terms regarding His commission. Servants obey. Why? Because they understand that He is Lord and they are not.

Putting boundaries around what we will and will not do puts us in control instead of allowing Him to exercise dominion over us. Granted, some just need to know what He desires and get a fix on what His will is and then they will pull up stakes and go. Without regard for what it will cost personally, they are willing to trust Him and leave the details up to Him. The Great Commission of Matthew 28:19–20 never asks us to figure out the details and, once we understand everything, go make disciples. He simply says go. Too many of us—pastors and church members alike—say no. We are willing to do anything He tells us to do—but only up to a point, and then we reserve the right to decline. By doing that, we demonstrate that our loyalties do not rest with Christ, but our hearts are divided between what we feel comfortable doing and what we prefer not to do.

Frankly, the state of missions in the church today would be radically different if people would just be honest about the question of lordship. If Jesus is really Lord, He gets to call the shots! He gets to determine how much we should give away and how much we should keep. He gets to decide who should go to the ends of the earth and who should stay in the local context. He gets to tell us what has ultimate value to Him and show us what we are doing that gets in the way of that. He gets to do all of that and much more because He is Lord and we are not!

With a passion for Christ comes a passion for the things He loves. If we are content to maintain a remote, arms-length relationship with Christ, His desires will never captivate us, and His glory will never motivate us. But once we dare to draw near to Him and allow His splendor to light our way, we will see a whole new world and way of living in it. Once you see His glory, no one will ever have to talk you into anything, convince you of any duty, or guilt you into doing what He wants. Your only desire will be for Him. The question of lordship and the concerns about our rights to a life of our own choosing fade into oblivion before the brilliant light of His radiant majesty. Problems with the will quickly disappear when the beauty and power of Christ converge in such a way that we cannot imagine wanting anything but what brings Him pleasure.

Do you want your heart to change regarding missions? Do you want the people with whom you serve to embrace the Great Commission? Pray what Moses prayed. "Lord, show me your glory!" Then the old hymn will make more sense than ever before, "Turn your eyes upon Jesus . . . and the things of earth will grow strangely dim in the light of His glory and grace."[7]

Pastors and churches often love their own local church more than Christ and His church, even more than Christ and His glory. They will not have a passion for the nations if they have no passion for Christ. They may sing and pray and proclaim their desire that "His glory may be known in all the earth," and that really sounds good! But it means little if there is no desire or commitment for the Lord to reveal His glory here and now. If there is no readiness or willingness to act in response to whatever He says, what will it take to overcome that formidable obstacle?

Many hurdles beyond those just discussed stand in the way of reaching a level of missions involvement in the local church that is worthy of Christ. But as we try to assess where we are currently as far as the state of missions goes, both in the sights of pastors and priorities of congregations, we cannot avoid the conclusion that where we are falls far short of where we ought to be. Our present state of affairs reflects badly on how well we are living out our present statements of faith. Poor stewardship, misplaced priorities, lifeless and indifferent pastoral leadership, denominational and local church bureaucracy, and many other telling indicators reveal a disturbing pattern of neglect of God's heart for the nations. His heart is toward the nations . . . His kingdom . . . the declaration of His glory in all the earth. How could we have missed that? Perhaps the next chapter, a brief summary and review of the biblical support for missions, should clear up any misunderstandings about what brings pleasure to the heart of God.

---

1. The Missions Conference of which we speak convened in New York from April 21, 1900 to May 1, 1900 and met in churches all over the city as well as Carnegie Hall. The chairman of the event was former president of the United States, Benjamin Harrison. On the program with him were William McKinley, the current president of the United States and Theodore Roosevelt, future president of the United States. But lest anyone write this off as a political showcase, the speakers included A. T. Pierson, pastor of churches in London and New York; J. Hudson Taylor, missionary to China; A. H. Strong, author of *Systematic Theology*; John G. Paton, Scottish missionary to the New Hebrides; and Ira Sankey led music for the conference!

2. Andrew Murray, *Key to the Missionary Problem* (Fort Washington, PA: Christian Literature Crusade, 1900), 11–12, quoting Dr. G. F. Pentecost.

3. Ibid., 39.

4. By the grace of God, I have been blessed in an unusual way by my association with two seminaries with strong emphases on missions— Gordon-Conwell Theological Seminary and Southeastern Baptist Theological Seminary. When I studied at Gordon-Conwell, I had the privilege of taking courses in missions under the tutelage of Dr. J. Christy Wilson whose heart and life breathed a passion for missions unlike anyone I have ever known. His influence, as a role model, on my life may never be measured this side of heaven.

Presently, I live only thirty minutes from Southeastern which has a strong commitment not only in curriculum and degree programs to missions but regularly sponsors trips and sends its faculty, staff, and students overseas to get hands-on experience in missions. Of course, I mention only two of the many seminaries fully engaged in missions modeling. I am sure you can suggest many others from your own exposure to their influential role in shaping how you look at your missions calling.

5. Christian Smith and Michael O. Emerson, with Patricia Snell, *Passing the Plate: Why American Christians Don't Give Away More Money* (Oxford: Oxford University Press, 2008), 13–18.

6. Ibid., 18.

7. Helen Lemmel, "Turn Your Eyes upon Jesus," written 1918, published 1922 by the British National Sunday School Union in *Glad Songs*.

CHAPTER 3 MISSING THE POINT

One of the common deficiencies in most churches is evangelism. Few followers of Jesus Christ would consider belonging to a church that was not committed to evangelism, as long as they get a free pass on it themselves! It is not necessarily that they don't believe the gospel, although that might be true for some who have been misinformed or confused by the pluralism of our culture. It is not that they do not care that people apart from a saving relationship with Christ are condemned for eternity to an actual place of everlasting punishment the Bible calls hell; they really do care, at least at some level. It is not that they have logical reasons for excusing themselves from this aspect of the life of discipleship—unless fear and uncertainty count as logical reasons. No, Christians generally understand that they should be active in personal witnessing and sharing their faith, and a vast number have been taught how to do that and why it is important. Yet something is missing. There is a disconnect between knowing and doing.

The same holds true for missions. We all want to belong to missions-focused churches, churches committed to take the gospel to the nations. The Great Commission makes sense to us. The plight of lost people stirs our compassion. The uniqueness of Christ as the only One who can save us from that plight is still largely believed and embraced. But if the previous chapters paint an accurate picture, something is woefully wrong because we are not acting like we get it at all.

The answer appears to be so simple. Christ commanded us to go, so we must obey. Because of lost people's horrifying future judgment and punishment, we should be filled with compassion. Since the Bible teaches that salvation can be found in no one other than Jesus Christ, we must believe. All these things make sense, so why is the church not seeing more of its members presenting Christ to others? Why are so many churches ignoring the nations in their strategic plans for ministry?

Two major issues account for much of the failure to embrace evangelism and missions as essential to the purpose and calling of the local church. We have lost our sense of *the place of the Great Commission* as an expression of the will of Jesus Christ for all His followers and *the power of the Holy Spirit* as the force behind our witness to the nations. Until these two resume their rightful place and receive their proper priority, the best we will ever see is occasional, arbitrary, ineffective, limited involvement in both missions and evangelism.

The Place of the Great Commission

One of the early problems regarding missions arose when the Great Commission was relegated to that category of Christ's teaching that was thought best left to the apostles and confined only to the apostolic age. As strange as it may seem now, many in the early church saw the command to go and make disciples of all nations as something directed specifically to the apostles and not applicable after that generation passed off the scene. In understanding the Great Commission as a unique responsibility of the first-century church, the argument against church involvement in missions resulted in the common practice and understanding that the church should no longer assume a primary responsibility for taking the gospel to the nations. In much the same way that many theological frameworks and systems limit certain spiritual gifts and signs and wonders to the apostolic age, the guiding principle during that time was that missions was a unique calling for a unique time and no longer holds relevance in the mission of the church. Over the centuries, perceptions began to change, and eyes began to open among the churches in broader circles sometime around the eighteenth century. But unfortunately the neglect of missions was so prevalent by that time that it has had a hard time regaining its place of biblical prominence. Even in the life of churches adamant about their convictions that the Bible is the true and reliable source of authority and practice in the lives of believers in the body of Christ, convictions about actively engaging in missions still holds a less prominent place in the life of the church than it does in Scripture.

One of the pivotal lessons learned since that time is that there will always be forces at work to diminish the biblical emphasis on missions. Too much is at stake if the whole world is to know the truth of the gospel and wonders of salvation through Jesus Christ. Several notable factors contribute to the general malaise within the church toward our responsibility to "go and tell" the good news of God's love and forgiveness. Although numerically the missions force is greater today than it has ever been, proportionate to the explosive expansion of the world's population, we go backward with each successive generation.[1] What kinds of factors contribute to this move in the wrong direction? Why are so few willing to accept God's call to go where He chooses and communicate what He desires.

Diluting and Dividing the Commission. The passage referred to as the Great Commission in Matthew 28:18–20 speaks of making disciples of all the nations by going to them with the message we have been given. "All authority has been given to Me in heaven and on earth. Go, therefore, and make disciples of all nations, baptizing them in the name of the Father and of the Son and of the Holy Spirit, teaching them to observe everything I have commanded you. And remember, I am with you always, to the end of the age."

Just before He ascended, Jesus gave more clarity to the Commission in Acts 1:8 when He told His disciples, "But you will receive power when the Holy Spirit has come upon you, and you will be My witnesses in Jerusalem, in all Judea and Samaria, and to the ends of the earth."

Two trends have emerged in response to the nature of these instructions from Christ.

Diluting the Commission. With a little shift of emphasis, we can effectively dilute the Great Commission to more manageable terms more suited to our preferences than to a genuine understanding of the scope of what Christ calls for us to do. Most students of Scripture are familiar with the teaching these days about the imperative nature of the command in Matthew 28:19. We have learned that the true imperative verb in that verse is "to make disciples," and not as it appears in English translations to include the word "go," which is actually a participle. The implication is that we are commanded to make disciples but not commanded to go. Therefore, the trend in most interpretations of this passage has been to make the point that a more likely translation of the verse would be, "As you go, make disciples." That translation lines up well with the recent emphasis on lifestyle evangelism in modern churches. As you go about your life, make disciples. That is a valid truth that would make a profound impact on local church evangelism if it were practiced. But is that translation consistent with the exhortation to make disciples of all the nations? For most Christians, as we go about the normal patterns of our lives, we will not encounter the nations as a matter of course. To make disciples of the nations, we will actually have to go somewhere besides where we typically would go in the daily routines of our lives.

In an enlightening article about this passage, Roy Ciampa, associate professor of New Testament at Gordon-Conwell Theological Seminary, contends that even in its participial form, the word *go* has the grammatical power of an imperative.

The first participle in Matthew 28:19 (the one that precedes the main verb, usually translated "Go") is a participle of attendant circumstance. . . . When translated into English the participle of attendant circumstance is translated as a finite verb, sharing the mood (indicative, imperative, etc.) of the main verb. . . .

We should note that the exact form of the participle used in Matthew 28:19 (*poreuthentes*) is used seven times in just that gospel and fifteen times in the New Testament as a whole (Matt. 2:8; 9:13; 11:4; 21:6; 22:15; 27:66; 28:19; Mark 16:15; Luke 7:22; 9:12, 13, 52; 13:32; 17:14; 22:8), and it is almost always used in this way. It never means "as/while you go." It is most often used, as here, in conjunction with imperative verbs, indicating that the hearers are to go (and do something which could not be done if they just sit there). Remember, the mood of the main verb casts its shadow over the participle of attendant circumstance so that when the participle introduces an imperative it gains an imperatival force as well, even though the main point is found in the main verb and the participle points to a first step that must be undertaken to accomplish the action of the main verb.

So what does all this tell us about Matthew 28:19 and the Great Commission? It means no ancient Greek would take it to mean "while/as you go, disciple the nations" but would understand, from intimate familiarity with this common usage, that the meaning was "Go and disciple the nations" and that the main point was not to go but to disciple the nations, but that the nations would never become disciples if the apostles and those converted by them did not take the gospel to them. Going is not the ultimate point, but it is a prerequisite, a necessary step towards the goal of making disciples of the nations and we must be intentional, deliberate, about going everywhere and leading all peoples to (willingly) obey the Lord Jesus Christ. Jesus never suggested that the nations would be discipled as long as we simply shared the gospel as we went about the normal routines of our lives. He indicated that we needed to be intentional/deliberate about making sure all nations got the message and were taught how to follow Jesus.[2]

Ciampa is not alone in his explanation of the force of the verb *go* in this passage. In *Salvation to the Ends of the Earth: A Biblical Theology of Mission*, Andreas Köstenberger and Peter O'Brien address the issue as well. While affirming that "make disciples" is the primary point of emphasis on the text, going is an integral part of how the exhortation is to be understood.

> Jesus' disciples are to "go and make disciples": the aorist participle "go" (*poreuthentes*) modifies the aorist imperative "make disciples" (*matheteusate*) as an auxiliary reinforcing the action of the main verb.
>
> [Then in the footnote, the explanation continues] What is stressed in 28:19 (contrary to popular notions) is not going, but the making of disciples (though the latter may well imply the former). Compare with this the use of the imperative of *poreuomai* plus a second imperative in 28:10 ("go and tell"), where proportionately more weight may rest on the going itself; and the use of the present participle of *poreuomai* plus an imperative in Matthew 10:7 ("as you go"), where the participial force may receive greater emphasis. . . . That we are simply to make disciples "as we go" rather than going somewhere for the express purpose of making converts is unduly extreme.[3]

The extreme limitation of the participle *poreuthentes* that translates simply "as you go" without its proper connection with the command to make disciples is not supported grammatically and certainly gives the wrong impression about the need to go somewhere if the intent is to make disciples of all nations. You cannot and will not be effective in obeying the Great Commission if your disciple-making efforts remain limited to where you find yourself "as you go" through your normal walk of life. To make disciples of all nations assumes and expects that those who follow His command will get out and go somewhere to do it—presumably not just where you presently live but also among all those nations still in need of hearing of His saving grace!

The impact of erroneous applications of that verse shows up in church after church, which defines its missions responsibility and calling in local terms. Many who love to speak of their "missional" identity as a congregation limit their application of the Great Commission to the proclamation of the gospel "as they go" through their lives within their own cultural contexts. Intentional strategies to go and send people to make disciples of all nations takes a backseat to a more localized emphasis. Certainly that is not at all true of all churches defining themselves as missional. In fact some of the strongest missions churches would speak of themselves as missional. But it does follow that those who prefer to see missional ministry as disciple making "as you go" would be less inclined to go somewhere else and make disciples. Adding a contemporary label does not change the traditional problem of churches' staying home when the nations need someone willing to go and make disciples.

As a point of clarification, understanding that the command to make disciples includes the need to go does not mean every follower of Christ has to go to all the nations with the gospel. But it does make clear that He intends to send witnesses to them who could never be reached if all He meant was for all of us just to be effective disciple makers and evangelists "as we go" about our business in our own culture. Therefore, we have to recognize a mandate to the churches to include a strategic commitment to go and send some of our own to the ends of the earth as well as to the end of the cul-de-sac.

Dividing the Commission. A second issue arises with this same general concern, this time in the context of Acts 1:8. When the power of the Spirit comes, He told His disciples that they would then be His witnesses "in Jerusalem, in all Judea and Samaria, and to the ends of the earth." Contrary to popular practice, this is not intended to be multiple choice! A proportional strategy targeting all those areas gives the church the opportunity to diversify its focus according to what Jesus laid out as the scope of our mission field. When efforts to highlight one to the exclusion of the others, such an inappropriate emphasis results in an imbalanced ministry.

Throughout the history of the church I pastor, missions has been given its rightful place in our budget priorities. By functioning as a principle-based ministry, our purposes have been clearly defined by biblical principles. Yet in the early years when money was scarce, some were ready to cash in on the missions money and redirect it to the constant needs present in our own congregation. The argument was simple—spend it on Jerusalem since there are plenty of lost people right here at home. If we would invest the same amount we were spending elsewhere on building up the local congregation's base, we could eventually do more in other places. In other words, why not choose Jerusalem, our home base, as the focus of our witness and outreach, and let someone else deal with Judea and Samaria, and yet another group deal with the ends of the earth?[4]

On the other extreme were what could be called missions zealots who wanted us to spend a dollar overseas for every dollar we spent at home. This group had no practical vision for people without Christ here at home but were consumed with zeal for those they would never meet and never have to tell about Jesus. The distance made it more comfortable to justify their enthusiasm for sending money and others to do the work of evangelism elsewhere and at the same time feel good about their role in world evangelization without ever having to be personal witnesses themselves. To be fair, some people had a genuine passion for the ends of the earth but could not see that Christ did not call us to be witnesses in *either* one of three places. He said we would be His witnesses everywhere—no exceptions, no improvising, and no easy ways out. Dividing the territory and picking our favorites do not satisfy the exacting demands of a commission that tells us to be faithful across the board, just as He said. So the reality is that many churches have decided to emphasize one and neglect the rest. Christ never offered us that as an option! His commission is to make disciples by going to all peoples in all places with all diligence.

Pentecost and the Power of the Holy Spirit

However, even when the Great Commission comes back into play as a motivator for missions, we have to admit that that alone is insufficient as an impetus for widespread and sustained involvement of the church in missions. The primary consideration of the modern missions movement of the eighteenth century and on to the present has been that we are commanded to take the gospel to the nations. The simple fact that Jesus told us to do it should hold sufficient force in our hearts and minds to stir us to obedience and send us to the ends of the earth for Him. For many thousands of missionaries through these past three centuries, the command to go has been compelling, and they went because He said so. Yet, as we have noted, comparatively few have stepped up to that level of obedience. Why might that be?

Perhaps another question needs to be considered first. Why do followers of Christ not obey Him in other areas? After all, our wholesale neglect of the command to go tell the nations about the love and forgiveness of Jesus Christ does not stand alone in the list of omissions on our part. To be sure, "if Jesus said it, we should do it" should be sufficient for us to take action. But I know from my own personal experience that He has issued many commands and offered much instruction that falls on deaf ears, even among His disciples. The Bible commands many things that disciples of Christ have never taken seriously in a consistent way: "Love one another." "Tithe." "If you marry, stay married." "Do not forsake your own assembling together." "Forgive as Christ has forgiven you," and so on. The issue is not so much that we don't think these things matter, or whether they are intended for us, but the concern is one of far greater importance. Before we came to know Christ, we could not obey the law of God; and even now that we do know Christ, we are still incapable of doing His will in our own strength. It is not that we do not understand or that we do not care; we do. The simple truth is, people who are spiritually powerless cannot accomplish what only those with spiritual power can.

In *Pentecost and Missions*, Harry Boer lays out a fascinating premise that states in part that the early church did not engage in missions because of the Great Commission, but because it was simply an overflow of the fullness and power of the Holy Spirit coming upon the church. The motivating force behind early missions in the church was the presence of the Holy Spirit, and that empowering presence moved the people of God to become vital witnesses for the glory of Jesus Christ. Although the apostles were certainly familiar with the Great Commission—it had been spoken to them by Jesus Himself—the chief concern for taking the message of Christ to the ends of the earth arose after the coming of the Holy Spirit. That fact does not nullify or in any way diminish the significance of the Great Commission, but it does raise an important point. Until the Spirit came as the Father had promised and as Jesus had told them, the information was in their possession, but the inspiration and motivation to take action were missing.

Bruce Ware offers this helpful insight into the vital connection between the coming of the Holy Spirit and the passion of believers to take the gospel to the nations.

> There is no saving revelation of the Spirit that is not the saving revelation of Jesus Christ and him crucified and risen. Hence, missions is necessary. The hidden peoples of this world are without hope apart from their learning about Christ and placing their faith in him alone for the forgiveness of their sin. We have allowed this concept of the necessity of the spread of the gospel slowly but surely to disintegrate. It's sort of like soap on the floor of the shower. Over time, without being aware of what's happening, it just sits there and vanishes. It gets soft and mushy and after a while it's gone altogether. The Spirit wants his people to know that he has come to empower them to be witnesses of Christ, and that apart from knowledge of and faith in Christ, people cannot be saved. May God grant us emboldened passions to yield to the Spirit, and to see the name of Christ proclaimed by every people, tongue, and nation. Yes, the Spirit has come to glorify Jesus, and this happens in part as the gospel of Jesus reaches the ends of the earth by the power of the Spirit.[5]

Should we be surprised by this? Of course not! Just as we could not keep the law of the old covenant making it necessary for Christ to come for us, neither are we capable of keeping the commands of the new covenant apart from the supernatural intervention of God. Therefore, the work of the Holy Spirit plays an indispensable role in a life committed to obey Christ in all things, including the Great Commission. Boer's conclusion is that the power, effectiveness, and breadth of the missionary movement of the early church arose from the coming of the Holy Spirit at Pentecost, not from a determination to fulfill the Great Commission. A brief consideration of the nature of the gospel underscores why that was true then and remains so now.

Living by the Law or Walking by the Spirit. None can claim to have a relationship with the Father on the basis of how effectively we obey the will of God. Our sin and the weakness of our human nature, our flesh, consistently get in the way of doing what God requires of us. Having been born to new life by the Spirit does not result in our having perfect ability to keep His commandments. We must rely entirely on the power of the resurrection of Jesus Christ through the abiding presence of the Holy Spirit if we hope to succeed in any manner in fulfilling the will of God. As Paul explains it in Romans 8:3–4, "What the law could not do since it was limited by the flesh, God *did*. He condemned sin in the flesh by sending His own Son in flesh like ours under sin's domain, and as a sin offering, in order that the law's requirement would be accomplished in us who do not walk according to the flesh but according to the Spirit."

So God does not expect us to fulfill either the requirements of the old covenant or the commands of Christ in the new covenant in our own strength but in the power of the Holy Spirit. We never could and now that Christ has come we never need to do so because our capacity for obedience rests in the strength of the Lord.

Neither does He expect that a command will compel what a heart does not commend. If our hearts are not held in the grip of a profound love for Jesus Christ and a deep appreciation for the treasure He is, we will not be motivated to continue in our commitment to speak of His glory among the nations for very long.

Occasional fits of duty and periodic bouts of guilt will produce temporary responses among many but seldom sustain any long-term transformation of our passions. Only by the overflow of hearts made full by Christ will His people maintain the intensity of devotion that will call them and keep them on mission for His name's sake.

Desire and Power. The role of obedience to the commands of God cannot be downplayed, but neither can the role of the Holy Spirit in empowering and shaping a desire for that obedience. Always powerless to obey the law in our own strength, we cannot sustain missions efforts by sheer force of will or tireless discipline on our part. Of course, determined people with strong wills can put on a good outward show and perhaps achieve some measure of success. But for the body of Christ to engage in a sustained, effective commitment to missions, we must have more than an obligation keeping us on target. Nor can we count on our compassion to remain constant as a sufficient motive to send laborers out into the harvest. No, Peter's sermon on the Day of Pentecost after receiving the Holy Spirit explains what must happen for the church to go and make disciples of the nations: "On the contrary, this is what was spoken through the prophet Joel: 'And it will be in the last days,' says God, 'that I will pour out My Spirit on all humanity'" (Acts 2:16–17). The role of the Holy Spirit in missions has been neglected to the extent that we should ask ourselves if the sending and going by missionaries, and the giving and supporting by churches can be traced more to human activity than to an undeniable movement of God. When the Spirit starts moving, the church and the people start going—no campaigns, no manipulation, no guilt—just a people abiding in Christ and walking by the Spirit.

Shaping Our Desires. The Holy Spirit builds a desire in our hearts, not for missions initially, but a desire for more of Christ. But once that desire ignites in us, the fuel that keeps it burning is consistent with what Paul says will happen in those who begin to walk in the light of Christ. They will never tire of "discerning what is pleasing to the Lord" (Eph. 5:10).

Coming to know Christ as Savior does not make us immune to the attractions of the world around us. On every front, what we desire and are inclined to think we must have has been shaped by temporal concerns more than eternal ones. Left to follow our hearts, who can honestly say that we would prefer the costs and the sacrifices involved in reaching the nations with the gospel over the comforts and conveniences of the familiar surroundings we have come to expect as our right? Entitlement and the American dream of worldly success have trumped absolute surrender and the kingdom value of eternal significance.

In an address to seminary students in the fall of 2009, Al Jackson, pastor of Lakeview Baptist Church in Auburn, Alabama, explained the impact of desires shaped more by the culture than the call of Christ:

> The greatest obstacle to the Great Commission is not our doctrine, or the willingness of candidates to go, but the American dream. . . . We have two options. Either we invest in earth, or we invest in heaven. We invest our resources in the American dream, or we invest our resources in the kingdom of God. . . . The American dream says, "Get more—more of everything." The American dream is to have whatever I want when I want it. . . .
>
> I have very little hope for my generation. I think my generation has bought into the American dream. But I have hope for your generation. My prayer for you is that you go and put some deep roots down in a church that is in a community, in a town, in a village—and not move up the corporate ladder to a large Southern Baptist church—to work in that church, to work with those finance committees and to fight those battles to mobilize your people to get the gospel to the nations.[6]

Something will shape your desires, mold your interests and command your affections. When we allow it to do so, the world around us will smother us into conformity with itself. But in Christ, a new life in the presence and power of the Holy Spirit promises us release from that inevitability. Paul challenges Roman believers to be diligent to avoid the shaping influence of the culture and to pursue a mind that is shaped by Jesus Christ. "Do not be conformed to this age, but be transformed by the renewing of your mind, so that you may discern what is the good, pleasing, and perfect will of God" (Rom. 12:2).

What does the Holy Spirit do? What can we expect if we turn our desires and affections over to Him? Jesus informed His disciples that the Spirit would come to shine glorious light on Him so that we might see Him as He is, that He would remove the veils from our eyes so that our spiritual blindness would be healed, that He would give us spiritual birth to new life so that as new creatures born of the Spirit we would be alive to all that God is—for us in Christ.

Therefore, as we awaken to this new life and see with new eyes, a new world opens up for us. When we see what God has done and the brilliance and brightness of the illuminating work of the Holy Spirit reveals just how glorious He is, our desires begin to be redefined as what we value most gets reshaped by hearts and minds conformed to be more like the Creator and less bound to the creation. The appeal and attractiveness of the Lord captures our affections, and what had been hidden in the shadows appears because of the work of the Spirit. All of this has been there all along; but until we live by the Spirit, walk by the Spirit, and are filled with the Spirit, we are oblivious to it all!

> But if, in fact, our gospel is veiled, it is veiled to those who are perishing. Regarding them: the god of this age has blinded the minds of the unbelievers so they cannot see the light of the gospel of the glory of Christ, who is the image of God. . . . For God, who said, "Light shall shine out of darkness"—He has shone in our hearts to give the light of the knowledge of God's glory in the face of Jesus Christ. Now we have this treasure in clay jars, so that this extraordinary power may be from God and not from us. (2 Cor. 4:3–4, 6–7)

The missing element in much of the missions deficiencies in the body of Christ is a clear view of the glory of God in the face of Christ. Rather than affections shaped by desires for more of Him, we have tried to summons some sense of duty to perform His bidding. People who have seen His glory do not have to be cajoled into service; they cannot imagine anything more wonderful than the privilege of doing so! David demonstrates this kind of desire when he cried out, "I have asked one thing from the LORD; it is what I desire: to dwell in the house of the LORD all the days of my life, gazing on the beauty of the LORD and seeking Him in His temple. . . . In Your behalf my heart says, 'Seek My face.' LORD, I will seek Your face" (Ps. 27:4, 8).

What would happen if pastors began to extol the beauty of Christ in their preaching and teaching? What if people could sharpen their focus and view Him as the ultimate vision of all that is glorious and worthy? When our hearts are filled with the Spirit, our eyes are absorbed with the picture of the perfection and wonder of Jesus Christ. That which occupies the highest place in my affections is what I value the most. Until a work of the Spirit reshapes our desires so that all our longings are in the Lord, the compelling interests of our lives will not be in declaring who He is and what He has done. If our desires are divided, the best possible response we can expect to the call of Christ will be compromised. But if we understand that we have this treasure in earthen vessels and grasp the immensity of His grace toward us, our perspective on taking that message to the nations or the neighborhood will be transformed. We will order our lives around that which commands our hearts, and we will open our lives up to any available opportunity to make His glory known.

One of the most telling indications of what shape our desires have taken is how and what we pray. We may fool others and even ourselves about the nature of our desires, but prayer tells the true story because it serves as a display window into our souls. The presence of the Holy Spirit serves to shape us, mold us, so that we want what God wants and then cry out to Him for those things. In his 1863 book, *The Mercy Seat*, Gardiner Spring, pastor of the Brick Presbyterian Church in New York City, explains this in a powerful way:

Prayer is the language of desire; it is the offering up of our desires to God. It is the devotional thoughts and affections of the soul expressed in words. No spiritual emotions enter more intimately into the experience of the Christian, or more truly form the character of his piety, than those which are felt and expressed in his habitual intercourse with God. If he has adoring views of his Maker, and humbling views of himself; if he hungers and thirsts after righteousness; if he has strong confidence and joy; if his desires go out toward the enlargement and beautifying of the Church of God on the earth, and the salvation of men; nowhere do these internal emotions and desires find utterance so truly as in prayer. Where these devout affections exist with anything like ardour and intensity, they are uttered by a sort of necessity. Such persons cannot help praying. It is not possible that emotions this deep and spiritual, this high-born and heaven-imparted, should remain silent and smothered with the bosom. The heart is too deeply affected by them not to seek this relief.[7]

When we desire Christ above all else, our prayer lives will demonstrate that as the Spirit saturates our thoughts and affections with all that brings pleasure to Him. Much that is lacking in the response of the church to the call of Christ to the nations shows up in the minimal mention of such things in the way we pray. Prayer really is the language of desire. Before missions takes hold of the church, a consuming desire for Christ and His passions must be shaped in our hearts by the Holy Spirit.

Unleashing His Power. The Holy Spirit unleashes the power of God in us when He comes to give us new life. All that we could not do on our own, once we are born of the Spirit, He comes to dwell in us and empowers us with all the fullness of God's strength. In his prayer for the Ephesians, Paul laid out his desire for them to grow to be mature in Christ when he prayed . . .

that He may grant you, according to the riches of His glory, to be strengthened with power through His Spirit in the inner man, and that the Messiah may dwell in your hearts through faith. I pray that you, being rooted and firmly established in love, may be able to comprehend with all the saints what is the length and width, height and depth of God's love, and to know the Messiah's love that surpasses knowledge, so you may be filled with all the fullness of God. (Eph. 3:16–19)

A major feature of the early church was the presence of supernatural power because of the indwelling presence of the Spirit. During their days with Jesus before His crucifixion, His followers were often confused, fearful, and inconstant in their devotion to Him. Even in the days after the resurrection while they were with Him, the promises were theirs, but the power was not. All of that changes on the day of Pentecost, just as Jesus had told them it would. In fact, He had prevailed upon them to remain in Jerusalem until they had been "empowered from on high" (Luke 24:49). The nature and purpose of that power could not have been clear to them at that point, but they did wait and pray just as He had instructed them.

Could they have misunderstood what that "power from on high" was supposed to accomplish? If today's conversations about the power of God offer any clues, it is likely that some might have hoped for the power to throw off the yoke of Roman oppression, others the power to take authority away from the religious establishment, still others the power to become healers and miracle workers and gain a following for themselves. Maybe others held out more mystical hopes of a new realm of spirituality, new dimensions of understanding divine mysteries, seeing extraordinary visions and dreams of a heavenly nature and other personal aspirations of drawing near in intimate intercourse with the Lord God.

But Jesus introduced a different idea. Not that those things were not possible, but He spoke to a much more practical manifestation of the power of the Holy Spirit. In His own words He told them that when the Holy Spirit came and they received His power, that power was not for show, but it was power to go. "But you will receive power when the Holy Spirit has come upon you, and you will be My witnesses in Jerusalem, in all Judea and Samaria, and to the ends of the earth" (Acts 1:8).

Of all the claims made in our day by those who speak often of their experiences with the Holy Spirit, seldom do we hear much about the power to be His witnesses. That seems too mundane, too tame, to a world that longs for sensational manifestations of spiritual power, but that was not the case for Jesus and the early church. His power to be His witnesses was high on His list of priorities in what He communicated about what the disciples should expect when they were "empowered from on high" (Luke 24:49). That power was intended to compel them to move out with the gospel and proclaim a message that was to be more than words but a message with power—the power to save, the power to give life, the power to transform.

This is not to suggest for a moment that the only reason for the power of the Spirit in us is for missions and evangelism, but since that element is so largely missing in much of the modern church's discussion of the manifestations of the Spirit's power, a renewed emphasis on this point is well deserved. The connection of the Spirit's power and the power of His message through His messengers shows up often in the early chapters of the book of Acts. Perhaps in one of the most obvious accounts in this regard, the response of the church to threats from the religious leaders in Acts 4 offers a wonderful example of power and witness:

> "And now, Lord, consider their threats, and grant that Your slaves may speak Your message with complete boldness, while You stretch out Your hand for healing, signs, and wonders to be performed through the name of Your holy Servant Jesus." When they had prayed, the place where they were assembled was shaken, and they were all filled with the Holy Spirit and *began* to speak God's message with boldness. (Acts 4:29–31, author emphasis)

No fear, no shame, no confusion—the disciples cried out to God for more power in order that they might speak the Word of

God with greater boldness. And that is just what happened when they were all filled with the Holy Spirit.

To the power of the Spirit, we owe so much—the power to see the glory of Christ, the power to live life as new creatures by faith in His name, the power to overflow with contagious joy in vibrant worship and adoration of the Lord, the power to love one another unconditionally and selflessly—all of these would be impossible in our own strength. But because we have become the dwelling place of the Holy Spirit, we also find ourselves transformed from meek, silent followers to bold, effective witnesses to the grace of Jesus Christ. God has unleashed us to take the gospel of Jesus Christ to the nations and empowered us to do so with power none of us has apart from the work of the Holy Spirit in our lives.

Commissioned with Authority and Clothed with Power

If our motivation to be His witnesses is just an obligation to keep a command, it cannot compare to what happens when our hearts are controlled and compelled by the inner workings of the Holy Spirit. A life wholly yielded to Christ and filled with the Holy Spirit sees and desires and goes all out for anything that promises to bring delight to the heart of God. And missions definitely delights the heart of God as people all over the world are introduced to the glory and grace of Jesus Christ!

---

1. With a world population in excess of 6.8 billion people and only 2.2 billion even nominally identified as Christians, the staggering reality is that more than 4.6 billion people are without the hope of eternal life through Jesus Christ. At the time of Christ, world population statistics estimate that about two million people occupied the earth. The one billion threshold was reached around 1800, two billion by 1927, four billion by 1975, and the eight billion mark should be surpassed by 2025. To put things in perspective, there are more lost people on earth now than there were people on earth in 1975.

2. Roy Ciampa, "As You Go, Make Disciples?" http://connect. gordonconwell.edu/members/blog_view.asp?id=190052&post=37543. "The most common use of the participle of attendant circumstance, the usage found here, is one where an (1) aorist adverbial participle, (2) comes before the

main verb, and (3) refers to an intentional action that had/has to take place as a prerequisite to the realization of the action of the main verb (adverbial participles that do not fit all the criteria do not fit in this category)."

3. Andreas J. Köstenberger and Peter T. O'Brien, *Salvation to the Ends of the Earth: A Biblical Theology of Mission* (Downers Grove, IL: InterVarsity Press, 2001), 103–4.

4. My answer was always that if we neglected all that Christ commanded us to do, we would have no need to spend more money at home because the Lord would have no reason to trust us with more people if we were not going to follow Him with those we already had! If we were not faithful with little, why would He trust us to be faithful with more?

5. Bruce A. Ware, *Father, Son, and Holy Spirit: Relationships, Roles, and Relevance* (Wheaton, IL: Crossway, 2005), 119–20.

6. Reverend Al Jackson, chapel address at Southern Baptist Theological Seminary, Louisville, Kentucky, September 15, 2009.

7. Gardiner Spring, *The Mercy Seat* (Morgan, PA: Soli Deo Gloria Publications, retypeset from the 1863 edition published in Glasgow, 2001), 2.

SECTION TWO
WHERE WE WANT TO BE

CHAPTER 4 ALWAYS ABOUT THE KINGDOM

The kind of person reading a book about missions usually has a confirmed interest in the subject already. Therefore, most of you already know and understand the theology and biblical mandate for missions, but allow me to give a brief overview of how God views the nations and how we are to view them as well. Without that context, we may be operating with different assumptions about what is at stake.

The Heart of God for the Nations

From the beginning of the Bible, God revealed that He has a heart that reaches out to the nations. In Genesis 12, the chapter following the dispersion of the nations after the debacle of Babel, the Lord issues a call to Abram in the land of Shinar (Mesopotamia) where the tower had been erected. The purpose of that calling was to enter into a covenant with Abram promising that he and his progeny would be blessed. Following the typical pattern of the people who have been called since then, Abram could have stopped listening after hearing that God would bless him. However, the blessing was not just for Abram, but a promise that in him all the nations would be blessed as well: "I will make you into a great nation, I will bless you, I will make your name great, and you will be a blessing. I will bless those who bless you, I will curse those who treat you with contempt, and all the peoples on earth will be blessed through you" (Gen. 12:2–3).

Choosing Abram to be the father of a great nation was never intended to produce an exclusive heritage but to provide a godly lineage called to live by faith in the promises of God and show "all the peoples on earth" that the Lord is God.

Subsequent promises to Isaac and Jacob confirmed this direction so that the patriarchs of the faith all understood that the blessing of God in their lives was not for their sake alone but as a means toward the end that all nations could know the Lord. To Isaac as he was settling into the land of Gerar, the Lord said, "I will make your offspring as numerous as the stars of the sky, I will give your offspring all these lands, and all the nations of the earth will be blessed by your offspring" (Gen. 26:4).

Then again to Jacob in a dream, the promise was once reiterated when the Lord told him, "Your offspring will be like the dust of the earth, and you will spread out toward the west, the east, the north, and the south. All the peoples on earth will be blessed through you and your offspring" (Gen. 28:14).

There was never any other intent. God chose Abram, Isaac, and Jacob as the heads of a growing nation that would serve His eternal purposes in showing the nations of the earth that there is only one God, and He can be trusted to keep His promises as we keep His word. The foundation of that relationship was faith, believing God and trusting Him in all things.

> Just as Abraham believed God, and it was credited to him for righteousness, so understand that those who have faith are Abraham's sons. Now the Scripture foresaw that God would justify the Gentiles by faith and foretold the good news to Abraham, saying, "All the nations will be blessed in you." So those who have faith are blessed with Abraham, who had faith. (Gal. 3:6–9)

So as we take note of the calling of Israel into existence, the purpose of God was to set apart a people for His own possession that through them all the nations of the earth could be blessed through faith in Him. By raising up a holy nation, His expressed desire was to set them high above the nations so that all peoples would see and long for what Israel had—a relationship with the only true God, one claimed by faith in the promises and grace of that one who is recognized as Lord of all. So it was that hundreds of years later, through Moses, the Lord once again repeated His strategy:

> "And today the LORD has affirmed that you are His special people as He promised you, that you are to keep all His commands, that He will put you far above all the nations He has made in praise, fame, and glory, and that you will be a holy people to the LORD your God as He promised." (Deut. 26:18–19)

Again, through the prophets, the Lord addressed the matter directly, especially through the words of the prophet Isaiah, when He said, "It is not enough for You to be My Servant raising up the tribes of Jacob and restoring the protected ones of Israel. I will also make you a light for the nations, to be My salvation to the ends of the earth" (Isa. 49:6).

In other words, how is it possible for God's chosen people to think that the scope of His mercy and the breadth and length and height of His grace should be limited just to one people among all the nations of the earth? Indeed, it is too small a thing to imagine of such a great and glorious God, rich in mercy, abounding in grace!

The Plan of God for the Nations

Since we see that God has always had a heart for the nations, we should also understand that He has a plan to reach them. Even as we saw the various representative texts supporting the premise that He has always had in mind a way of salvation for all nations, we saw a pattern that indicated some of what was involved in His plan. Briefly stated, the plan calls for a people to be called out as His own and then by His faithfulness, power, and love prove without a doubt that there is no God like Him. As other peoples see what He is like, they will be drawn to Him themselves and embrace Him by faith as well.

The emphasis in the New Testament on taking the gospel to the nations is broadly understood and does not need to be reviewed in great detail. However, the presence of this same message in the Old Testament may not be as obvious and definitely not as widely known. Consider this series of examples of how this was understood and stated among the early leaders of His people in Israel according to various accounts in the Old Testament. Abraham, Isaac, Jacob, and Moses have already been noted, so here are some others:

- When Joshua and the Israelites crossed over the Jordan River into the land God had promised, God told him to place a memorial there to remind the people of Israel and the peoples of the earth that God is awesome. "This is so that all the people of the earth may know that the LORD's hand is mighty, and so that you may always fear the LORD your God" (Josh. 4:24).
- When David penned the words to Psalm 2 (what Charles Spurgeon calls a "sublime psalm . . . the psalm of Messiah the Prince"), he saw the nations forsaking their defiance and mockery against the Lord and bowing in worship before Him: "Ask of Me, and I will make the nations Your inheritance and the ends of the earth Your possession" (Ps. 2:8).
- When Solomon prayed in dedicating the temple to the Lord, he asked for the name of the Lord to be seen by the foreigner who came near:

> Even for the foreigner who is not of Your people Israel but has come from a distant land because of Your great name and Your mighty hand and outstretched arm: when he comes and prays toward this temple, may You hear in heaven in Your dwelling place, and do all the foreigner asks You for. Then all the peoples of the earth will know Your name, to fear You, as Your people Israel do and know that this temple I have built is called by Your name. (2 Chron. 6:32–33)

• When Elijah confounded the prophets of Baal on Mount Carmel, it was not God's design to exalt Elijah's prowess as a prophet but to show everyone present that He alone is the Lord.

> Then Elijah approached all the people and said, "How long will you hesitate between two opinions? If Yahweh is God, follow Him. But if Baal, follow him." But the people didn't answer him a word. . . . "Answer me, LORD! Answer me so that this people will know that You, Yahweh, are God and that You have turned their hearts back." (1 Kings 18:21, 37)

• When Isaiah added his voice to the others it was with a clear view that the salvation of the Lord was being offered to the nations.

> The LORD has displayed His holy arm in the sight of all the nations; all the ends of the earth will see the salvation of our God. (Isa. 52:10)

> Arise, shine, for your light has come, and the glory of the LORD shines over you. For look, darkness covers the earth, and total darkness the peoples; but the LORD will shine over you, and His glory will appear over you. Nations will come to your light, and kings to the brightness of your radiance. (Isa. 60:1–3)

We could go on and include many others among the prophets whose voices would echo the same theme. God wants to call the nations of the earth to Himself, and He has chosen to model covenant faithfulness and reveal His word and will through a people, Israel, chosen to be a conduit for His mercy and grace.

Once the promised Messiah had come, the plan moved into higher gear as the church assumed the responsibility for taking the message to the nations. The New Testament record is full of exhortations to the people of God to move out with the story of God's plan of salvation for all who would believe. The pronouncement by Simeon at the temple repeated what had been revealed by the prophets when he held Jesus in his arms and said, "For my eyes have seen Your salvation. You have prepared it in the presence of all peoples—a light for revelation to the Gentiles and glory to Your people Israel" (Luke 2:30–32).

Then at the beginning of His ministry, John the Baptist made the connection between the One who was to come with Isaiah's prophecy "and all flesh will see the salvation of God" (Luke 3:6 NASB). These introductions to Jesus Christ again emphasized that God was concerned for the salvation of Israel but also of "the Gentiles" and "all flesh."

If you are familiar at all with the life and ministry of Jesus Christ, you already are well acquainted with His focus on offering eternal life to all who would believe in Him. Right at the start of his gospel, John noted that when Jesus came into the world, He came first to the people God had chosen. The promise to Abraham was thus fulfilled that through his seed the Savior would come. But as had been true throughout God's dealing with Israel, His own people did not get it, would not accept Him, and turned away from Him: "He was in the world, and the world was created through Him, yet the world did not recognize Him. He came to His own, and His own people did not receive Him" (John 1:10–11). So He spoke to the breadth of His Father's plan in sending Him into the world when He told Nicodemus "that whoever believes will in Him have eternal life. For God so loved the world, that He gave His only begotten Son, that whoever believes in Him shall not perish, but have eternal life" (John 3:15–16 NASB). These two wonderful uses of the word "whoever" made the purpose of God clear to all who would hear this great news of salvation because it opened the door for those beyond the nation of Abraham and Moses to receive His forgiveness and find eternal life in Him.

Toward the end of His ministry, Jesus once again honed in on this theme so that there could be no mistake about His intentions. After several references to the inclusion of the Gentiles, or the nations, in the kingdom of heaven, He declares that the world of humanity is His target and His people would be charged with taking the message to everyone everywhere.

This good news of the kingdom will be proclaimed in all the world as a testimony to all nations. And then the end will come. (Matt. 24:14)

Then Jesus came near and said to them, "All authority has been given to Me in heaven and on earth. Go, therefore, and make disciples of all nations, baptizing them in the name of the Father and of the Son and of the Holy Spirit, teaching them to observe everything I have commanded you. And remember, I am with you always, to the end of the age." (Matt. 28:18–20)

But you will receive power when the Holy Spirit has come upon you, and you will be My witnesses in Jerusalem, in all Judea and Samaria, and to the ends of the earth. (Acts 1:8)

The continuation of the plan God had from the beginning was central to the coming of Christ, a plan to offer forgiveness and acceptance to all who would believe in Him.

The balance of the New Testament bore witness to how that was understood and applied in the life of the early church. Paul explains to the Romans how grateful and careful non-Hebrew people should be for the privilege of being grafted in as a branch of the olive tree, God's chosen people, to his challenge to his fellow Jews to welcome a holy jealousy which sees the salvation of the Gentiles and makes them long to know the same for themselves (Rom. 11:11–24). Peter's encounter with Cornelius from Caesarea forced him to see that Christ had not come only for the salvation of the Jews but for the Gentiles as well. Prior to that time, he had not understood what had been in the Scriptures from the beginning but had escaped him. After watching the Spirit work, he went back to Jerusalem and reported what had happened as the Lord had called those who had once been excluded and made them His own. Upon hearing Peter's report, the church in Jerusalem marveled: "When they heard this they became silent. Then they glorified God, saying, 'So God has granted repentance resulting in life to even the Gentiles'" (Acts 11:18).

Soon after, the church began to undergo severe persecution, believers were scattered throughout the world, and with them went the gospel. Paul accepted his calling as apostle to the Gentiles as a matter of simple obedience (Rom. 1:5) but also as a continuation and fulfillment of the design of the Father's heart all along.

We who are not from a Jewish heritage owe our place in the family of faith to this initiative from the Lord to introduce His grace through His people Israel but then to carry it through them to the rest of the peoples and nations of the earth. Now it is our turn. We have not received this message and this hope as an end in itself but as a treasure to be shared with all. Imagine the surprise awaiting many believers when we all come before the throne of God one day, and people from all over the earth are standing shoulder to shoulder praising Him because they were also redeemed by the grace of Jesus Christ.

> And they [the multitude] sang a new song: You are worthy to take the scroll and to open its seals; because You were slaughtered, and You redeemed people for God by Your blood from every tribe and language and people and nation. You made them a kingdom and priests to our God, and they will reign on the earth. (Rev. 5:9–10)

But what if? What if the patterns of inactivity and isolation continue and believers choose to remain in the church house instead of going to the nations where every tribe and tongue and people and nation are waiting to hear?

> Now the Scripture says, No one who believes on Him will be put to shame, for there is no distinction between Jew and Greek, since the same Lord of all is rich to all who call on Him. For everyone who calls on the name of the Lord will be saved. But how can they call on Him in whom they have not believed? And how can they believe without hearing about Him? And how can they hear without a preacher? And how can they preach unless they are sent? As it is written: How welcome are the feet of those who announce the gospel of good things! (Rom. 10:11–15)

CHAPTER 5 MAJOR OBSTACLES TO A KINGDOM-FOCUSED MINISTRY

Knowing that God desires for the nations to come to know Him and seeing the biblical plan He has outlined to reach them gets us moving in the right direction. But if it were that simple, I believe we would have made more progress by now in getting the gospel where it needs to go. We understand that we are commissioned to go and that the Holy Spirit empowers us to go, but some issues stand in the way. Paul told the Corinthians that "a wide door for effective ministry has opened for me—yet many oppose me" (1 Cor. 16:9). The same is true today. Because the Lord is preparing the way to reach the nations, the door is opened wide by His hand. But we cannot assume that wide-open doors mean there are no obstacles or adversaries blocking the way. In order to understand the task before us, we need to recognize the realities at hand.

Five Roadblocks We Face

1. **Inward-Focused Churches.** Somewhere between the early church in the New Testament and the modern church, God's plan and purpose for the church has been obscured. A shift in emphasis here, a redefining of intent there, and soon the church began to conceive of itself as an entity that exists for its members. A church

subculture emerged along the way that bears little resemblance to the accounts of the church in Jerusalem in the days after Pentecost.

In fact, something like that nearly always happens when God's people begin to develop their own identity and invent their own unique culture apart from Christ. What happens is what has happened for thousands of years: we get so absorbed in our own little world that we forget about the rest of the people on earth. From the day the ark landed on Ararat to the present day, people called by God to be His own have tended to climb on board their own boats, pull up the gangplank, and sail away, oblivious to everyone outside in the rising waters. For some reason we have found it easier to close doors and keep others out than to open doors and invite people in. Absorbed with concerns for our own well-being, we lose sight of the big picture—the kingdom focus that lifts our eyes from the immediate circumstances of life as we know it to a broad perspective that addresses the exhortation from Christ to "seek first His kingdom and His righteousness" (Matt. 6:33). The natural tendency of human beings drives them to be self-focused and egocentric, whereas the call of Christ elevates our passions to a higher calling with a kingdom focus centered on the desires and purposes of the Lord.

Throughout the history of the church, different approaches have shaped our response to God's call to reach out to the nations and develop a kingdom mentality in our ministries. In the New Testament, we are introduced to various groupings of people who held strong worldviews that defined their understanding of what it meant to be the called-out people of God—Pharisees, Sadducees, Essenes, and Zealots. From Pharisees to modern-day fundamentalists, rules of disengagement have been created and upheld scrupulously, even if it means doing so callously. The force behind their movement is separation. When confronted with the poison of the Sadducees and the current version of them, theological liberals, we who believe the Scriptures wince at their disregard for biblical truth and their dismissal of the supernatural power of God. We also find Essenes and their contemporary counterparts who prefer retreats into asceticism and isolationism looking for the latest spiritual and emotional experience to carry them until the next one comes along. Then there were the Zealots who plotted takeovers and advocated aggression in the secularized culture wars in order to impose, or at least preserve, their way of life by force. Again this group is mirrored in our day by activists whose only real kingdom concerns involve fighting for their rights to live as they please without interference from others, primarily anyone in authority. These groups come across as fanatical so we stay as far away from them as possible so that we do not become identified with their brand of faith and practice. These four distinctive groups from the New Testament era had agendas that had nothing to do with the kingdom of heaven or the values of the King of heaven.

Where was their kingdom focus? Do we not see the same tendencies in the church today warring against any real desire to get out of the house and extend our influence to reach the nations? What seems to be largely missing among all these movements is the call of God to engage the nations in a meaningful way to reveal to them the light of the gospel and help them come to the knowledge of Jesus Christ as Savior. But we have to look hard to find balanced, biblical men and women who love Christ and refuse to hide His light in a dark world desperate to see and have hope. The combination of a passion for Christ and His glory, and a heart of compassion for the unreached people and nations of the world establish a solid foundation for building a kingdom-focused ministry in the local church.

The Old Testament also offers a fascinating study of Israel's travails, bouncing back and forth, on the one hand wanting to forget their identity as God's chosen people and assimilate into the surrounding cultures and nations and on the other hand wanting to resist the voices of the prophets calling on them to rise up and shine the light of the Lord so that the nations of the earth would be drawn to Him. Sometimes they wanted to be like the world, and other times they wanted to keep the world out, but seldom was there any indication that they understood they were to be God's messengers to the world so that the world might come to know that the Lord is God.

So the question before us is this: Does God really want people from all nations included in His kingdom, or does He only intend for those who were blessed by providential design to be born with access to His promises and provision of eternal life to know and belong to Him? Put more directly, did God choose Israel alone to be His people, or was it His plan to speak to and through them and call all nations to Himself? Does the church as it exists now have exclusive rights to the gospel; and now that we have been brought in, can we pull up the gangplank and close the doors of the ark?

Stated in such a blunt manner, every believer knows the answer to that question. But examining what we do as an indication of what we believe, one would have to conclude that we may have embraced a faulty view of how God sees His people. From all the evidence I can find in Scripture, He chose us and now calls us His own, but does so with every intention of sending us back into the world around us, to the nations, so that He might reach more and more to be a part of His everlasting kingdom.

So for those who think that once the church is comfortably full, the building debt retired, and the budget met, we have reached our destination and fulfilled our purpose, the Bible presents an entirely different picture of what the Lord wants us to do as long as He leaves us here. Just as He never intended for the revelation of Himself to remain an exclusive claim of Israel, so He does not intend for the church to become satisfied when we have come to know Him ourselves. As long as the nations remain unreached with the good news of Jesus Christ, our calling is clear. It is always about the kingdom. It is always focused on what He is doing to spread abroad the glorious light of Christ through us to the ends of the earth.

Developing a kingdom mentality rather than merely focusing on feathering the nest of the local congregation requires an honest assessment of what we believe and what we are willing to do with the knowledge that God has the nations on His heart and in His purpose for the church.

2. A Trend Toward Isolationism among Nations. Several years ago, as the Soviet bloc nations were released from their subjugation to the imposed will of the Soviet Union, I was in one of the central European countries beginning to enjoy its new freedom. One of the pastors I met made an astute observation, one which I have come to understand with even greater clarity over the past eighteen years. He said that most of the conflicts between nations and most of the clamoring for independence and autonomy did not arise from nationalism but from tribalism. The concept of "tribe" in Scripture usually refers to "a body of people united by kinship or habitation"[1] and consists of a smaller unit of people within a larger whole with whom there is a closer affinity for the same values, traditions, beliefs, and cultural heritage.

With national boundaries drawn and redrawn by politicians, the existing cultural, ethnic, and tribal distinctives of an affected people are not always reflected within the borders of the redefined states. Some of the most volatile conflicts and least resolved animosities over the past hundred years make much more sense in the light of this problem. A brief recollection of some of the most brutal atrocities in recent history demonstrate the nature of this powerful force of resistance against the imposition of foreign forces, beliefs, and authorities from outside the "tribe."

The inexplicable horrors of Rwanda in the spring and summer of 1994 were not the result of an invading nation forcing itself into the sovereign state of Rwanda but the result of tribal antagonism between the Hutu and Tutsi people. The international community was shocked as hundreds of thousands were slaughtered because of nothing more than tribal hatred. Even today, civil war in the neighboring Congo traces its roots back to the population shifts and refugee movements of various tribes seeking to escape the slaughter fourteen years ago.

In Central Asia, the Kurds have an ethnic identity that transcends national borders, a tribe unto themselves, but they are prohibited from establishing their own homeland and instead have been assimilated into the culture of the nations of which they have been forced to be a part. Efforts to establish themselves as a recognized people have resulted in systematic genocide at the hands of unscrupulous rulers like Saddam Hussein, the former dictator of Iraq.

The devastation in what once was Yugoslavia stemmed from passions forced to remain dormant under the days of communist leader, Josip Tito, but unleashed with a fury in 1991–1992 when once again the ethnic identities emerged as stronger than any artificially created nationalism. Serbs (from an Orthodox Christian culture), Croats (from a Roman Catholic tradition), and Bosnians (consisting primarily of a Muslim population) went to war against each other, set up independent nations for themselves, and suffered unthinkable crimes at the hands of those who were only recently identified as one nation, Yugoslavia, proudly hosting the 1984 Winter Olympic games together in Sarajevo.

The pattern has repeated itself *ad nauseam* throughout our lifetime—Palestinians and Jews, Hindu militants in India fighting the encroachment of Muslims and Christians into their territory, Sri Lankans suppressing Tamils, Kenya's political conflict rooted in animosity between the Kikuyus and the Luos and their allied tribes. There is clear evidence to support the premise that tribalism plays a dynamic role in the attitudes toward protection and isolation within many nations and people groups. When people are threatened by outside forces, they resist and try to isolate themselves as a means of preserving what has inestimable value to them.

All of the turmoil created by trying to blend cultures and violate values and traditions generates a passionate longing to remove the offending influences—peaceably if possible but at all costs when necessary. Therefore, nations and people groups tend to become more and more isolated from one another by choice, or by force if warranted. Persecution arising from those passions has become standard news these days—if the reports even make the news at all.[2]

People have determined to carve out a place in the world for themselves, isolated from those who either threaten them or impose on them and their way of life. Policies of nations have led them to abandon entire people groups to vicious dictators without so much as lifting a hand to help. Politicians demonstrate either racist or ethnocentric tendencies by advocating rescue and intervention only when the victims are enough like their "own kind" to merit their interest, or who might be useful in perpetuating their own culture. I have been fascinated to hear opposition to wars in Bosnia, Iraq, Rwanda, Sudan and other places, not on the basis of principled pacifism but because it is deemed unthinkable that "people like us should give up our lives for people like them." Normally liberal media outlets and left-of-center politicians have frequently opposed actions in the Middle East because they could not justify the loss of American lives to save Arab lives! Such is the nature of ethnic and tribal isolationism.

After the devastating attacks on the World Trade Center and Pentagon on September 11, 2001, a profound sense of instability seized the citizens of the United States. For generations the isolation of two oceans provided a buffer of insulation from any perceived vulnerability from enemies outside our borders. But now as the world grows smaller due to advances in travel and communications technology, threats to our security are more tangible. Therefore, more attention is now focused on protecting ourselves with growing tendencies toward closing our ranks instead of opening our arms. So instead of advances in technology broadening our horizons about the possibilities of reaching every "tribe and tongue and people and nation" (Rev. 5:9), isolationist tendencies become more pronounced as we become more aware of the increased threat posed by the growing encroachment of competing values and beliefs and even violence against our own tribe.

The church has adopted some of this isolationist mentality and developed patterns of behavior that betray our tendencies. Knowing the commission we have to reach out to the nations, we still find a compelling interest only in seeing people reached with the gospel who are most "like us" and a limited commitment to risk going outside our comfort zones to an increasingly frightening world. We seem to be able to sleep easily enough without any apparent concern for the billions of people not like us who have no access to the gospel of Jesus Christ.

Add to that reluctance a subtle preoccupation in Western churches with the "satisfied-customer mentality," and we discover that many churches in the United States are more inclined to invest themselves in themselves than they are to see the rest of the world as worthy of their best efforts and resources. Megabucks go into building megachurches and state-of-the-art facilities for people who have virtually unlimited access to the truth, but only token efforts are made to bring financial resources and our best people to the overwhelming task of taking the hope of Christ to unchurched people in the rest of the world. We demonstrate that we are willing to go to great lengths for the comfort and preservation of our own tribe but gladly accept our isolation from the rest of the world without pausing to consider that cutting ourselves off from them leaves them without anyone to speak to them of the love and glory of Christ.

3. Magnitude of the Task. Rather than seeing the biblical assignment as simple a task as one person at a time, the sheer numbers of people who need to hear the gospel of Jesus Christ makes the calling to missions overwhelming. When we hear of population growth worldwide and the burgeoning nations of China and India with over a billion people each, we can become paralyzed by the massive scale of the task before us. What difference can we possibly make in accomplishing such a monumental mission? So instead of taking the initiative in small steps to do what we can, it becomes easier for everyone to assume that someone else will step up, and so we wait.

The math alone is disconcerting when you think of how much it would take for each person to hear the gospel just once. Yet the genius, the brilliance, of the plan given to us by Christ calls for a multiplication plan, not an addition plan. Although everyone is familiar with the model by now, it is instructive to repeat it here. If you alone were the only Christian willing to fulfill the Great Commission and were willing to lead one person per year to Christ, train and disciple them, and then both of you do the same the next year, each repeating the process—that process of multiplying by two each year would see the entire world have a chance to hear and respond to Christ in only thirty-five years. In fact, the multiplication-by-two factor would result in over 8.6 billion people impacted in that time.[3] Of course we all know the obvious—the attrition rate factored in with the numbers who failed to succeed in actually seeing someone trust Christ as Savior, in spite of their faithful witness, and many other intangibles make such a scenario unlikely. But the task becomes more manageable when it is noted that our starting point for that mathematical progression is not just one but millions who already profess faith in Christ.

Research done by missiologist Ralph Winter actually shows that we are making great gains proportionally in the ratio of unbelievers to believers. Starting with the book of Acts and the earliest church, consider these statistics:

AD 100	360 unbelievers for every 1 believer
AD 1000	270:1
AD 1500	85:1
AD 1900	21:1
AD 1970	13:1
AD 2000	9.3:1

Now when that is viewed in the context of the number of congregations of believers, or the number of churches to the number of known people groups who are still unreached with any gospel message, we should be even more encouraged about the provision God is making to reach those who are lost without Christ.

AD 100	1 church for every 12 unreached people groups
AD 1000	1:5
AD 1500	1:1
AD 1900	20:1
AD 1970	150:1
AD 2000	650:1[4]

The sheer size of the global population intimidates us until we take into consideration the unfolding plan of the Lord to make sure all people have access to the gospel. At first glance, the task appears to be impossible. But once we assess the resources the Lord has assembled and called to the mission of making disciples of all nations, we can reasonably get excited about His wisdom and about our part in fulfilling His work. The challenge is to start with the basics of sharing Christ right where we are, praying about what role He wants us to play in building His kingdom, and then moving out at His direction to take Him to the nations.

The problem is not with the plan but with the execution of the plan. Whether the failure to meet the challenge is due to lack of training, low levels of commitment, absence of any strategy to identify and share with unbelievers, or any number of other possible reasons, we are not taking responsibility for what Christ has commissioned us to do. There may be ways to sugarcoat that reality, but the fact remains that few members of the body of Christ have ever, or will ever, lead anyone else to know Him as Savior. And that has become such a normal state of affairs that no one seems bothered about it.

So our negligence on the small scale of our local mission field does not bode well for our commitment to extend our efforts to the masses beyond our immediate reach. The prospect of making the sacrifices to take the gospel to the ends of the earth with its billions when we have not proven any significant commitment to taking it to the neighborhoods where we live is not promising. All of this leads to the next point.

4. Compromise of Conviction about the Message and the Masses. Evangelical theology holds a fixed commitment to the uniqueness of Jesus Christ and the biblical truth that salvation is only by grace through faith in Him. In our day the implications of those commitments and beliefs typically influence individualistic applications of those truths. In other words we are convinced that when we realize our need for salvation from sin, the only means of receiving God's forgiveness, being accepted into His presence and gaining eternal life is to place our trust in Christ alone. That is personal. "Blessed assurance, Jesus is *mine*! . . . This is *my* story

. . . this is *my* song."[5] We hold firmly to that as an unshakable conviction. But do we apply that truth on a broader scale? Does it really apply in all times and in all places and with all people groups?

Exhaustive statements of faith, carefully constructed apologetics in defense of the gospel, theological arguments dissecting the various possibilities of how justification can be explained, adamant affirmations of the authority of Scripture, and even the power of the gospel are all important, necessary, and foundational. But what happens when there is a puzzling divide between our intellectual declarations about the gospel among the redeemed and our practical proclamation of the gospel among the nations? Why is there such a wide gap between what we profess to be true and what we intend to do with that truth? Two issues present themselves as potential explanations for this disconnect.

First, we may not be as certain about the exclusive nature of the gospel as we claim. Under some circumstances, when forced to say so, a substantial number of believers cave in when asked if they think that everyone apart from saving faith in Jesus Christ stands condemned before God. The surrounding culture has so conditioned us to be politically correct in what we say that we compromise our convictions about the gospel when confronted with the direct question about those who have never responded by faith to the gospel. Not wanting to sound narrow, too often the answers we offer back away from stating what our official doctrines affirm and what we say the Bible teaches. So do we believe that every human being is a sinner in desperate need of a Savior or not? And do we believe that every one dying apart from the forgiving grace of Jesus Christ is forever lost, condemned to everlasting punishment, or not?[6] If we hesitate to admit in debate and informal dialogue what we affirm in doctrine and formal declarations of our faith, we cannot hope to be captivated by watered-down appeals to enlist people to go tell the world that they may or may not be lost apart from Christ.

If we have lost our convictions, then we need to return to the unchanging truth and get reacquainted with the glory of God in the gospel of Jesus Christ. Until then, if we somehow just hope it will all work out for those who have never heard, we will never form any attachment to the heart God demonstrates for lost people in His command for us to go and tell the whole world the good news. Nothing less than an earnest conviction that Jesus Christ is the only way of salvation will provide sufficient motivation to take His message to the ends of the earth.

In a similar vein, doubts about the power of the gospel plague the church in what we believe will actually be accomplished when the message is simply proclaimed. Do we have confidence that there is sufficient power from on high that accompanies the word of Christ to break through the barriers that normally would thwart the effectiveness of the life-changing truth of the gospel? Paul made clear that he had no such doubts, nor was he in any way embarrassed to tell anyone the truth about Jesus Christ. In Romans 1:16, he wrote, "For I am not ashamed of the gospel, because it is God's power for salvation to everyone who believes, first to the Jew, and also to the Greek." We need a generation of men and women who believe that God's power does back up the declarations of His truth in Christ. On one of our college ministry's beach outreaches, our students came back amazed by what happened. Accompanying the students on the trip was a veteran pastor, a man over seventy years old, spending his time with college students and sharing Christ during spring break at the beach! As they watched him lead one after another to faith in Christ, one of the kids observed, "When he shares the gospel, he *expects* people to respond!" In cross-cultural settings, we have to believe that when Paul said, "To the Jew first and also to the Greek," he anticipated the hesitation among many in the church over the years who would question whether there is sufficient power in the word to transcend all obstacles to faith in Christ.

By affirming the power of the gospel, we do not nullify the need to prepare a sound and persuasive explanation of what God has said and done through Christ. We still have to be "ready to give a defense to anyone who asks you for a reason for the hope that is in you. However, do this with gentleness and respect" (1 Pet. 3:15–16). But we can have every confidence that the message itself brings conviction when we act as witnesses for Christ and allow the Holy Spirit to accomplish what we never can. Bold proclamation begins with trusting assurance that there is power in the message.

Second, we may not be as concerned about the eternal destiny of unbelieving people as we would like to think we are. The missing element is love, love that takes action and refuses to be confined to rhetoric. Without a God-given, inspired love for others, we cannot work up enough of our own compassion to care that people we do not know will be lost forever without the life-transforming good news about Jesus Christ. If we can keep our view of the world to nameless, faceless, meaningless people, our cool, detached response to their spiritual condition will remain indifferent. But if we allow our hearts to engage at a personal level and begin to see each face as an individual created in the image of God, each life as an unfolding story that will end in tragedy or glory, our indifference cannot help give way to a loving concern for and compassionate connection with potential brothers and sisters with whom we might share an eternal home.

Whether our theology is wavering or our compassion is weak, those of us who love Christ cannot compromise our convictions by neglecting the masses of people whose lives are desperately hopeless until they have opportunity to respond to His offer of new life by faith in His name.

5. General Spiritual Apathy. With all the other issues, we have to factor in the general lack of commitment so common in churches around the nation. A condition of spiritual anemia has left the body of Christ looking for someone to step up and lead the way, to see if anyone will overcome the lethargic spiritual attitude that characterizes too many who profess faith in Christ. When statistics reveal that 20 percent of the members do 80 percent of the ministry in most churches, no one seems alarmed or disturbed. What that means is that a significant number of those who say they follow Christ are in reality living essentially secular lives, knowing and understanding the call of Christ to biblical discipleship but allowing a disconnect to persist between faith expressed and faith practiced.

With that situation dominating the landscape in so many churches, is it any wonder that the kind of extraordinary sacrifice involved in the pursuit of missions is only rarely found? From basic biblical stewardship to consistent intercessory prayer to compassionate and fervent evangelism to daily time in the Word of God—when these things are missing from the daily disciplines of church members, missions has a hard time fighting its way to the surface. How can we expect to see the nations gathered under the lordship of Christ when we are not even sure how to see our own lives surrendered to His lordship? Should we expect a response to the call to missions from the same people who have only a marginal commitment to the call to serve Christ in their own homes, churches, and communities?

Practical Implications for the Church

As we come to grips with these issues acting as barriers, or deterrents, to fulfilling the Great Commission, change has to take place if the culture of missions in the local church is to take root in any meaningful way. Business as usual has not been effective in developing a missions mentality among the vast majority of churches in the United States. Therefore, if anything is going to be different, steps will need to be taken to make the necessary shifts toward a Christ-centered, biblically focused, Spirit-led missions mind-set in our churches.

1. A Principle-Based Approach. As with every aspect of our ministry, each part of our calling should be defined and developed according to the biblical principles which impact that particular ministry. When we look at the missions calling of the church, we realize that the Bible is filled with instructions and examples, exhortations and encouragements, to make Christ known among the nations.

One of the primary roles of pastors is to teach and equip the people under his care so that they are prepared to walk humbly and faithfully in doing the will of Jesus Christ. As that role is accomplished, the people will come face-to-face with the priority of missions in God's plan. That will then press the question: If God has made missions such a priority, why do we not devote more of our life together as a congregation in the pursuit of what is clearly one of His passions? So for missions to ascend to prominence in people's minds and gain the priority position it has in Scripture, we as pastors must step up to our responsibility to teach, equip, encourage, challenge, pray, and send members of our own families and congregations out among the people of the world who need to know Christ. If we do not make it a priority of our ministry, why should they?

Once it has assumed its place as a priority in the life of our churches, it will become apparent that without a strategic plan you will waste a lot of time, energy, and momentum. Therefore, develop a missions strategy based on the principles you find in Scripture as to where and how you will focus your attention in reaching beyond your own borders with the gospel. We have found that we need to shape our missions focus strategically so we do not spread our efforts too thin. Yet at the same time, we recognize our need to give proportional emphasis to the Acts 1:8 triad— Jerusalem, Judea and Samaria, and then to the uttermost parts of the world. A strategy that fails to take into consideration any one of those becomes unbalanced and one dimensional. The strategy you develop helps shape the precision of your effort and allows you to focus your ministry funds and personnel in specific ways. Of course the strategy will include more than just where. It will anticipate questions as to how, when, how much it will cost, who will go and how they will be challenged and identified, and a host of other recurring questions concerning your focus. A principle-based approach to missions will give you both the biblical priority and the strategic clarity to keep missions before the church in a healthy way.

2. A Sending Mentality. Strange as it may be, many churches who consider themselves strong supporters of missions seldom measure the level of their willingness to be a sending church. If we have it right, the commission to make disciples requires a commitment to go. And how will they go if they are not sent? Missions as an emphasis in a local church demands the cultivation and development of this sending mentality in at least three areas:

- *We need to send our best people, not the marginal ones.* At some point the idea emerged that only those who were not suited to successful ministries locally were the primary candidates for missions. The suggestion that such an unstated assumption existed should make us shudder at the thought. Both the example of Scripture and demanding realities of what is required of those being sent to the ends of the earth stand together to denounce such a strange notion. When we begin to think of who should go, our first thought will always have to be one of self-examination and personal surrender to see if the Lord might have chosen us to go. Before we can give thought to sending someone else, we first have to ask Him if He wants us. Then as we pray and lay out the challenge to our churches, we do not look to those whose gifts are meager, whose effectiveness is limited, or whose influence for Christ is minimal. We look for the best available and ask the Lord to allow us to have a part in sending them. When the church in Antioch prayed and asked the Lord whom to send, they understood correctly when He led them to set apart Saul and Barnabas, their primary teachers and leaders! Dare we hold back our best for ourselves when the demands of the call to missions deserve those who can serve Christ in the best possible manner.

- *We need to send our best funds, not the leftovers.* How does your church decide on what to give in the area of missions? Recently I have discovered that many congregations place nearly everything else in their budget in line ahead of missions. After all their local priorities are addressed, if anything is left over, then at the end of their fiscal year, that portion can be contributed to support missions. Many of these same churches would be quick to complain about the failure of their members to practice biblical stewardship in the gift of their tithes and offerings, but do not recognize that their own practices fail in setting a good example! If a church wants its members to be faithful in sacrificial giving, the priority given to missions giving should demonstrate what that kind of giving looks like first. We are called as individuals to give firstfruits when we give, not what is left—if anything. The same priority must be given to missions giving in the allocation of our financial resources as a church.

- *We need to give our best attention, not our afterthoughts.* If a church wants to develop a missions mind-set throughout the congregation, they must give it a place of consistent emphasis at the time members join and all year long every year after that. A missiological mind-set must be evident in the vision of the church, the content of the prayers in corporate worship and in small groups, the ordering of the annual calendar of the church, the annual ministry plans presented to the congregation, and the reports that come back from the implementation of the plan. Keeping missions in front of the church reminds everyone that this calling cannot be relegated to the bench until the last few moments of the game. Missions thinking, strategizing, giving, sending, and challenging should be such an integral part of the life of a church that it would feel empty and incomplete without it.

When we choose active obedience in the area of missions, we cannot go halfway. God's calling deserves God's best resources so we find great satisfaction in accepting the role of a sending and going people among a praying and giving people.

An Eternal Purpose Restores and Energizes Missions

One of the challenges facing many churches is how to achieve and maintain a level of passion for missions over the long haul. The occasional missions emphasis and spotlighting devastating human needs around the world succeed in motivating people for a while, but sustaining an appeal to the emotions and heartstrings wears thin, and people eventually can develop an immunity to the pleas. Compassion is a wonderful gift from the Lord, but that alone will not be sufficient to keep us on task in fulfilling the Great Commission. We need a great, more satisfying purpose that compels us even when we are not aware of the immediate needs of others—something that burns in our hearts all the time, not just when we are "guilted into" a feeling that we should do something! The more I understand of God's eternal purposes, the more I see that I embrace missions more fully and comprehensively as a way of life as a Christian when I do not anchor it in human need but in God's glory.

The greatest and most compelling reason to engage in missions is that God is glorified when we do what He has called us to do! Compassion for the lost is a great purpose and leads many into missions involvement, but a passion for the glory of God in all the earth is an unending source of motivation, inspiration, and consistency in making the name of Jesus Christ known to everyone everywhere! Compassion for the lost is a great reason to engage in leading your church to be a missions-focused church, but the greater glory of Jesus Christ is *the* reason to make it your highest honor and greatest desire to do all that He has commanded us to do.

We must keep the priority of missions intact, the proportional emphasis on missions in balance, and the purpose of mission in perspective if we hope to stay on point as missions-focused congregations.

1. Norman Hillyer, "Tribe (*fulh*)," *NIDNTT*, Vol. 3 (Grand Rapids, MI: Zondervan, 1978), 871.

2. Another young woman was just reported killed in the international news as I write. Her story is all too familiar. She was a Christian serving the people of Afghanistan in charity work and the radical group, the Taliban, decreed that she must be killed for influencing the people to take seriously the love of Christ as practiced by her. A leading official in India was arrested for fomenting violence against Christians in the state of Orissa, and intimidating local police officials into doing nothing to quell the attacks. Those two accounts have been reported in the news media in just the past twenty-four hours.

3. Any church committed to that progression of evangelism person to person, "each one reach one," would find that the congregation would double each year if everyone committed to reach just one other person for Christ each year.

4. Based on data from the Web site of U.S. Center for World Missions. *The Amazing Countdown Facts*, compiled and written by Ralph D. Winter, Phil Bogosian, Larry Boggan, Frank Markow, and Wendell Hyde, http://www.uscwm.org/mobilization_division/resources/resources.html.

5. Fanny J. Crosby, "Blessed Assurance."

6. Much to my dismay, I was actually present at a meeting when a preacher stated confidently that our task in missions and ministry was simply to tell people that they are *already* saved. In his view, everyone is already in God's family and only needs to be informed of that fact. No faith required, no repentance or forgiveness necessary, not even an acknowledgement that God exists—just tell everyone they are already just fine! What a radical contradiction of the gospel!

CHAPTER 6 THE VALUE OF MISSIONS MODELS FROM THE PAST

D id the modern church just discover missions? Has the missions mandate always been about the kingdom? If that is true, and the biblical evidence supports that it is, then missions has a history of over two thousand years. Apart from an occasional sermon illustration at a missions conference, most Christians have little knowledge and even less intellectual or emotional connection with much of the godly heritage of missions preceding our arrival on the scene here at the beginning of the twenty-first century. As one would expect, there have been down times over the centuries when the church virtually dropped out of the race to win the nations for Christ. Little if any record can be found of her ventures into the unreached parts of the world to carry the gospel. Of course, some of that can be traced to the absence of much gospel witness within the church itself. A renewed commitment to missions always starts with a renewed interest in the gospel, a gracious response to the gospel, and a compelling vision of Christ in the gospel.

Rather than chronicle the failures of the church over the centuries and assess the forces at work to undermine the integrity of the body of Christ, the factors contributing to the decline and corruption of her soul, the purpose of this chapter is to reach back and discover periods of great advance for the gospel. We want to be aware of what can produce deadness and lethargy toward the command of Christ to take the gospel to the nations but focus instead on those influences and dynamics at work when the church was particularly effective in reaching out to introduce Jesus Christ to a world without hope.

Therefore, we ask what common denominators we can find over the course of missions history that can inform our agenda today and offer encouragement to our efforts. The promises of God in His Word give us all we need. Yet remembering how those promises worked out in the lives of those who have gone before us can be profitable for those of us longing for an awakening and strengthening of missionary zeal in our generation.

Before we look at specific cases, from Antioch to America, a brief overview of what those common denominators are should provide a helpful context for our journey into the past. What factors played a role when the church had the greatest impact in missions? Just to name a few, whether we take a look at the birth of modern missions with William Carey in the late eighteenth century, a study of the first international efforts going out from the church in Antioch in the first century, or a review of the forces at work in the resurgence of interest in missions in our day, many consistent elements are shared by all, just as you would expect:

- Power from on high as the Holy Spirit's work flowed freely
- A passion for Christ
- Prevailing prayer
- A rich soaking in the Scriptures and sound doctrine
- Unwavering faith that trusts God to be faithful in all things
- Holiness and purity of life (together with deep repentance and an abhorrence of sin)
- Eyes willing to see and have compassion on others
- A supportive, sacrificial, and generous sending community
- Persecution and opposition

These and many other factors appear in every movement God has stirred up among His people when they believed His promises, obeyed His commands, and went where He sent them, proclaimed what He told them and gave others what He gave them.[1] Obviously this is not intended to be an exhaustive list but representative of the circumstances in which missions thrives among any people, regardless of the century or the geography or the culture. Not all of the missions movements were strong in all areas equally, but the more of these factors present and in force, the more effective and lasting their impact for missions seems to have been. The more these dynamics came into play, the greater the reach of missions moved and prospered in seeing people come to know and worship Jesus Christ.

In the following pages we will look at the biblical model for each of these nine criteria for becoming an effective church where missions shapes the mission. The first four form a foundation of fundamentals needed for any endeavor to glorify and honor the Lord. Once they have been developed within the culture of the ministry, as the people mature, the practical implications of these four lead to the development of the next five which will be presented in the following chapter.

After looking at the biblical model for each, we will then see how some of these characteristics contributed to the growth of missions in various historical contexts over the centuries.

Power from on High

In a conversation with Nicodemus in John 3, Jesus said that no one can see the kingdom unless he is born again. Confused by this statement, Nicodemus asks, "How can anyone be born when he is old?" (v. 4). The response Jesus gave at that point has led to many debates and disagreements but the simple explanation was, "Whatever is born of flesh is flesh, whatever is born of the Spirit is spirit" (v. 6). Each of us is born according to the flesh when we come into this world. But only by putting our trust in Christ and believing in His name can we be born of the Spirit. Until that happens, we are spiritually dead with no capacity for understanding or living out the new life Jesus gives because that life is spiritual, available only in those who have been born of the Spirit.

New life in Christ is the life of the Spirit at work in us. He makes us alive and empowers us in a way only He can. Therefore, Jesus took time to address His disciples one last time in the Upper Room before He was crucified to prepare them for what was still to come. Following Him wherever He went and going wherever He sent them was not a matter of personal discipline and determination. What awaits every one of His disciples is a path that cannot be followed without a power and strength from beyond us.

> And I will ask the Father, and He will give you another Counselor to be with you forever. He is the Spirit of truth. The world is unable to receive Him because it doesn't see Him or know Him. But you do know Him, because He remains with you and will be in you. . . . I have spoken these things to you while I remain with you. But the Counselor, the Holy Spirit—the Father will send Him in My name—will teach you all things and remind you of everything I have told you. (John 14:16–17, 25–26)

> I am the vine; you are the branches. The one who remains in Me and I in him produces much fruit, because you can do nothing without me. (John 15:5)

> Nevertheless, I am telling you the truth. It is for your benefit that I go away, because if I don't go away the Counselor will not come to you. If I go, I will send Him to you. (John 16:7)

The fact that Jesus was no longer going to be with them had still not connected with His disciples, but Jesus prepared them by teaching them that One would come who would never leave them but would dwell within them—not just alongside them but actually inside them. Such a notion was beyond their ability to comprehend at this point, but this truth became critical in the days just following His resurrection.

In two distinct encounters with His disciples after He rose from the dead, Jesus anticipated one of two responses from those who loved Him and wanted to live for Him. Either they would be so discouraged by His departure that they would give up and go back to the life they had before they met Jesus; or, perhaps worse, they would try preaching and teaching a good way to live but without the power and authority of the One who spoke as no one ever had before. How pitiful either of those courses of action would have been!

So Jesus precludes such things by telling them to do something that was counterintuitive. He told them to wait—to do nothing right away but to stay where they were, together in Jerusalem. But He wanted them to wait with a purpose, to receive the promise He had been making all along.

> Then He opened their minds to understand the Scriptures. He also said to them, "This is what is written: the Messiah would suffer and rise from the dead the third day, and repentance for forgiveness of sins would be proclaimed in His name to all the nations, beginning at Jerusalem. You are witnesses of these things. And look, I am sending you what My Father promised. As for you, stay in the city until you are empowered from on high." (Luke 24:45–49)

In the first part of this statement, Jesus reiterated what He had already said to them and gave them the Great Commission again. But now there is a difference—all the difference! No longer would their success in proclaiming His name be tied to their skills as eloquent speakers and convincing apologists. Until they were "empowered from on high," they could do nothing of eternal consequence; but after receiving the promised Holy Spirit, look out! The empowering presence of the Holy Spirit takes a message of marginal interest and infuses it with fire, igniting the hearts and minds of those who are awakened to its truth. So much that passes for ministry and missions in our day lacks the one component that would awaken spiritually dead people and give them radically new life! The mechanics of ministry and missions, no matter how sophisticated or clever, how imaginative or relevant, cannot overcome the absence of power from on high. Just before His ascension to heaven, Jesus once again sets forth the terms of engagement for those who would follow Him: "But you will receive power when the Holy Spirit has come upon you, and you will be My witnesses in Jerusalem, in all Judea and Samaria, and to the ends of the earth" (Acts 1:8).

Every movement blessed by God in the history of missions has begun with the power of the Holy Spirit being poured out upon and through those He chooses to use. Many organized efforts have failed without any logical explanation. Gifted people have fallen flat when everyone just knew they would find great favor and effectiveness. Well-funded and fully staffed endeavors have accomplished nothing even though, according to the wisdom of the world, they should have flourished. But any hope of success in missions depends entirely on the empowering presence of the Holy Spirit, clothing His people with power from on high and carrying the truth of His Word straight to the hearts of those who hear with such penetrating capacity that it pierces the soul and produces reverence, awe, and conviction. So you can count on it, every major move of God to produce a resurgence of missions passion begins with the people being clothed with power from on high.

A Passion for Christ

Once the beauty of Christ has captured our hearts, the glory of Christ has left us in awe, and the grace of Christ has won our love, motivating us to tell others about Him does not take much! When our passion for Jesus Christ takes over, we gladly embrace His lordship and accept His instructions. To hear Paul speak of Christ, the compelling love he has for Him explains so much of his motivation for going to the nations with the gospel so that others might discover his greatest treasure. The familiar language of 2 Corinthians 5 regarding our calling to be ambassadors for Christ, appealing and imploring people to be reconciled to God, flows out of Paul's description of Christ in the previous chapter. Because of his passion for the beauty and glory and wonder of Christ, Paul could never be silent about Him, nor could he be satisfied staying home in Antioch cultivating a personal, private, deeper knowledge of Him while the nations had yet to hear of Him.

> The god of this age has blinded the minds of the unbelievers so they cannot see the light of the gospel of the glory of Christ, who is the image of God. For we are not proclaiming ourselves but Jesus Christ as Lord, and ourselves as your slaves because of Jesus. For God, who said, "Light shall shine out of darkness"—He has shone in our hearts to give the light of the knowledge of God's glory in the face of Jesus Christ. Now we have this treasure in clay jars, so that this extraordinary power may be from God and not from us. (2 Cor. 4:4–7)

When the motive for missions arises from a *sense of guilt* that we ought to do more to help people in need, that may suffice for a while as long as our compassion holds steady. When the motive is *gratitude* to do something good for God as a way to "pay Him back" for His mercy on us, all we are demonstrating is that we do not really understand grace. When the motive is to *impress* others with the depth of our commitment to Christ, the superficiality of that needs no comment. When the motive is to *produce humanitarian change* through a better way of living, the success will only be temporal and not eternal.

The only impetus that will sustain a missions movement is an overwhelming love for Christ and a passion for His glory to be made known as widely as possible. Until He is our most valued treasure, as He was for Paul, His message will be no more than a logical explanation of how people can escape God's judgment, not an impassioned introduction to the infinitely radiant splendor of seeing, loving, and knowing Jesus Christ.

Until Christ is our priceless treasure and His beauty fills our souls, all efforts to worship or serve or obey Him will be like half-filled cups trying hard to overflow. Obeying His commands to make disciples of all nations flows freely only when our love for Christ overflows fully. Therefore, sending churches must be savoring churches that adore Christ as most precious. As we learn to "taste and see that the LORD is good" (Ps. 34:8), the delight we find will lead us to savor and be satisfied with all that He is. The impact on missions, then, is substantial. People will not rally to action until they have learned how to rest in adoration. "I have asked one thing from the LORD; it is what I desire: to dwell in the house of the LORD all the days of my life, gazing on the beauty of the LORD and seeking Him in His temple" (Ps. 27:4).

When Christ has become everything to us, nothing else holds the value to us that it once did, nor can it keep us in its power the way it once did. As long as Christ simply holds a place in our affections but not the highest place, we will be content to acknowledge Him but never committed to forsake all for Him. "More than that, I also consider everything to be a loss in view of the surpassing value of knowing Christ Jesus my Lord. Because of Him I have suffered the loss of all things and consider them filth, so that I may gain Christ" (Phil. 3:8).

History records a few occasions of what happened when Christ became the "surpassing value" in someone's life. One of the most memorable accounts is the story of Hudson Taylor, an Englishman whose love for Christ led him to choose a radical direction for his life so that he could make himself completely available to follow His Savior without hesitation. If you have had any exposure to the history of missions in the modern era, more than likely you have heard of Taylor and his groundbreaking labors for Christ in China at the end of the nineteenth century. By his death in 1905, more than 205 mission stations had been established all over China through the efforts of this man for whom Christ was more than the centerpiece in a message of salvation but was the compelling passion of His life. What would motivate a young man to do what he did? What would prompt a twenty-one-year-old medical student in England to leap at the chance to suspend his training and board a ship for Shanghai where he fully expected to live and die for Christ?

In a biographical work by Dr. Howard Taylor, second son of Hudson Taylor, some of those answers may be found.

What was the secret, we may well ask, of such a life? Hudson Taylor had many secrets, for he was always going on with God, yet they were but one—the simple, profound secret of drawing for every need, temporal or spiritual, upon "the fathomless wealth of Christ. . . ." We want, we need, we may have Hudson Taylor's secret and his success, for we have Hudson Taylor's Bible and his God.[2]

Later in the book, Taylor describes the work God did to enlarge his heart and increase his capacity to love Christ and trust Him more. As a young man, he had come to know Jesus Christ and soon learned what a glorious and wonderful a Savior He is. In his journal he wrote of an afternoon encounter with the Lord which characterized so much of his spiritual life:

> Well do I remember how in the gladness of my heart I poured out my soul before God. Again and again confessing my grateful love to Him who had done everything for me, who had saved me when I had given up all hope and even desire for salvation, I besought Him to give me some work to do for Him as an outlet for love and gratitude. . . .
>
> Well do I remember as I put myself, my life, my friends, my all upon the altar, the deep solemnity that came over my soul with the assurance that my offering was accepted. The presence of God became unutterably real and blessed, and I remember . . . stretching myself on the ground and lying there before Him with unspeakable awe and unspeakable joy. For what service I was accepted I knew not, but a deep consciousness that I was not my own took possession of me which never since [has] been effaced. . . .
>
> I saw Him and I sought Him, I had Him and I wanted Him.[3]

The more I have read of the deep affection Taylor had for Christ, the more I see what stirred his heart. For those to whom Christ is radiantly beautiful and a person of infinite worth, the gladness and joy that comes from learning what He desires and doing it without pause is of inestimable value. When the opportunity to leave for China came, it appeared at an inopportune time—before his medical training was complete. But depending, as he had learned to do, on the leading of the Lord, Hudson Taylor prepared for the service God had put on his heart. Even though he had placed himself in rigorous training and had somewhat isolated himself from dependency on his family, the reality of his departure appears to have hit home as indicated in a letter he wrote to his mother just prior to the time he must leave for China:

> If I should be accepted to go at once, would you advise me to come home before sailing? I long to be with you once more, and I know you would naturally wish to see me; but I almost think it would be easier for us not to meet, than having met to part again forever. No, not forever! . . .
>
> I cannot write more, but hope to hear from you as soon as possible. Pray much for me. It is easy to talk of leaving all for Christ, but when it comes to the proof—it is only as we stand "complete in Him" we can go through with it. God be with you and bless you, my own dear Mother, and give you so to realize the preciousness of Jesus that you may wish for nothing but "to know Him" . . . even in "the fellowship of His sufferings."[4]

As I read that, I find that my heart as a parent cannot separate my emotions from the pain his mother and father must have experienced to see him go, knowing that they might never see him again in this world. However, do you hear the degree of confidence he has in the sufficiency of Christ, not just for himself but for his parents? Speaking of forsaking all out of love for Christ is one thing, but when the time comes for that proof, he reminds his parents that the "preciousness of Jesus" will be more than enough to see them through. When their hearts ache with longing to see their son, when his heart aches with loneliness on the other side of the world, the sufficiency and splendor of Christ must be so real, so tangible, so personal that all will be able to stand firm having been made "complete in Him."

Nearly ten years ago our oldest son flew to South Korea to spend ten weeks teaching during his summer break from college. When he was about the same age as our son, Hudson Taylor spent five months on board a ship making his journey to China while our son spent only the better part of two days flying to his destination. Rather than have to wait for months to hear from him by mail, he was able to call us the night he arrived and assure us that he had made it. From the home of his Korean hosts, he wanted to let us know that all was well (even though their limited English reduced their early communication to a lot of nodding, bowing, and smiling!). We were thrilled to hear his voice, and then it happened— that catch in his voice stifling a little emotion welling up from within. When he almost choked up, I was "done in" for a moment realizing that Christ would have to be enough for him since there was nothing I could do, no way I could be there for him inside of two days of travel, and no reason to think that what I had to offer could compare with the lessons to be learned of the "preciousness of Jesus" when we learn to stand complete in Him. So to read that letter from Hudson Taylor to his mother connects my heart to theirs, across the decades and the circumstances, to unite us at a place unlike any other. Christ is every bit as awesome and precious and has the same surpassing value today for you and me as He did then for them.

Who would dare venture forth to the ends of the earth with the gospel of Christ if the glory of Christ has not captured your heart? But for those who have learned that He really is all we need, nothing else matters but to give Him all that we are. So one last look at Hudson Taylor's heart in 1854 and we move on to the next point. In a letter to his sister, Amelia, just before leaving, his passion for Christ shines through so brilliantly that his extreme devotion to his missionary calling makes more sense to modern, indulgent Christians who need what Christ offers and what Taylor had.

> When we look at ourselves, at the littleness of our love, the barrenness of our service and the small progress we make toward perfection, how soul-refreshing it is to turn away to Him; to plunge afresh in the "fountain opened for sin and for uncleanness"; to remember that we are "accepted in the beloved" . . . "who of God is made unto us wisdom, and

righteousness, and sanctification, and redemption." Oh! the fullness of Christ, the fullness of Christ.[5]

Such a passion for Christ and a confidence in His worthiness, the unspeakable awe and joy he felt in His presence were all Hudson Taylor needed to give His entire life in serving Christ by taking the gospel to the people of China.

Prevailing Prayer

Christ Himself established prayer as a precedent for missions. "Then He said to His disciples, 'The harvest is abundant, but the workers are few. Therefore, pray to the Lord of the harvest to send out workers into His harvest'" (Matt. 9:37–38). Whenever the church joins together to pray for God to send workers, He does. The more mature a congregation, the more that maturity is demonstrated in selfless, sustained, even systematic prayer for missions. When our concerns are kingdom concerns instead of self-focused concerns, our prayer life will reflect a growing desire for all that brings delight to the heart of God. In his book on prayer, Gardiner Spring speaks of prayer as the "language of desire."[6] In other words, prayer serves to showcase whatever is on our hearts and reflect whatever drives our passions. If we do not pray consistently and fervently for the nations, pray for workers for the harvest, pray for the reach of the gospel, pray for Christ's glory to be made known in all the earth, we have every reason to believe that none of those things has made it to a place of prominence in what we long for and truly desire.

In the model prayer Jesus instructs us to pray for the coming of the kingdom, "Your kingdom come" (Matt. 6:10), followed by a prayer for our daily bread. One could easily draw the conclusion that for Christ, the natural desires we have for God to provide daily bread should parallel the desire we have to see His kingdom extended throughout the earth. Even at the beginning of the Psalms, the Lord tells us to pray for the nations when He said, "Ask of Me, and I will make the nations Your inheritance and the ends of the earth Your possession" (Ps. 2:8).

Prayer that captivates our hearts and consumes our desires arises from deep conviction and fervent love for the will of the Father. So when He burdens a people with a longing to pray for missions, He lights a fire that is not easily extinguished. Churches and their people begin to pray, then to give, and then to go. That pattern has been repeated often over the centuries as God keeps lifting our eyes to see all that He has prepared for us and wants to do in and through us. Prevailing prayer always precedes great missions movements.

The first missions endeavor on record emerged from a period of worship, prayer and fasting among the members of the church in Antioch. Actually, the initial followers of Christ took Him seriously when He told them to stay in Jerusalem until they were "empowered from on high."

As the book of Acts begins, they were gathered together in prayer, waiting for the promise of the Holy Spirit. Christ had made the promise that the Holy Spirit would come and empower them to be His witnesses, but that promise did not relieve them of the need to pray and ask the Lord for the fulfillment of His word. So prayer preceded the sending of the Holy Spirit, the development of a vital, witnessing community of worshippers called the church, the first evangelistic outreach of that church on the Day of Pentecost in Jerusalem, and the introduction of a kingdom vision in the hearts and minds of the earliest disciples. Although in the early months, the new church was content to stay right where they were in Jerusalem and the flavor of their ministry was decidedly sectarian because it did not move far from its Jewish roots in the synagogue and with strict adherence to the law. Still, they prayed, they preached, and they served as the Lord built a community of faith that was born by grace and sustained in that grace by the power of prayer.

If you are familiar with the history of modern missions, you are already aware of the way God chose to work through a group of men and women in the early eighteenth century from the regions then known as Bohemia and Moravia (modern-day Czech Republic and Slovakia). After centuries of persecution, dating back before the martyrdom of John Hus and many others in 1415,[7] attempts to find a peaceful home to practice their faith in many other locations, a small remnant of believers were finally offered asylum on the estate of Count Nicholas Louis von Zinzendorf near Berthelsdorf, Germany, in 1722.

These members of the Moravian church, the *Unitas Fratrum*, or "Unity of Brethren" as they were originally named in 1547, fled continued persecution from agents of the Roman church and the rulers of Bohemia and Moravia. A small community began to emerge on the estate that became a haven of religious freedom for them and was soon called Hernnhut, the Lord's Watch, or the place God will guard. During the next few years, as the numbers swelled, many from other theological perspectives added diversity to the community, but a diversity that led to distrust and conflict over time. Rather than sit by and watch the work of the Lord be fractured by contentions, Count Zinzendorf, a young man of only twenty-seven, prayed and asked the Lord to use him to bring healing and unity. He visited, prayed for, and prayed with every family in the community and at a special Communion service on August 13, 1727, God did a mighty work by His Spirit. People who had suffered from broken relationships were reunited. Old wounds were forgiven, and a spirit of repentance and brokenness swept through the community in a way that could only be attributed to the Holy Spirit. Prevailing prayer had preceded this outpouring, and now in the aftermath of such a gracious work of the Lord, the people determined to continue in prayer.

What followed is nothing short of miraculous. The "Brethren" began the "Hourly Intercession," a plan for every hour of the day and night to find at least two members of the community in prayer. Little did they know with that small start that these hourly prayer times would continue for more than one hundred years. Think of it! Pairs of believers were praying around the clock for one hundred years!

The result? Well, initially the results were felt within the community itself as people were on fire in their love for Christ and one another. But fervent, persistent prayer will always find its way into a passion for what is on God's heart. So yes, God put the nations on their hearts as well, and within four years two young men from Hernnhut sensed that God was calling them to take the gospel to the slaves of the West Indies. As John Greenfield's 1927 book, *Power from on High*, describes what took place, he quotes Evelyn Hasse: "Prayer of that kind always leads to action. In this case it kindled a burning desire to make Christ's Salvation known to the heathen. It led to the beginning of Modern Foreign Missions. From that one small village community more than one hundred Missionaries went out in twenty-five years. You will look in vain elsewhere for anything to match it in anything like the same extent."[8]

Prevailing prayer stirs the heart and opens our eyes to see what God sees, to love what He loves and to long for what He longs for. Spending time in the presence of One who loves and seeks the nations cannot help but be contagious. In the examples of the Scriptures and the Moravians, prayer ignited a missionary movement. The same is true for today. We cannot expect to see godly results if we do not employ godly means. If we want to see a resurgence in the sending posture of the church in our day, we must pray importunately—being shamelessly persistent in asking the Lord of the harvest to send forth laborers.

A Love for Truth

People can easily forget what you and I say. What they cannot disregard so easily is the powerful truth of God's Word. That is one of the reasons we place such a high priority on making the Bible available to those to whom we are sent. Missions depends on an authority source far greater than your word or mine if it transcends cultures and ages, races and nationalities. Debates about the worth of Scripture and the value of having a trustworthy message have left many confused people in the pews who have been asked to support the work of the church with no compelling reason. I remember hearing leading churchmen and scholars in the 1970s and 1980s declare that the resurgence of interest in upholding an infallible and inerrant Word was ill advised and without historical precedent. Their argument was simple: the church had never believed the Bible to be inerrant, and those who raised such concerns were in danger of the sin of bibliolatry. A flawed book filled with inconsistencies and errors, in their estimation, inspired confidence in the themes and lessons to be learned without having to believe it all to be true and treasured. One never finds that to be the case in any movement of God that resulted in a powerful outreach to the nations with the message of hope and truth in the gospel of Jesus Christ!

In the words of A. T. Pierson near the end of the nineteenth century, we hear a clear voice declaring why we love the truth of God's Word, when he said:

> And I pray you to notice that while we want to emphasize the human element in missions, God emphasizes the divine element. God's greatest missionary is not men, but it is the Book—the infallible Book; the Book that never grows old or weary, never needs a vacation, and never dies; the book that goes everywhere, and if it only speaks to every man in his own tongue wherein he was born, it becomes the living and immortal missionary of God.[9]

With the church in Ephesus, Paul not only did the work of an evangelist in leading many to become disciples of Jesus Christ, but he stayed among them for two years teaching them the Word of God. When he gathered the Ephesian elders at Miletus to leave them his parting sentiments and challenges, he reminded them that his ministry there had consisted largely of a ministry of the Word.

> I did not shrink back from proclaiming to you anything that was profitable, or from teaching it to you in public and from house to house. I testified to both Jews and Greeks about repentance toward God and faith in our Lord Jesus. (Acts 20:20–21)

For I did not shrink back from declaring to you the whole
plan of God. (Acts 20:27)

His missions passion was to anchor each church in the eternal
truth, and he knew that only a steady diet of biblical preaching
and teaching could accomplish that purpose. Later on in his
instructions to fellow missionary Timothy, he charged his young
friend with these words: "All Scripture is inspired by God and is
profitable for teaching, for rebuking, for correcting, for training in
righteousness, so that the man of God may be complete, equipped
for every good work. . . . Proclaim the message; persist in it whether
convenient or not; rebuke, correct, and encourage with great
patience and teaching" (2 Tim. 3:16–17; 4:2).

A missions calling does not send disciples of Jesus Christ to
the ends of the earth to share ideas and build rapport in order to
instill a higher social order. Missions sends people to the nations to
proclaim the truth of the Word of Christ so that they might come
to Him, put their faith in Him, and know Him and His glorious
salvation: "So faith comes from hearing, and hearing by the word of
Christ" (Rom. 10:17 NASB).

By accepting the responsibility and embracing the privilege of
taking the truth to the nations, everyone who goes needs to love
that truth as the accurate account of God's revelation of His own
nature and will. No church has prepared for the Great Commission
that has not first grounded its people in the immutable Word of
God. Then as we go, we proclaim the Word and allow the Holy
Spirit to make it alive in the hearts of those who hear so that the veil
is taken away, and the truth transforms by revealing the matchless
wonder of Christ!

Belief in the trustworthiness of the Bible builds faith. Love
for the God of the Bible inspires devotion. Confidence in the
power of the Bible generates boldness. Many revivals and missions
movements have been launched when the Word of God has
captured the affections and aspirations of a people and excited their
creativity and imagination to find new ways to take the hope of

Christ to the nations by making the Scriptures available to as many people as possible.

Such was the case with Watkins R. Roberts, a Welsh chemist in his early twenties back at the beginning of the twentieth century. In the midst of the Welsh Revival, God captured his heart and changed the course of his life and of millions of others for generations to come. A unique movement of the Lord swept through Wales during the years 1904-1906 with some estimates placing the number of new believers in the range of 150,000 people. Another young man, Evan Roberts, only twenty-six years old, had been praying for eleven years for a revival in his country. God chose to use him as the instrument through whom many thousands were transformed by the gospel of Jesus Christ. The impact of the revival was profound and extensive. Social structures felt the reverberations as so many thousands put their faith in Christ and into practice—pubs closed, debts were repaid, cursing and foul language were all but abandoned, and even the courts were closed for lack of criminal cases—it was an amazing demonstration of the power of God to take a simple message from His Word and change the course of people's lives. Starting with a meeting with young people in his own church, Evan Roberts traveled all over Wales and preached a four-part sermon, a basic biblical message he delivered frequently over the next couple of years:

1. Confess all known sin.
2. Deal with and get rid of anything "doubtful" in your life.
3. Be ready to obey the Holy Spirit instantly.
4. Confess Christ publicly.

Although the revival came to a conclusion after about two years, the long-term effects extended across the world and across the years. Several years ago I stayed in the home of a family in Wales and asked what they knew about the 1904 revival. Since it had taken place over eighty years earlier, I did not expect any personal connection but hoped they might have some stories to tell. The grandmother told me that she recalled in her early childhood years churches throughout Wales still referred back to those days and occasional "aftershocks" of revival continued during her younger days. Sitting in the balcony of her church as a little girl, she remembered church meetings when the power of Christ was so great that the entire room was filled with a sense of His presence, and people responded with great fervor and passion. Years had passed since the first waves had died down, but the strong movement of God was clearly not diminished in the church she knew as a little girl.

The impact of the revival not only reached across the years but also traveled around the world. While revival was sweeping Wales, the young man Watkins Roberts sensed that God was calling him to a work in India. Colonialism in the British Empire had created a troubling series of incidents in the nations where their dominion was building resentment among nationals. In one portion of northern India, British troops found themselves stymied by the resistance of tribal groups whose determination not to fall under the rule of outsiders created a dangerous situation for the occupation forces. Reports of the violence in the tribal regions came back to England, noting in particular the brutality involved in the ongoing conflicts.

Inspired by the revival in Wales and informed by the reports from India, Roberts responded by committing himself to extend the reach of the gospel to the tribes who were so violently opposed to the presence of the British strangers in their land. His plan was not complicated, nor did it require a large financial support base. He determined that he would travel to India, find someone who spoke the language and work with them to translate the Bible into the tribal languages. Such was his confidence in the power of the Scriptures, that he believed if he could just get the Bible into the hands of the people, they would want to know Christ and give their lives to Him.

His initial contacts in the tribal regions were with the Lushai tribesmen, and soon the Gospel of John had been translated into their language. As he waited on the Lord for the next step, the arrival of a simple gift of about twenty-five dollars from a woman back in England enabled Roberts to print several copies of the Gospel of John and send it to the chiefs of as many tribes as he could. The simple strategy was put into practice—provide the Word of God in the language of the people and let the Holy Spirit act through the power of the Scriptures.

One particularly hostile tribe was the Hmar people. They had been known to raid British-held tea plantations and kill as many people as possible—one raid resulting in the death and beheading of nearly five hundred! A copy of the Gospel of John was given to the chief of the Hmar; and with the help of a Lushai tribesman, he heard a translation of the Word prompting him to want to know more. Especially important to him was what this book said about being "born again." Against the warnings of the British military leaders in the region, Watkins Roberts accepted an invitation from the chief of one small Hmar village to come help him and his people understand more of what they had heard. Rather than losing his life at the hands of this violent people, Roberts soon had the joy of seeing the leaders of the Hmar come to know Christ through the powerful influence of Scripture.

One of the first to come to know Christ was a man named Chawnga. Through his new faith in the Lord, he saw the power of the Bible and the message it told and began to pray that his son would be used by the Lord to translate the Bible for the Hmar people. At age ten he told his son, Rochunga Pudaite, that when he was born, he had been dedicated to the Lord as one who would bring the Bible to many people. Chawnga took him to a high mountain and pointed to the horizon and, as Pudaite wrote later, "If I were to go to the next mountain, he told me, there would be another, then another beyond that, for the horizon never ends. 'God's love,' he assured me, 'will go with you, my son, beyond the horizon.'" Soon he was sent away to a mission school so that he could learn how to translate the Bible and make the Scriptures available to his people. While his father and other tribal preachers went throughout the region taking the Bible to the other villages, Pudaite studied and eventually played a part in answer to his father's prayer, his dream for his people. The impact of the Bible was extraordinary on their lives—far beyond their initial experience of coming to saving faith in Christ. Over the next generation the Hmar people became "one of the most advanced ethnic groups in all of India" according to Pudaite.

> Since the Hmars got the Bible they have become one of the most advanced ethnic groups in all of India. At least ninety-five percent are Christians, worshiping in over 200 churches. Except for Mr. Youngman (the name the tribe gave Watkins Robert because of his age when he came to them), the only missionary they have had is the Bible.[10]

The love for the truth of God's Word led a young man from Wales to take the Bible to a dangerous tribal group and let the power of the Word, attended to by the presence of the Spirit, do its work. The son of a tribal leader devoted his life to making the Scripture available to anyone, anywhere in the world as the horizons expanded far beyond the little villages of the Hmar people. In his book *My Billion Bible Dream*, Rochunga Pudaite explains his desire and his plan to send a Bible to every home in the world with an address listed in phone books of cities everywhere. After seeing what the truth did among his own people, in his own family, he decided to carry out the vision of taking the message of hope to the ends of the earth by getting the Bible into the hands of people who might not otherwise have access to God's Word.

Since it was founded in 1971, his organization, "Bibles for the World, Inc." has mailed more than fifteen million Bibles to addresses found in the phone books of nearly forty nations. In their primary focus area, northern India, they have also planted more than three hundred schools and churches during that same period. As of this writing, "Bibles for the World" is planning a special Scripture distribution back in the same regions in which his native tribe, the Hmar, lived to celebrate the one hundredth anniversary of the arrival of Watkins Roberts in 1910. When Roberts came, he brought with him a love for Christ, a love for His Word, and a love for people who need an opportunity to learn of the grace of God in Christ. One missionary with one book, the Bible, made the difference in the lives of untold thousands among the Hmar and from that small tribe to millions more around the world. The impact of that single act of obedience continues to make its mark among the nations as the Scriptures do what the Lord promises they will do: "So My word that comes from My mouth will not return to Me empty, but it will accomplish what I please, and will prosper in what I send it to do" (Isa. 55:11).

Love for the truth of God's Word stirs a passion for missions in the hearts of those who have experienced firsthand the liberating power of the gospel in the Word of God. What could happen if you are the next one God calls to embrace that passion? From Evan Roberts to Watkins Roberts to Chawnga to Rochunga Pudaite to millions of homes—and now to you who are reading this amazing story—God's Word makes the difference as the light of the truth of the gospel is made known through its God-breathed words.

These four characteristics of a missions-focused church will radically change the perspective of any congregation as they view their calling and purpose. Once these take root in the hearts and minds of the followers of Christ, missions will become a prominent desire and a priority effort in any church. When pastors and Christian leaders dare to emphasize the *importance of the power of the Holy Spirit, a passion for the beauty and glory of Jesus Christ, a faithful, fervent dependence on prevailing prayer and a growing confidence in and love for the Word of God,* they will not be able to contain the resulting enthusiasm for missions in their flocks!

----

1. "The ideal missionary must have four passions: A passion for the truth; a passion for Christ; a passion for the souls of men, and a passion for self-sacrificing." A. T. Pierson, *Ecumenical Missionary Conference, New York, 1900,* Vol. 2 (New York: American Tract Society, 1900), 328.

2. Dr. and Mrs. Howard Taylor, *Hudson Taylor's Spiritual Secret* (Chicago: Moody Publishers, 1989, 2009), 16.

3. Ibid., 20–22.

4. Ibid., 47–48.

5. Ibid., 49.

6. Gardiner Spring, *The Mercy Seat* (Morgan, PA: Soli Deo Gloria Publications, retypeset from the 1863 edition published in Glasgow, 2001), 2.

7. Hus preached in Prague each week at Bethlehem Chapel, a building capable of seating three thousand, and because of the power of his message of salvation by grace through faith in Christ, it was consistently filled. It also was dedicated to the proclamation of the truth in the Czech language, not Latin as the Roman Catholic church insisted. People longing for truth flocked to hear Hus, among them the king and queen of Bohemia. One can understand why the established church of Rome was threatened by his biblical messages and why they eventually branded him a heretic and burned him at the stake when you hear the essence of his message. He cried out to the throngs gathered in Bethlehem Chapel, "A man can receive the pardon of his sins only through the power of God and the merits of Christ. Let who will proclaim the contrary, let the pope or a bishop or a priest say, 'I forgive thy sins, I absolve thee from their penalty, I free thee from the pains of hell'—it is all in vain and helps thee nothing. God alone, I repeat, can forgive sins through Christ, and He pardons the penitent only." Quoted by Allen W. Schattschneider, *Through Five Hundred Years* (Bethlehem, PA: Comenius Press, 1956), 19.

8. John Greenfield, *Power from on High* (Warsaw, IN: John Greenfield, 1928), 26.

9. Pierson, *Ecumenical Missionary Conference*, 326.

10. Rochunga Pudaite, *My Billion Bible Dream* (Nashville, Camden, New York: Thomas Nelson Publishers, 1982), 14.

CHAPTER 7 **MARKS OF PAST MISSIONS MOVEMENTS**

When Providence Baptist Church began back in 1978, we were determined to lay a solid foundation for biblical ministry. Having observed many other church plants as well as seeing patterns develop in existing churches, we knew that without agreement upon some fundamental issues, we would find ourselves constantly addressing the recurring issues facing all churches. Therefore, we agreed upon and established each of the four foundational issues outlined in the previous chapter as fundamentals of our life together. By doing that, we avoided a host of concerns that are resolved effectively by an affirmation of the importance of aspiring to give practical expression to each one: *the centrality of Jesus Christ, the authority of the Scriptures, the need for the power of the Holy Spirit, and a thorough undergirding of life and ministry by prevailing prayer.* Without realizing it at the time, we were following a course that would lead us not only to become a church designed to fulfill God's purposes but also to be shaped by God's call to be engaged in missions. Once God anchored those commitments in the life of the church, the base was in place that would be necessary for building a kingdom-focused ministry.

Since each of those four foundations play such an important part in the spiritual health and vitality of a local church, it is not surprising to see them playing a critical role in every major movement in the history of missions. Previously we looked into each of those four foundational elements of a church seeking to fulfill its role in the greater work of the kingdom. In this chapter we want to explore five other criteria evident in unusual periods of missions intensity and progress in the life of a church.

An Unwavering Faith that Trusts God to Be Faithful in All Things

When the apostle Paul took the gospel to Corinth, he did so with a conviction on his heart. This Greek city was a prosperous center of international trade, and the new converts in the church could easily have contributed to support his labors among them. But Paul chose not to allow that. Whether he was concerned that they might confuse their support with the notion that they could claim credit for the work God was doing among them or Paul himself wanted to allow churches elsewhere to share in the blessing of investing in others, his reasons do not need to be understood. What is important to understand is that he had an unfailing certainty that God would provide everything necessary for His work to be funded and faithfully supported. In one of the most comprehensive statements in all of Scripture about God's trustworthy provision for those who labor in His name, Paul says, "And God is able to make all grace abound to you, so that always having all sufficiency in everything, you may have an abundance for every good deed" (2 Cor. 9:8 NASB).

With that truth resonating in his heart, Paul would not ask the Corinthians for anything but chose instead to rely on the ability of God Himself to make sure there was a sufficient supply for everything needed for an effective ministry to be carried on among them. In order for them to be encouraged to be generous themselves, Paul asks them to step up with gifts for the needs of the church in Jerusalem. Rather than developing pride in what they could do for themselves, they were asked to give generously for the sake of others so that God would get the greater glory as He prompted His people to support the work He was doing in other places. In doing this, Paul provided a model for missions support.

Although there are many ways to engage in going, sending, and supporting missionaries and missions causes, the two primary ways are through traditional organizational structures and through what has been loosely called "faith missions." The first way recruits candidates and trains them by appealing to the constituency most closely connected to the sending agency. For example, a denominational missions board would appeal to its colleges and theological schools as well as its churches to challenge men and women to embrace the Great Commission and respond to God's calling to missions. The second way, faith missions, in its pure form, would only appeal to the Lord and ask Him to raise up laborers without going directly to anyone to ask them to respond. The same difference would be true regarding the funding of missions. Organizational efforts would work to establish a funding method which would produce a steady stream of reliable income upon which a trustworthy budget could be built in sending forth missionaries. Faith efforts would rely primarily on prayer. George Mueller of Bristol made this approach more well known by resolving not to ask for funding for his orphanage but to rely on prayer and ask the Lord to put the desire and impulse to give directly on the hearts of those who were intended to support the work. Hudson Taylor, although occasionally making his needs known to friends and supporters back in England, for the most part followed the same practice in preparing for his calling to China and later on in the daily rigors of his labors while in China. During his time in London before leaving for China, Taylor tested this principle by speaking to no one about the needs of the mission except the Lord. He wrote, "When I get out to China, I shall have no claim on anyone for anything. My only claim will be on God. How important to learn, before leaving England, to move man, through God, by prayer alone."[1]

Perhaps one of the most avid followers of this faith missions principle was Johannes Evangelista Gossner. The history of missions includes people whose names are well known in heaven but little known on earth. Gossner was one such man. He was a Roman Catholic priest who discovered the gospel of grace after many years serving as a parish priest in various cities in the Bavarian regions of Germany. Through the example and teaching of an influential group of Christian leaders who were determined to live what they believed, Gossner's ministry underwent a radical transformation. His superiors within the church of Rome could not overlook what he was teaching and modeling before his parishioners so after a time of imprisonment for what they perceived as egregious error on his part, his credentials were taken away as a priest. He moved naturally toward a Protestant tradition and eventually at the age of sixty-three became the pastor of Bethlehem Church in Berlin.

Missions movements had been springing up all over Europe, and longing to reach out to "heathen people" all over the world had given rise to a wide variety of missionary sending agencies and boards. Discouraged by the growing bureaucracy he saw in how missionaries were being prepared and deployed, Gossner advocated what came to be known as "faith missions," an approach already modeled by George Mueller and William Carey. Instead of launching vast organizations and sophisticated campaigns to raise support for missions, Gossner believed that the work of missions would best be accomplished through prayer and an unswerving trust in the provision of the Lord.

> Here I sit, he would say, in my little room: I cannot go here and there to arrange and order everything; and if I could, who knows if it would be well done? But the Lord is there, who knows and can do everything, and I give it all over to Him, and beg Him to direct it all, and order it after His holy will; and then my heart is light and joyful, and I believe and trust Him that He will carry it all nobly out.[2]

There is something exhilarating about hearing accounts of what happened when men like Gossner, Taylor, and Mueller demonstrated faith by relying on prayer to move the hand of God to move men to give, go, and pray. What a reminder in practical terms of what Paul said, "And God is able!" Churches shaped by their missions calling understand that and rest in His perfect and abounding provision.

Distinctive, Holy Lives

When the church and its members look no different from the world around us, they can be excused for not taking us seriously when we speak of a God who has transformed our lives. Even within the body of Christ, if there is nothing distinctive about us, nothing that speaks of holiness or sets us apart as those who have been with Christ and are much like Him, those around us will not be motivated to anything more. But when we see the beauty of holiness and long for the righteousness of the Lord to be ours, the Spirit dwelling within us spurs us on and gives us an appetite, builds up a desire, and cultivates an aspiration in our hearts to be faithful to Christ in every way. Peter offered encouragement in that direction when he wrote, "But, as the One who called you is holy, you also are to be holy in all your conduct; for it is written, 'Be holy, because I am holy'" (1 Pet. 1:15–16).

Although preaching and teaching on holiness have often been neglected in modern churches, true holiness of life presents an appealing and attractive manner of living because the light of Christ shines brightest through a clean window. In the early days of my pulpit ministry, I preached a message on holiness in the church where my parents and grandparents were members, the church in which I grew up. After the message my grandmother noted that she had not heard a sermon on holiness since she was little girl; she assumed it was only emphasized among those from churches in the "holiness" tradition, associated with a legalistic worldview and an eccentric code of behavior and dress unique to people from that background. In her mind holiness was not appealing but appalling. Primarily it lacked attractiveness as a lifestyle because it was connected more with being peculiar than with being like Jesus Christ. Holiness of character seldom overcame the emphasis on abiding by rules and regulations arbitrarily established by cultural traditions.

What do you consider to be winsome and attractive about true, biblical, Christ-centered holiness? Can you see why a genuine likeness to Christ would present a compelling model for others to follow so that they would want to become like Him and to live for Him? In his 1879 classic, *Holiness*, British pastor and author J. C. Ryle expressed the same concerns he observed in nineteenth-century churches that we still find today.

> The subject of personal godliness has fallen sadly into the background. The standard of living has become painfully low in many quarters. The immense importance of "adorning the doctrine of God our Savior" (Titus 2:10), and making it lovely and beautiful by our daily habits and tempers, has been far too much overlooked. . . . Sound Protestant and Evangelical doctrine is useless if it is not accompanied by a holy life. It is worse than useless; it does positive harm.[3]

Ryle goes on to say,

> True holiness, we surely ought to remember, does not consist merely of inward sensations and impressions. It is much more than tears, and sighs, and bodily excitement, and a quickened pulse, and a passionate feeling of attachment to our favorite preachers and our own religious party, and a readiness to quarrel with everyone who does not agree with us. It is something of "the image of Christ" which can be seen and observed by others in our private life, and habits, and character and doings (Rom. 8:29).[4]

When "the image of Christ" makes its appearance in the lives of His followers, who can resist the urge to follow in the footsteps of holy people who are living dynamic lives of radical distinctiveness and radiant joy? The motivation to pursue Christ's calling to the nations is accelerated greatly when the nature of changed lives offers all people a glorious hope for a better life—a Christ-centered, God-glorifying, Spirit-led life.

The evangelistic power of a transformed life, filled with awe and wonder at the greatness of God, cannot be discounted. When lives begin to display a genuine shift in priorities and passion, from the routines of this world to the glories of the kingdom of Christ, the pull is stronger than gravity and draws people to come to the One who is responsible for the change, Jesus Christ being the author and finisher of our newfound faith. Perhaps one of the most wonderful descriptions of this is found in the book of Acts soon after the Holy Spirit came upon the early church:

> Then fear came over everyone, and many wonders and signs were being performed through the apostles. Now all the believers were together and had everything in common. So they sold their possessions and property and distributed the proceeds to all, as anyone had a need. And every day they devoted themselves to meeting together in the temple complex, and broke bread from house to house. They ate their food with gladness and simplicity of heart, praising God and having favor with all the people. And every day the Lord added to them those who were being saved. (Acts 2:43–47)

Holy living is not natural. Holy people are not normal. Therefore, when we stumble upon folks who match the biblical design, we take notice; and unless we are spiritually dead and blind, the Spirit within us produces a longing in us to become like them— imitators of them as they are imitators of Christ.

How does this influence missions in the local church? First, those who wake up to what it means to live for Christ in all things soon see the world through His eyes. Holy lives reflect the character of Christ but also a desire to please Him in all respects. As the saints (as the "holy ones" are called in Scripture) see themselves as set apart in character, they realize that they can also trust the Lord to set them apart in where He calls them to serve Him and in what He calls them to do. If we are not open to be *set apart* in the way we live, how will we ever be willing to be *sent away* to introduce people from every nation to the holiness that is required to see the Lord

(Heb. 12:14)?[5] A heart for being sent as a faithful witness awakens first to a call to be set apart as holy servant.

Second, when members of the church recognize holiness of life and a willingness to go among their peers, God makes that kind of life contagious to others. Once it gets started, it is hard to predict where or if it will end! Year after year in our own church, we watch with awe as God continues to call out individuals, young couples, families, retired people, recent college graduates, successful business people, medical professionals, and on the list goes. Had they been surrounded by sour-faced, disenfranchised, joyless people who could find no place to fit in here and had no choice but to take the heroic route of a career in mission, would they have been attracted to join them? Although those unattractive kinds of Christians may flatter themselves into thinking their attitude and demeanor are holy, no one else who knows and treasures Christ would ever reach that conclusion. When my grandmother remarked that her only exposure to teaching on holiness was confined to a small group from an eccentric tradition, I sensed in her words that she had found their ideas of holiness far from appealing. One friend of mine refers to folks who view holiness as a joyless, separatist form of self-righteousness as people who have been "weaned on a sour pickle." Nothing about that kind of people adorns Christ's call to a life of distinction.

No, instead of seeing a negative model of imposed external regulations, those who watch the steady stream of people saying yes to a missions calling have witnessed a parade of joyful, excited, godly, appealing people who demonstrate a remarkable likeness to Jesus Christ. They see people who are leaving what they know for what they cannot predict for the sake of the One whom they never want to disappoint. Happy, holy people becoming missionaries draw others in the same direction because everyone can see that the distinctive nature of their holiness gives the call to missions a beautiful luster as they "adorn the doctrine of God our Savior."

Compassion for the Lost

The primary motivation for missions is not lost people. "Missions exists because worship does not," as noted in the introduction to this book. Missions' first passion is for God to receive the highest praise and the greatest glory, so our preeminent design does not stem from the needs of people but from the essential worthiness of God to be worshipped.

But with that properly noted, no one can argue that God does not have compassion for lost people. And if God has compassion for them, so must we. Any church that diminishes the reality of what *lostness* means either has little enthusiasm and involvement in missions now or will soon lose whatever it might have had. Throughout the Gospels, Jesus speaks to the condition of lost people and even explains the nature of His ministry with reference to them: "For the Son of Man has come to seek and to save that which was lost" (Luke 19:10).

Therefore, it only makes sense that when a church comes to the conviction that lost people matter to God and should matter to us, evangelism shifts from a specialized ministry of elite witnesses to a core commitment of the entire congregation. Once that shift takes place, it is a logical move to expand the scope of the evangelistic field to include the nations, not just the neighborhood. Compassion for those apart from Christ leads us to develop a strategic plan to reach them. For that plan to be biblically sound and sensitively constructed means that we as leaders have to become serious students of both God's Word to discern the eternal principles behind the plan and students of the nations and cultures where the gospel will go to understand the unique challenges of making the message clear in a loving, gracious manner.

The driving force is love—love for God and love for others. Having been loved and redeemed, the proper response of those who know Christ is to want others to benefit from the infinite measure of that same love. Multitudes of aimless, helpless people all around Him stirred compassion in the heart of Jesus:

When He saw the crowds, He felt compassion for them, because they were weary and worn out, like sheep without a shepherd. (Matt. 9:36)

As He approached and saw the city, He wept over it, saying, "If you knew this day what would bring peace—but now it is hidden from your eyes." (Luke 19:41–42)

People who care enough about the spiritual condition of others to weep as Jesus did will find a way to reach them with the hope of the gospel. If we find ways to insulate ourselves from their pain and their hopelessness, we can ignore them and neglect them. But once we have seen them with compassion through the eyes of Christ, our hearts will be moved to join in the movement of God to do whatever it takes to make sure they have an opportunity to hear the good news of His redeeming love through Christ.

The first time I went to India, the prospect of facing massive poverty and the constant flood of people honestly frightened me. How would I respond? Could I keep my emotions in check and my wits about me in the midst of this wave of human need? In preparation for the time, I went about the business of preparing my messages and getting the teaching material together for the pastors' conferences and meeting. But I also was steeling myself and unconsciously put up an emotional defense system to guard my heart from being completely overwhelmed. The net effect was that I saw it all but chose to view it from a remote distance, personally detached and disengaged. I did not allow myself to react or to respond; cool indifference kept me from grieving over their lostness and prevented me from feeling any compassion (or feeling anything for that matter).

When I returned home, people asked how it went, and I felt a sense of pride that I could say that it went well, and I had not allowed the hopeless situation of the people to bother me or get in the way of a good trip. In fact, I secretly congratulated myself that I had not been like another team member who had been so devastated by the condition of the people that she could not sleep at night and ended up suffering the health consequences of sleep deprivation. She just did not know how to handle it like I did, I told myself.

How long it took for me to realize how calloused and coldhearted I had become, I cannot say. For the sake of my reputation, I would love to say conviction came right away, but I have to admit that what I had done only became apparent many months later. When it hit me, I was embarrassed before the Lord—all the while I had been telling Him how much I loved Him and was willing to go anywhere and do anything to serve Him. But in all honesty there was an obvious disconnect between that professed love for Him and His love for a lost world. My calculated indifference to those He had called me to love in His name went undetected far too long. Eventually, the Lord showed me and by His mercy forgave me for not caring. Life seldom gives many opportunities for a "do over," but since that first visit, the Lord has given me several chances to go back to India and each time I have prayed before going that He would guard my heart but that He would also engage my heart by giving me His compassion for those I would see and meet. He has been faithful to do that each time!

Back in the days of Hudson Taylor, stories from China were reported through regular correspondence to churches back in England. As Christians read of the plight of millions of Chinese people without Christ and no hope of ever hearing of Him without outside help, they responded because their hearts were filled with compassion. The support for Taylor's labors was widespread and extensive because the Lord gripped the hearts of His people when they heard the heartbreaking news of a lost people. Today communications are so much improved that we not only can read of great need; we see it dramatically unveiled for us on the nightly news with video evidence of what we have heard. But in many circumstances the constant barrage of images has almost inoculated our culture, even within the church, and made us immune to the massive amount of human need rolled out before our eyes. The result is that we often ignore the pain and neglect the calling to respond compassionately, and lost folks remain unreached. Missions-minded people refuse to turn away and instead ask the Lord to grow their compassion and feed their desire to find a way to offer help and hope.

When a church develops a love for people who do not know Christ and a compassion for them, missions flows easily from an idea to a mandate. In an 1869 hymn Fanny Crosby wrote, "Rescue the perishing, care for the dying, Jesus is merciful, Jesus will save." Knowing that and seeing a world filled with desperation and people who are broken and helpless should fuel the fires of our missions passion.

The Support of a Sacrificial, Generous Community

The best environment for sending missionaries is a healthy community of believers who have demonstrated a strong commitment to the Great Commission and a growing evidence that they are walking by the Spirit. Out of such a context, the support base builds confidence for those aspiring to go. When missions becomes normal instead of rare, something positive begins to take place among people seeking to live for Christ. The church can become a virtual nursery for cultivating a missions environment in which God continues to call out folks to go and even more to give and pray.

Yet we also see what can happen when supportive words are not accompanied by supportive action. For example, many believing parents pray for laborers for the harvest but pray that God will not call their own children or grandchildren. Imagine the unnecessary obstacles that crop up when young people hear their parents pray one way and then object when they declare their intentions to go! Mixed signals from church leaders can also create confusion. If the pastor preaches missions from the pulpit but joins leaders in cutting back funding for missions in the budget, what are potential candidates supposed to think? No, we cannot send mixed signals about our commitment to missions. The missions culture in the local church should give consistent signals of support and offer constant indications of encouragement to those who are processing the stirring within their hearts to go and make disciples from among the nations.

When the community has consistently made personal sacrifices on behalf of others who have answered God's call to missions, that spirit offers encouragement for those still sorting out what they should do. Since one of the biggest hurdles to get over for most of those considering their role is how they will survive the funding needs of going to the corner of the globe God has in mind for them. They know He will provide, but if they have not seen evidence of generosity among those in their own network, it is difficult for them to imagine how it will work. But if they have come to terms with their calling in the context of a generous, sacrificial people, they already have some level of understanding that helps them overcome their fears.

Everyone says they pray for missions and missionaries, but if missionary candidates come from a faith community where that prayer support is largely invisible and behind the scenes, can they expect something different on their behalf? No one wants to launch out by faith without knowing that there is a base of prayer covering them and a financial commitment undergirding them as they go.

The biblical model of generous giving for the sake of others is not directly related to missions but in fact is in reverse. The church in Jerusalem had fallen on hard economic times during the days of prime missionary activity in Asia Minor and across the Aegean Sea along the coast of what is now Greece. Paul and some of the churches he had founded developed a plan to gather funds to send back to Jerusalem from those congregations which had benefited so greatly from the prayers and people sent out by them, mostly by way of the church in Antioch.[6]

In the 2 Corinthians letter, Paul appealed to the church there to demonstrate both gratitude and generosity by making and keeping a commitment to contribute to the needs of their brothers and sisters in Jerusalem. As a missionary and church planter, Paul was supported in his ministry by the gifts of churches up the coast from Corinth as well as his own bivocational work as a tent maker.

Even though he introduced the gospel to Corinth and stayed there teaching and preaching for a year and a half to get them firmly established in the faith, Paul refused to accept financial support from them.

> Did I commit a sin by humbling myself so that you might be exalted, because I preached the gospel of God to you free of charge? I robbed other churches by taking pay from them to minister to you. When I was present with you and in need, I did not burden anyone, for the brothers who came from Macedonia supplied my needs. I have kept myself, and will keep myself, from burdening you in any way. (2 Cor. 11:7–9)

The Macedonian churches were generous in supporting Paul as he moved on from their community to continue the work of the gospel in declaring Christ and establishing churches. But eventually Paul wrote back to Corinth to challenge and encourage them to give freely in order to meet needs back in Jerusalem. Missions money from other churches had made it possible for them to grow and prosper, and now it was time for them to imitate their generosity. Offering the Macedonians as an example of true liberality in giving, Paul urges the Corinthians to join in the gladness of a generous spirit.

> We want you to know, brothers, about the grace of God granted to the churches of Macedonia: during a severe testing by affliction, their abundance of joy and their deep poverty overflowed into the wealth of their generosity. I testify that, on their own, according to their ability and beyond their ability, they begged us insistently for the privilege of sharing in the ministry to the saints. (2 Cor. 8:1–4)

Paul presents an appeal to the Corinthians to show their love for Christ and the work of the church by giving generously themselves. As they had received, now they should be not only willing but should be faithful in fulfilling their commitment to support the people of God in other places in the work of the gospel. After Paul had explained further what he was asking them to do, he makes clear that God loves cheerful giving, generous giving, sacrificial giving. Through trust in His provision, there will always be plenty to go around so that we all get a share of the blessing because we participated in our share of the giving.

> It is not that there may be relief for others and hardship for you, but it is a question of equality—at the present time your surplus is available for their need, so that their abundance may also become available for your need, that there may be equality. As it has been written: "The person who gathered much did not have too much, and the person who gathered little did not have too little." . . . Now the One who provides seed for the sower and bread for food will provide and multiply your seed and increase the harvest of your righteousness, as you are enriched in every way for all generosity, which produces thanksgiving to God through us. For the ministry of this service is not only supplying the needs of the saints, but is also overflowing in many acts of thanksgiving to God. (2 Cor. 8:13–15; 9:10–12)

Looking out to recognize and give to meet needs in others runs counter to our natural tendency to take care of our own situations first. Then if any is leftover, others are welcome to it. The trouble is that there is seldom any leftover and that the Lord asks for the firstfruits, not the leftovers!

Most pastors expect obedient, faithful members of their churches to give generously as an indication of the disposition of their hearts toward God. A tithe, or 10 percent, of their income usually defines the standard for good stewardship. But what happens when a tithe is given to support a church that neglects their responsibility to practice what they preach? If the church does not give away at least a tithe of its income to support the Lord's work beyond its own walls, the message delivered to the members is clear—home matters more than elsewhere. To that they have every right to say, "That is why I spend it at *my* home rather than give at church!" The lesson is obvious. If we want to generate a giving attitude in the members, they need to see generosity in how the church treats its calling to support the work God is doing elsewhere. Churches need to be committed to give at least 10 percent of their income away—and hopefully that goes to support missions! We cannot expect tithing from our members if we do not model it throughout our ministry.

When missions gets its due from the local congregation, the spirit of generosity overflows throughout the church. Whatever amount is budgeted in our church giving plan is always exceeded significantly by designations over and above what is allotted. In fact, most years the designated gifts to missions are well over half again the amount in the budget. A generous support of missions from the local church excites and creates enthusiasm for doing more to make it possible for more missionaries to go and more work to be supported.

Receiving gifts for missions and then reporting on the results when possible serves a dual purpose. First, it reassures those who give that their gifts are going where they intended. Second, it provides visibility for what God is doing through the gifts and encourages others to join in because they can see for themselves the fruit of missions generosity. The joy of watching an appeal for a worthy cause capture the hearts of the people makes me grateful and glad I get to be a pastor. Beyond the normal giving to support missionaries, when a project comes up that will benefit evangelism and church planting somewhere in the world, people dig deep into their pockets and surprise themselves with what can happen when a congregation works and gives together.

Rebuilding homes after floods in eastern North Carolina, sending work teams to the Gulf Coast after Hurricane Katrina, rebuilding a small island village on the coast of India after the tsunami, constructing schools in the slums of Nairobi, hosting a major regional conference for laborers in much need of refreshment and renewal because of the intense struggles in their field of service—these and many other projects captured the imaginations of our congregation over the past several years as I witnessed incredible generosity and sacrifice. From those investments we have watched in wonder as scores of our own families have been made confident that a home sending base with that kind of track record for missions will support them as they go. The sacrificial and generous home church should not be surprised when the attitude results in greater reassurance among their members that if they sense God's call to go, they will surely see God's hand moving their own church family to provide graciously and generously in support of their needs.

Persecution and Opposition

By the time Peter wrote his first epistle, Christians were already scattered across the Mediterranean community of nations. He addressed this letter to the "Diaspora," or the "Dispersion," or to the sojourners, "temporary residents of the Dispersion in the provinces of Pontus, Galatia, Cappadocia, Asia, and Bithynia" (1 Pet. 1:1). Because of the persecutions taking place in Jerusalem (Acts 8:1),[7] many of the earliest believers were forced to flee for their lives; and when they relocated, they planted not only their families but also the gospel in new fields where the Lord intended to reap a bountiful harvest. Right from the start, the church needed a push to move out with the message. Persecution and opposition have always proved to be useful tools in compelling the people of God to relocate and to take the hope of the gospel with them as they go. Sometimes fear produces results that faith does not.

No church lays out a missions strategy that includes ways to invite persecution so that people will have to move out! However, whenever in the history of the church it has happened, the results have been for God's glory and for the greater good of the expansion of the kingdom as the gospel goes wherever the "diaspora" go. Even in the Old Testament, the record of God's faithfulness to His work is seen in the way He accomplishes good from what appeared to be complete disaster. After years spent in Egypt as a slave and then a prisoner because of the cruelty of his brothers and the malicious accusations of scorned woman, Joseph was elevated to the second highest position in the land. When famine forced his brothers to come to Egypt to seek food and relief from imminent starvation, they did not realize the official to whom they were speaking was the brother they betrayed and sold into slavery. All the years of suffering, all the years of desperation and loneliness, must have come to mind when Joseph recognized these men, but his response to their fear when he discloses who he is sets him apart as a man who now knew and trusted a sovereign God. "But Joseph said to them, 'Don't be afraid. Am I in the place of God? You planned evil against me; God planned it for good to bring about the present result—the survival of many people'" (Gen. 50:19–20). While others could not see any good, only the evil consequences of wrongdoing, God prevailed and produced a glorious result. And Joseph was wise and mature enough to recognize it.

Persecution in England and across the continent of Europe produced such hardship for Christians in the seventeenth century that they sought refuge and a place to find religious liberty. Driven from their homes, cut off from their countries, imprisoned, martyred, and persecuted in a multitude of ways for their faith, followers of Christ suffered great cruelty and systemic opposition to their biblical faith and fervor. Looking back now, we can see that the Lord was preparing the way for the gospel to have a place from which to launch new endeavors in missions and church planting. The new world of the Western hemisphere provided a climate for spiritual freedom and expressions of faith unknown to many who made their way here. Now nearly four centuries later, the church that was established on the western side of the Atlantic Ocean largely because of persecution and opposition on its eastern shores seem to have forgotten the value of enduring hardship for the gospel.

Some have observed that the church in the West could use some good old-fashioned persecution to shake things up and get people out of the church houses and into the world. The message of missions which once was so powerful and revolutionary has become so anemic and institutionalized that more Christians are interested in preserving the peace and maintaining the *status quo* than they are in seeing a worldwide explosion of interest in the good news about Jesus Christ. If history teaches us anything on this point, it is that when the church starts settling in, it seldom is shaken unless crisis forces its hand. Persecution has often been the only instrument capable of pushing people out the door and into less comfortable places, places they would never have chosen but places in need of the hope of Christ.

Whereas I am grateful for those times when God brings conviction for missions with a gentle nudge from His Word, or a quiet commitment in response to the stirrings of the Spirit, I believe there are times when drastic measures, which result in great missionary zeal and fervor, are necessary. Few church members in the Western world would want to suffer what Chinese Christians have endured for their faith, but the truth is that the church and its message of salvation through faith in Jesus Christ have flourished better in the midst of strong opposition and sometimes fierce persecution than we have in peace. The church does not do well when it prays and cries out for protection from tough times when in reality those might be the circumstances God will use to get His message on the move again. Reluctant though we may be, and resistant as we are to struggling for our faith, those days may indeed be nearer than we think. Will we welcome the opportunity to suffer for Christ's sake and give power to our message by our steadfast witness, or will we insist that God keep us safely ensconced within the walls where no evil can touch us but also where the message cannot get out?

The promise of peace is not intended to foster a retreatist approach to church life but is an assurance from God Himself that whenever we go in His name and do His will—as we certainly do when we embrace His call to missions—He will cause us to find our rest in Him even in the middle of the storms we are so desperately trying to avoid. Anyone can have peace when nothing challenges it; but when persecutions and pain and opposition come our way, do we then know the "peace of God, which surpasses every thought," which will "guard your hearts and your minds in Christ Jesus"? (Phil 4:7). Missions often travels best in just such circumstances as would meet great resistance in those who prefer comfort to faithfulness.

Will These Shape Our Mission?

Not every missions church has all nine of these characteristics, nor is it reasonable to think that they should. But where they do prevail, missions will shape the heartbeat of that congregation as an overflowing response to the revealed glory of God in Jesus Christ. Missions then becomes a part of our "spiritual worship," and we become the kind of people who love to present themselves as living and holy sacrifices pleasing to God (Rom. 12:1).

Are any of these prominent in your church, your ministry, your family, your life? God wants to build us into a kingdom-focused people for whom missions is a normal way of life. Until we are ready either to pursue or to welcome these developments and/or convictions, missions will remain a peripheral issue for us. But once we aspire to see the character of our lives and ministries embrace these marks of missions ministries, God will do more than we can imagine to set us free to go in His name and make disciples of all nations!

---

1. Dr. and Mrs. Howard Taylor, *Hudson Taylor's Spiritual Secret* (Chicago: Moody Publishers, 1989, 2009), 33.

2. Reverend William Fleming Stevenson, *Praying and Working* (New York: Robert Carter & Brothers, 1863), 316–19.

3. J. C. Ryle, *Holiness* (Old Tappan, NJ: Fleming H. Revell, 1979), vii.

4. Ibid., x.

5. "Pursue peace with everyone, and holiness—without it no one will see the Lord" (Heb. 12:14).

6. When persecution hit the church in Jerusalem, many of the believers there were scattered and went into exile. Some ended up in Antioch, which was the sending church for Paul, Barnabas, and many others who had been recognized and set apart as missionaries (Acts 11:19–26).

7. "Saul agreed with putting him to death. On that day a severe persecution broke out against the church in Jerusalem, and all except the apostles were scattered throughout the land of Judea and Samaria" (Acts 8:1).

SECTION THREE
HOW TO GET THERE

CHAPTER 8 **A SURVEY OF BEST PRACTICES**

Chances are great that you have read this far with an increasing desire to do something to increase the level of missions involvement of your congregation and a growing conviction that this desire is rooted in a biblical mandate which cannot be ignored. But the purpose of this book is not to weigh you down with guilt about what you should be doing. The reason for making this information available is to assist pastors and churches as they dare to make a major step of faith to take the gospel to the nations as well as to the neighborhood. So what can you do? What are some practical steps to help you figure out where you go from here? The next few chapters are designed to lay out for you several ideas that have been tried and proven to be effective in leading a congregation to be more effective in allowing missions to help shape its mission.

Thousands of churches across the nation have discovered how to cultivate a missions focus and a missions culture in their congregations. There is so much to learn from those who have already pioneered the way, so in the next couple of chapters, we want to ask them what they are doing and why that is important. After identifying over three hundred of these churches from a variety of denominational settings, geographical locations, diverse demographic contexts, size, and other criteria, we asked them to help the rest of us figure out what can make us alike in our passion and pursuit of missions. Well over a hundred responded* and gave us some great information and ideas that challenge the veterans and encourage the rookies. In an effort to keep these chapters lean, we will only highlight some key thoughts here.

The main question we asked them to answer was this: What are the top ten practices in your church which foster the missions culture you enjoy? In other words, what has God used to shape the character of your congregation as a missions-focused church? Using our own church as a starting point, we asked if other churches practiced some of the same ideas and then asked them for details of how they did it. Then we asked for other practices they had found helpful which were not among our suggestions. The result was that the churches responding to the survey identified the top ten practices that were common among them.

The nine characteristics of effective missions churches over the centuries explored in chapters 5 and 6 provide the historical backdrop for us; but when we get down to particular cases in our own culture and time, we tend to focus on practices more than principles. In fairness to the responding churches, we asked for their best practices, what they did in the life of their churches that contributed to their present missions culture. After examining what these practices have in common, we can then look at the current practices alongside the historic characteristics and see if there are discrepancies between the two lists. The goal is to identify both our aspirations and our practices from a biblical point of reference in order to help churches and pastors in our day and in the years to come find and sustain the kind of missions effort consistent with what Christ has called us to pursue.

---

* A list of those who responded is provided in an appendix at the end of the book.

Historic Marks of Effective Missions Movements	Present Best Practices of Effective Missions Churches
Power from on high as the Holy Spirit's work flowed freely	Designated leadership responsibility for missions
A passion for Christ	High value for partnering with indigenous works
Prevailing prayer	Maintaining consistent contact with supported missionaries
A rich soaking in the Scriptures and sound doctrine	Emphasis on missions and evangelism from the pulpit/preaching ministry
Unwavering faith that trusts God to be faithful in all things	Use of both budgeted and outside of budget funds to support missions
Holiness and purity of life (together with deep repentance and an abhorrence of sin)	Emphasized both long-term relationships and short-term trips
Eyes willing to see and have compassion on others	Employ an assessment process in order to send those best suited and called
A supportive, sacrificial, and generous sending community	Involvement in international church planting
Persecution and opposition	Highlight missions at an annual conference to raise the visibility and priority of missions
	Adopt a people group or focus on a particular nation or region

Placed side by side like that, the current characteristics raise some interesting questions. Is the modern church more inclined toward pragmatism than principle? Is there room in our consideration for recapturing the catalysts for missions movements over the centuries? Can a church do all the right things and fill in all the right practices and still be largely ineffective in mobilizing its people to reach the nations with the gospel? For the moment let's postpone the answers to those questions and look at what and how churches are investing in the cultivation of a missions context in their congregations:

1. Assign clear leadership responsibility for missions (someone devoted to that effort).
2. Place a high value on indigenous works.
3. Maintain regular contact with their missionaries.
4. Emphasize missions from the pulpit/preaching.
5. Use both budget and nonbudget funding for missions.
6. Emphasize both long-term relationships and short-term trips.
7. Employ an assessment process.
8. Become involved in international church planting.
9. Highlight missions festivals (large churches).
10. Adopt a people group. A very narrow majority of small churches do not adopt a people group.

The churches responding to the survey were from all over the geographical spectrum, from new church plants weighing in as well as well-established, traditional congregations, and from a wide range of evangelical perspectives. Their answers proved to be a fascinating confirmation of the creativity of God's plan in developing unity in the midst of diversity. From churches with extensive global focus to churches with more of a local flavor to their outreach, there is much to be learned from this unscientific survey because of the wealth of wisdom present in those who answered and due to their willingness to take the time necessary to invest in people like you and me. So before getting into the specifics, let me express my profound gratitude to those churches and their leaders for pulling back the curtain and allowing us to see what is inside! The practices fall into three basic categories: *Building a Vision for Missions, Adopting a Strategy for Missions,* and *Sustaining the Support for Missions.*

Category One: Building a Vision for Missions

A vision for becoming a missions-shaped church must begin somewhere. Left to themselves, any church will tend to drift toward self-serving practices and invest inordinate amounts of time, energy, and money in keeping the home fires burning brightly. In order for an entire congregation to leave all that behind and rally behind a vision to reach the nations with the gospel, something has to happen to awaken them to that which is far better.

Therefore, in the process of finding out what effective missions churches do to generate a missions climate, it was heartening to discover that significant thought had gone into the building of a vision for missions. The best practices of such churches included answers to two critical questions: Who owns the missions vision in your church? Where does the church as a whole catch that vision? Four of the ten best practices addressed these two questions.

Who Owns the Missions Vision?

Perhaps a better way of asking this question is, "Who is directly responsible for developing, casting, and implementing the missions vision for your church?" In most church governance the pastor bears the primary responsibility for the oversight needed to make sure missions holds its rightful place in the priorities of the church's ministries. As he casts an overall vision for ministry, missions must be part of the comprehensive plan to fulfill the purpose of the body of Christ. But if the pastor is the only one carrying that vision, with all the competing responsibilities that typically fall on a pastor's shoulders, it will be difficult to give it the kind of sustained attention and care biblical missions requires. Worse still, if the pastor has no sustained interest in or passion for missions, a vital component of church life will be neglected, and I might add, to the detriment of the people and the spiritual health of the congregation.

Practice 1. Clearly Defining Leadership Responsibility for Missions

Effective missions-focused churches assign responsibility for missions to someone in addition to the pastor. Although the pastor in most cases casts vision for the ministry as a whole, a wise pastor delegates responsibility to those who can serve as specialists in particular areas of emphasis. Even in smaller congregations, no one thinks it unusual to assign responsibilities to specialists in the areas of music, children, students, finances, and so forth. Therefore, it should not be a stretch to consider adding missions as a specialty area.

Although some church leaders have suggested that every church member should be taught to understand the need for missions and take personal responsibility for it, experience tells us that when *everyone* is responsible, usually *no one* is responsible. When we defined *mission, missions,* and *missional* at the start of this book, one of the reasons we did that was to head off the mistaken notion that a "one size fits all" approach to leadership in those areas will suffice. Because they are different, each needs the best thinking, dreaming, and strategizing from the most qualified and committed advocates for each. When that does not happen, some pastors and Christian leaders equate their concern for the local evangelistic mission of the church with the more comprehensive global vision for taking the gospel to the nations. One respondent to the survey demonstrated this succinctly when he stated that "as a missional church we are all missions pastors." In the best possible light, that point of view holds an optimistic estimation of what church members understand or a limited appreciation for what a missions pastor does. In a more realistic light, missional or missions both get diluted; the people do not have access to the breadth of experience and insight available in both categories and both end up as woefully underdeveloped. Expressing it yet another way, one wrote, "We don't have a 'missions' or 'evangelism' department in the church but believe each person is to be a missionary, and we train them all to be that." In a perfect world that possibility certainly exists.

But in that same world there would be no need for a preaching pastor, worship pastor, or any other kind of specifically targeted pastoral ministry. All the saints would get it, and then they would get it all done without the need for pastoral leadership at all (an idea embraced as a good thing by some!). Missional thinking can be healthy for the church, but thinking that *being missional* stands as the equivalent of *pursuing missions* puts significant restrictions on the breadth of the Great Commission.

Perhaps it would be helpful here to restate the difference between missions and missional as noted in the introduction to this book:

> A missional church is committed to "adapting and refor-mulating absolutely everything (it does) in worship, disciple-ship, community, and service—so as to be engaged with the non-Christian society around it."[1]

So *missional* speaks specifically of the missiological mind-set of a congregation in how it seeks to engage the surrounding culture in meaningful ways so as to build bridges for the gospel. This is a much needed corrective to the isolationist tendencies of churches in general, cutting themselves off from informed dialogue with an unbelieving, unchurched, disinterested populace. For the record, I am an advocate for missional thinking and ministry. However, it cannot serve as a substitute for *missions*. If anything, being missional is simply a local manifestation of the kinds of gospel work that is to be done in all the earth; but on its own it seldom sees its purpose in terms that would pierce the darkness of unbelief in the world beyond their immediate locale.

> Missions is God's plan for reaching all nations with the good news of Jesus Christ by sending His people to tell them and show them the gracious, redeeming love of a glorious God.

So if pastors or Christian leaders confuse the two, or make them the same, it is understandable that the idea of having a separate focus in leadership would not make sense to them. But if they are different, as we have pointed out, the strategy and implementation plan for how to engage the church in both will need to be distinctive. Although the two have much in common regarding the manner of gospel ministry, the field in mind for each requires that churches give each specialized focus.

Therefore, the overwhelming majority of churches with effective missions ministries noted that one of the top ten best things they do is designate someone, or a group of people, to lead the charge, own the vision, and accept responsibility for providing biblical direction in showing the way from the pews to the nations.

Two primary approaches are practiced by effective missions churches—a pastoral staff member provides missions leadership, or an individual or a team of nonpastors accept the leadership role. As you might suspect, without sufficient funds to budget a full-time, or in most cases even a part-time, staff position, the latter option will be the most likely option for most churches. Of the churches surveyed, 68 percent of churches with attendance larger than 750 had a pastor on staff with at least a portion of his position description dedicated to missions leadership. Among the smaller congregations, approximately 70 percent of them assigned the responsibility for missions leadership to either an individual or group (committee, council, team, etc.).

Think for a moment of what that means for you if you are a local church pastor and still bear the weight of that responsibility on your own. Not only is it unwise stewardship of your time, if you hope to become an effective missions-minded church, you need to ask yourself if that is likely when less than one-third of such churches are attempting a solo leadership role by the lead pastor. What became evident in the survey is that the practice of designating someone to assume this role plays a big part in seeing a church become more effective in its missions task. If you do not have anyone designated to take the lead on missions, if missions should have the prominent role in your church that it has in Scripture, is it not time to consider making that move? Or if you have someone in that position but the effort is still in its earliest stages of development, are you ready to look into expanding what you are already doing? Perhaps a look at the energy and diversity of ideas that surfaced when we asked a survey question about this will whet your appetite for more than you are currently doing in your pursuit of the Great Commission.

When given the opportunity to describe what this person, or persons did, the range of ideas that emerged in response to this question was overwhelming! Some included just a position description, others just answered yes they did or no they did not have anyone assigned to take this responsibility. But as helpful as those pieces of information were, I was delighted to see how much information came in that I believe can be added to the growing pool of ideas as to how best to use this means of growing a strong missions culture in your church.

As people step into this arena of leadership, the attention they can give to the details of the task allows them to focus and tune in to creative and innovative ways of moving the church toward fresh new initiatives. Common sense tells you that if no one has direct oversight of missions, or if their efforts are divided by several other responsibilities, they will not be able to generate the kind of thinking, dreaming, and envisioning that someone can who can devote themselves fully to it. The responses we received indicate that some good, progressive, and creative thinking is going on.[2] Among the wealth of good ideas, we discovered five distinct benefits provided by having the right people dedicating their energies to explore possibilities and pursue the best ways possible to lead the church into a more active and aggressive posture toward missions. For churches choosing a less intentional path of leadership for missions, the results are dramatically different. But as the unique character of missions becomes clear, having people leading the way proves to be beneficial in the following ways.

1. Casting a Leadership Vision. Once the pastor or the board determines the general approach most consistent with the biblical principles for missions, the development of the particulars is best left to someone who can devote attention to the why, how, and what of a specific vision. As a senior pastor myself, it would be impossible for me to conduct the work of my primary responsibilities and give my best effort to the multiple levels of details needed for the work of missions to move ahead in an orderly, logical, and imaginative manner. In the early years of the life of our congregation, we established a missions team and charged them with coming up with guidelines and policies to carry out our missions calling. When we were eventually able to add part-time staff leadership to the mix, the effort improved considerably; and when a full-time pastor for missions was called, the jump was exponential! We were making some progress in casting a vision for missions before, but having someone who "owns the vision" has been of immense value to me and to the church. Using the team approach, the missions pastor capitalizes on a wide range of resources in capturing and casting a vision that is biblical, strategic, current, and compelling.

2. Mobilization and Inspiration of the Congregation. Involving hundreds of volunteers in missions events opens the door for many voices to articulate the vision for missions. Rather than the pastor beating the drum from the pulpit periodically, having a leader directly responsible for missions keeps people from all over the church plugged in to the effort—everything from praying to giving to going to dreaming! When that happens, people are inspired to dig deeper and see what else the Lord may have in mind for them. Mobilizing people to engage in missions has become a part of the culture of our congregation as friends and families watch others taking bold initiatives to do things I would never have dreamed of years ago. But now, due to regular updates and reports from those who have been involved in missions, amazing stories of God's faithfulness in providing means whenever there has been a willingness to go, prayer teams and active prayer support for missions as a normal part of small groups and classes have led to great awareness of what God is doing. Those things are promoted by a missions pastor and a missions team who are seeing extraordinary things happen in the lives of ordinary people who caught a vision from someone passionate enough to keep it in front of them!

3. Establishing and Maintaining Meaningful Partnerships and Relationships with Missionaries and National Partners. There is a nuts-and-bolts side to an effective missions ministry having to do with budget support, assessments, and reports; but the best service for keeping missions alive and active comes from meaningful relationships with missions partners and missionaries. As I have thought about the profile for someone in this position, the obvious qualities of missions vision, biblical passion for the proclamation of the gospel, administrative skills, team building and such things, an intangible quality may be as important as all of those combined. If the position is filled by a missions pastor, or if the person is not on the paid staff of the church, the quality that is indispensable is the ability to communicate love and care through relationships. Otherwise, the work can go forward in a mechanical, efficient manner; but the sense that someone really cares about the missionaries and their families will be missing. Phone calls, e-mails, visits, packages, prayer—all of these flow freely from people who care deeply but become a duty for those who are just "doing the job." When people know that you care, they are more inclined to care about what you know. Partnerships and relationships that begin with genuine care for the individual are more likely to result in an environment conducive to sustained effort over the long haul. As our missions pastor George Tissiere expresses it, we are simply holding the ropes that keep our colaborers connected to their ministry family back home.

4. Regularly Recruiting/Training/Coaching Folks from the Congregation to Be Sent Out and Supported as Missionaries. The visibility of missions is strengthened when it is associated with people, not just a concept. The more members of a congregation recognize the presence of others who represent all that is good and challenging about missions, the more likely they will be to want to learn more. As people are talking about missions, praying about missions, seeing people go on mission trips, hearing reports of

God's faithfulness, the task of recruiting them to take part is much easier. A climate for ministry which includes a natural presence of men and women who are engaged in missions personally tends to generate interest in a way that simply reading about it cannot.

Then when a missions pastor or team can step up with encouragement for those sensing that the Lord may be stirring them to action, that bolsters them with the confidence that this is not going to be a lonely venture into the unknown. They can be reassured that someone will be training them, walking with them, coaching them, and helping them navigate the complexities they will face as they move ahead with their pursuit. Obviously the Lord can do that without having an identifiable missions leader in the church, but surely you can see the advantage of having people in house who are knowledgeable and helpful as they seek to understand what to do next, why those things are important and who they can count on to accompany and support them along the way.

5. Advocating for Financial Support through Regularly Budgeted Funds and Special Giving Efforts. Anyone who has ever been involved in the budgeting process of an organization knows how important it is to have an advocate involved in the process. Granted, having percentage goals and financial targets can make a big difference in the outcome, but having someone who is passionate about their requests available to present the case personally does matter. Also, knowing that the funds represent the interests of people and the expanding influence of the gospel can sometimes get lost in budget meetings without a voice to speak up by way of reminder that these concerns are critical to the effectiveness of missions launched and supported by the local church. In still another way missions leaders provide creative thinking to place occasional appeals before the congregation to invite their generous support for extra projects and new initiatives. Protecting the people from too many of these appeals depends on established credibility from missions leaders who have not been overly persistent in placing too many concerns before them. But they also serve the congregation well when everyone knows a response is needed but depend on someone to show them the way.

Two such cases in our church stand out in my mind. One was the tsunami that hit the east coast of India in 2004. Worldwide support poured into the areas affected by this devastating natural disaster. Because of the presence of a missions pastor, our people rallied to the cause in unprecedented ways, giving generously to provide resources for relief efforts we knew about because of relationships on the ground prior to the tragedy. An entire village was rebuilt consisting of seventy new homes, a community center, and fishing boats to provide employment for the families on this small island. The challenge to our people did not come across as an imposition or manipulation but for what it was—a careful, organized strategy to make a difference where a tremendous need existed and a plan to match resources with need.

In a similar manner, flooding in the eastern part of our state caused by Hurricane Floyd in September 1999 provided another opportunity for our people to demonstrate generosity when given the chance. An organized effort was initiated by our missions leadership team, and untold thousands of dollars and volunteer hours were invested in helping rebuild the lives of people in a small town an hour or so from our own city. Ideas and responses to needs like these need to arise from someone who is taking care of such business—Gulf Coast relief efforts, school facilities in the Kametha slums of Nairobi, missions tithes from a capital fund-raising campaign—all these ideas and many like them had to come from someone. And if everyone is responsible, generally speaking, no one is. Pastors cannot be expected to do all of that and fulfill the rest of their responsibilities, so it is vital to the life and health of the funding of missions endeavors that they have the support of others who can shoulder those responsibilities well. Again, speaking of our own missions pastor, his description of his work is simply to "be an extension of our pastor's heart around the world." That is honestly giving me far too much credit, but I am grateful for someone who owns this vision and carries out this calling!

Occasional attention to missions as a sideline of ministry cannot compare with the targeted, focused priorities of people who understand and are excited about what can happen when God gives a vision and His people catch it.

So, who owns the vision? Ownership begins with the pastor but must then be delegated with his blessing and wholehearted support to specialists from within the congregation who can give the kind of direct attention and breadth of leadership required for such an extensive portion of the life call of the church.

---

1. Keller, "The Missional Church," 5.

2. For an excellent statement of vision and example of creative thinking regarding what can develop out of careful, prayerful concentration on the role of missions, see Appendix A on page 238. Mike Murphy from Elmbrook Church in Wisconsin provided one of the best descriptions I have seen of what the role of missions pastor can develop within a local church context.

CHAPTER 9 **CATCHING THE VISION**

Once the responsibility for overseeing the missions vision of the church has been clearly assigned and a person or team is in place to develop the strategy, build the leadership team and advocate the cause, what is to keep missions from becoming an eccentric focus of a few fanatics on the fringe of church life? That in fact is what happens in some churches. Missions has a place, the people understand, but not a central place, a prominent place, in the big picture. Contained respectably in that place, the rest of the church can go along its merry way, satisfied that someone is taking care of that and equally content to let them do it! But for missions to move into a more formative role in the culture of the church, missions must play a significant role in shaping the mission of the entire body of believers. To prevent isolation of and a subtle condescension toward those who are passionate about missions, a vision for missions must flow freely within the mainstream of church life. The survey of best practices fell into three categories, the first of which we introduced in the last chapter—building a vision for missions. After seeing the value of defining who owns that vision, the survey then revealed three major means of establishing that vision within the overall ministry culture of the church. Like most visions, missions is more caught than just taught.

Where Does the Church Catch the Vision?

Without a compelling vision for missions, a church cannot expect to cultivate a climate in which missions passion is the norm. The greater their understanding of the vision, the greater the likelihood they will catch it and then reflect it in the character of their ministry priorities and passions. So where does a church get that kind of vision? What can pastors and leaders do to paint a vivid picture of what can happen when we trust God for a missions mind-set for the church? When asked questions related to those issues, three answers emerged as the most common means of leading in that direction.

Practice 2. Informing and Inspiring the People—Missions Festivals/Conferences

Missions Conferences have gained a wonderful place among the best practices effective missions churches employ. Just as any event planned to emphasize something special, missions conferences can become routine and mundane, even "ineffective" as one respondent said. Others were even more direct in their opinion and were actually opposed to them.

Negative Feedback. As you would suspect, not everyone warms up to the idea of such special emphases on missions. One response offers a perspective consistent with a growing number of church leaders who seem to be looking at a different picture than most of the others represented in this survey. The confusion mentioned in the previous chapter regarding missions and missional thinking seems to be behind this leader's objections when he wrote, "We think these (conferences) facilitate the idea that missions is primarily a global event. Missions is the job of all people, and America is equally in need of missionary endeavors. Equipping the body with 'missions means far away' mentality seems to stem from old-school fundamentalism and doesn't really translate well to modern people who have a different cultural narrative than thirty years ago." How would you respond if you had the opportunity to dialogue with proponents of this perspective? Frankly, you probably do not have to look far to find someone who shares those convictions, perhaps right within your own congregation.

Is it true that America is "equally in need of missionary endeavors" when over 90 percent of the missions resources in the world are invested here and 90 percent of the world receives less than 10 percent of the resources? If missions is nothing more than "missions means far away" then shame on us, but if we define it as Jesus did in Acts 1:8, then shame on us for not cultivating a vision that begins locally and then strategically and practically extends to the ends of the earth! As far as relying on a throwback to "old-school fundamentalism," history actually shows that old-school fundamentalism largely abandoned missions in favor of local revivalism. As far as not getting a favorable translation of missions, both local and global, with modern people, the overwhelming response to the call to take the gospel to the nations is coming from twenty- and thirty-somethings. So as much as I can appreciate the idea that all church members are supposed to serve functionally as missionaries where God sends them, I must also point out that if they are never exposed to the biblical expansiveness of the field to which He sends His people, they will only see what they are shown. Dare to see the vision as both/and—local *and* global—the focus of most of the missions conferences as practiced by the majority of respondents indicate that they are doing a great job of that.

The Conference as a Best Practice for Imparting Vision. For a missions vision to be caught by the broadest number within the church population, it needs to be presented in the widest possible contexts. The overwhelming majority of the larger churches surveyed indicated that a missions conference or festival plays a large part in their vision casting. Such an undertaking is by no means easy, nor is it inexpensive, but the results are undeniable in that approximately 81 percent of larger churches sponsor such an event. It is also understandable that because of the logistics involved, smaller churches are less likely to do so; the survey showed that only about 35 percent of them did. But if you pastor a smaller congregation, do not be discouraged by the statistics or by the complexities of the conferences of some of the larger churches. By wise planning, you can design a conference scaled to suit your congregation.

As a church plant back in 1978, we had our first missions conference in the borrowed basement of another church before we even had our own facilities. I can still remember the enthusiastic response of our people and their excitement as they saw and heard and dreamed of the place missions would have in the future growth of our new congregation. So it need not be extravagant to be effective in casting a compelling vision and making a definitive statement that you are going to take missions seriously and give it a place of prominence in your ministry plans and purposes.

Not only can the size be adjusted, but the nature and frequency of the conference can be directly shaped to suit your own congregation. Reading through the ways different churches across the country do missions amazes me. The creative minds behind such things prove once again that the Lord does not call us to conformity but embraces our diversity of ideas behind a wonderful unity of purpose.

Just to give you a glimpse and perhaps stir up your imagination, here is a random sampling of some of the ways your colleagues in church missions engage their congregations in communicating a missions vision:

> *From Minnesota.* Host the missions conference the week after Easter to catch the momentum of the message of the Resurrection and the power of the gospel.

> *From Tennessee.* Set aside three weeks in the spring for international missions focus and three weeks in the fall for local and domestic efforts.

> *From North Carolina.* Spring global and fall global concentrations, each comprised of two Sundays to raise missions awareness and highlight significant global needs.

From Texas. Host an annual global outreach conference to encourage missionaries and educate/inspire the congregation.

From Illinois. Annual conference to raise awareness for missions, offer a homecoming environment for visiting missionaries, engage the next generation and raise their sights to see the nations.

From Connecticut. Host annual conference as pivot point for Faith Promise giving, cultivating interest in short-term and long-term trips, and educate the congregation on current missions trends.

From Colorado. Set aside five missions and outreach Sundays every year with each Sunday highlighting a different aspect of the missions focus of the church.

With all the good thinking behind all of these conferences, certain trends come to surface regarding the main purposes behind the special emphases.

Three Primary Purposes behind the Conference. Although the variety of what takes place at these conferences is impressive, the efforts usually include at least three primary purposes.

1. Information, Education, Awareness, and Exposure. The old saying, "Out of sight, out of mind," certainly applies as far as missions goes. Therefore, effective missions churches have found that the people need to be informed about the nature of the task, the results of their efforts so far in the form of status reports and stories from those personally involved, and an outline of plans for future engagement. Seminars, preaching, meetings with missionaries to explain their work, videos, and a host of other resources available promote the kind of environment that give people a chance to ask questions, pursue areas of special interest, and get a broader understanding of what it can mean to engage in missions. One of the highlights of many of the conferences is the informal discussion that arises from giving missions organizations and missionaries a place to set up booths or displays to give visibility to what they are doing and make themselves available to anyone who wants to talk. Not only is it educational, but it frequently breaks down the barriers people sometimes have that place missionaries on pedestals as different from the rest of us. A few brief conversations are usually all that is needed to see that those who go and those who stay are equally committed to following Christ but simply have been called to serve in a unique setting—sometimes involving a geographical move, and at other times just a reorientation to embrace a missiological mind-set for the culture in which you already find yourself.

2. *Inspiration, Motivation, and Mobilization.* When the days of emphasis reach their conclusion, whether a weekend or several weeks, the dream of conference organizers is that the missionary force will have grown both in understanding and in a new team of mobilized, motivated, inspired men and women ready to do whatever God wants and go wherever God sends. Hearing people tell the story of what God did in their lives to get them into a place of missions obedience inspires and motivates, but doesn't satisfy the goal of mobilizing a greater force for missions from the local public housing project to the farthest point of the globe. Inspiration and motivation without mobilization produces frustration. Aspirations of those investing time and energy and prayer into these conferences are that God will effectively call out from among us some of our best and brightest and that they will respond by going wherever He sends them to do whatever He asks of them.

A church in Mississippi wrote to say that God has raised up ten missionary families from their congregation, and all ten attribute to a past missions conference the first stirring of their hearts as the starting point for understanding and responding to their calling. A smaller church in New Hampshire put together a missions conference and watched with wonder as the Lord prompted their people to commit over $20,000 to missions that year. A young couple met some missionaries they fell in love with at the missions conference in their church in California, visited them in South Africa where they served, and within three years of their meeting now serve alongside them—all as a result of relationships established at a missions conference. At the end of a missions conference in a church in Massachusetts, the speaker asked for a commitment from those who were ready to give themselves to go wherever God called them, and ten people stood to their feet in response. A missions pastor from a church in Minnesota described the impact of their 2009 missions conference where 205 people from their three campuses and eight services made commitments to pursue at least two years of cross-cultural missions service. The conference was obviously gloriously effective, but it had the additional benefit of being the focal point of a praying congregation. He noted, "I believe the number one difference was the people praying for our conference and the fervency and concentration of the prayers. God really moved in a way for which no amount of planning could have taken credit."

In our church we pray and we plan, and each year numbers of people make life-changing commitments during our missions festival, scores of whom are "in the pipeline" now preparing for deployment. In the past decade, more than 125 have responded by going out with the gospel to the nations, some close by in domestic ministries, but the majority to places considered by most definitions to be the ends of the earth. Stories like these abound, and people love to tell them so if you know someone who hosts missions conferences, you will be inspired, motivated, and perhaps even mobilized yourself just by asking them about it.

3. *Encouragement and Support for Visiting Missionaries.* Knowing that you are not alone makes all the difference in the world to families situated all over the world serving as missionaries. Therefore, one other primary purpose of the missions conference is to offer an oasis for those who have been laboring in some pretty dry and dusty places. Each year many of the churches who host these conferences invest in getting families off the field of service back to the supporting churches so they can be refreshed and rejuvenated. Life in ministry anywhere is hard—not without its rewards but still hard. How important we have found it to be to provide the kind of

safe place for those serving in missions to come and be cared for! Knowing that somebody remembered you have small children and treated them with tenderness and concern can mean the world to a young mother and father who struggle just to survive as a family. At the conference these families and singles are grafted into the church family and flooded with genuine affection and appreciation, as members pay attention to their needs, pray for their pains, and rejoice in their victories. If you never hosted a missions conference for the first two primary purposes but simply determined that you wanted to love on and encourage some tired, frontline warriors in ministry, you might want to consider this as your starting motivation. Every year at the conclusion of the conference, some of our guests confess through tears how discouraged they had been, how exhausted they had been when they came, and how alone they had felt before they arrived—only to express the recuperative power of being in the presence of the Lord with His people for those few days. That certainly is not the expectation, nor is it the measure of a good conference, but when you see how the Lord encourages and builds up through the collective efforts of His people, you cannot wait for the next time.

Ending on a personal note, we call our conference our Annual Missions Festival, and it has become one of the greatest events of the year. Families and singles alike sign up early for our banquet with the result that we have a long waiting list of people who would like to attend, but space limitations prevent them from coming. A steady stream of new missionaries has emerged, many because they either caught the missions vision at the conference or saw the flames fanned to the point of saying, "Lord, send me!" He has, and we rejoice in the full-time missionaries who are commissioned each year to go. But we also find that there is a growth in passion for missions for short-term ventures, and thousands of our people have participated in trips over the years. Our prayer is that at least a tithe of those who go on short trips will one day make the commitment to go into missions as their primary vocation. So far the Lord has been answering that prayer and then some. So the missions conference plays a strategic role but also an inspiring, motivating, and encouraging role in the life and health of our identity as a church family. If you try it, I believe you will like it, especially if you follow the footsteps of some of the great churches who are leading the way in how to do it right.

Practice 3. Visibility, Equipping and Teaching—Pulpit Emphasis (Preaching and Platform Time)

Evangelical churches are churches designed to be gospel-centered ministries. Therefore, it should come as no surprise that effective missions churches with the high value they place on taking the gospel to the nations base that value on the authority and teaching of Scripture. More to the point, churches that preach the Bible thoroughly and faithfully are more likely to see, understand, and respond to the call of Christ to missions. As best practices were identified, it became apparent right away that most of the churches contacted are biblically focused in their pulpit ministry, hence their effectiveness in integrating biblical principles about missions into the fabric of their ministries. One cannot preach the Bible without encountering Christ's emphasis on missions.

However, the practical implications of that show up in different ways according to the preaching styles and approaches of each church. As much as supporters of church-based missions might prefer another approach, the churches most effectively engaging their people in missions do not do so by a steady stream of missions sermons. In fact, one missions pastor responded to the question: "Do you or your pastor preach entire series on missions?" by writing, "In my dreams!" And yes, there are people who love missions who would love to hear sermons about it all the time.

But the majority of respondents to the survey seldom preached specifically on missions as a topical sermon but rather preach through the Scriptures and take missions texts as they encounter them. That does not mean they never preach topically on missions. Most indicated that they do but only periodically and seldom more than a time or two a year. Guest and conference speakers address the topic in the context of missions conferences and emphases, but the majority of the time we discovered the pulpit ministry devoted little concentrated effort to promote missions. Most of the churches responding have at least one or two specific messages on Sunday mornings on missions themes, and some even had a missions emphasis once a month. Among the missional groups of respondents, their approach is to consider every message a missions message.

But as surprising as that finding may be to some, I find it refreshing. Missions should not be isolated from the normal Christian life, so neither should there be an artificial emphasis that raises it to a level beyond the balance of what the Scriptures teach about walking with Jesus Christ. In my own pulpit ministry, as much as I love missions, I seldom preach on it as a topic unto itself. Usually it arises by way of illustration of another point or the application of a broader principle. Then there are the times when it appears in the course of exposition while simply preaching through a book of the Bible and receives its appropriate emphasis in its context within the flow of the author's line of thought. Some pastors and churches divide their preaching year into a series of special Sundays, leaving everyone clamoring for a shot at the pulpit time—Sanctity of Life, persecuted church, Veterans and Memorials Days, Mother's and Father's Days, stewardship, election week, marriage and family, missions, denominational offering days, and so on! Did I leave out your favorite? Everyone wants to get in line to get your voice to advocate their cause from the pulpit! So I find it refreshing that most of the respondents incorporate missions teaching and preaching as they find it in the texts they are preaching. As they work their way through the "whole counsel of God" and as they "rightly divide the Word" through their weekly labors to equip the saints through sound teaching from the Bible, they invariably must address God's passion for the nations.

Therefore, giving attention and emphasis to missions from the pulpit contributes to a healthy, effective climate of missions in the local church. Topical, needs-based preaching that tends to major on a few themes each year seldom produces a passion for missions because when operating from a "felt-need" approach to topic selection, missions is not likely to surface as a key to a successful life or an effective church ministry. The effective missions churches surveyed followed a decisive pattern of biblical preaching that follows a systematic path toward consistent exposition of books of the Bible. As one pastor wrote, "When it comes up in the text, we deal with it!" That is good news for missions because God's Word is filled with His heart for the nations and His desire to send laborers out into the harvest via missions.

One of the side benefits of the lead pastor's preaching or at least mentioning missions in the context of other messages is that the congregation gets a sense of the heartbeat of the pastor for missions. If the subject never comes up unless a conference speaker or outside guest comes in to introduce it, the wrong idea may be given. By bringing missions into his pulpit ministry as a normal part of his preaching regimen, the pastor provides a model to be followed. When that emphasis is then undergirded by his absence from the pulpit to go overseas himself, the presence of someone in his place so that he can participate personally highlights missions in ways that cannot be calculated. If the pastor is content to leave missions in the hands of others, it may be that the signal he sends to the congregation is that he approves of missions but does not personally pursue missions. Whether it is in a sermon preached, a principle upon which ministry priorities are affirmed, or taking his place in active missions involvement by getting on a plane and going, the pastor often sets the tone for missions in ways he may never know or understand. What message is your approach communicating about the value of missions to you?

Nonpreaching Emphases. Preaching may be the most obvious way that the pulpit ministry gives visibility to the vision of Scripture for missions, but there are other helpful ways as well. Since most churches struggle with all the elements competing for time during worship services, limitations have to be placed on what can and what cannot be included. Of course, everyone has an idea about those things. Recently someone even suggested that we take five to seven minutes in each worship time to "get to know the people around you," based on the assumption that no one will want to bother to do that on their own time before and after the service. With all the events going on in the life of a busy church, pulpit time to "advertise" for them is viewed as a major perk, and I fully understand since that is where the largest group is assembled at one time. But if time were devoted to all that would benefit from such visibility, there would be little time for worship!

So what to do about missions? Are we speaking out of both sides of our mouths to laud the value of missions but unwilling to give it a prominent place of visibility in our corporate worship services? How do we maintain a proper balance in such things? Making the problem even more difficult is the proverbial "catch-22" whereby the more effectiveness your missions ministry enjoys, the more people and causes and issues lay claim to the spotlight. By way of illustration, any church would consider itself blessed to send out missions teams on short-term trips and missionaries on full-time assignments. But over the course of fifty-two Sundays a year, where do you fit in commissioning services for a dozen or more missionaries, prayer send-offs for a dozen or more teams and testimonies from those you have sent and prayed for who are at home and whose stories deserve to be heard? All of those take pulpit time, or they do not get it and feel neglected, unappreciated, or that the church/pastor does not really support missions as much as publicly affirmed! Yes, that is the proverbial spot between the rock and the hard place, protecting worship and the proclamation of the Word while giving room for expanding the vision of the congregation by exposing them to regular doses of missions inspiration, education, and motivation.

Some churches have found a way to incorporate brief "missions moments" into the service with great success while others find that it interrupts other priorities in worship if it is included too often. Striking the right balance is tricky, but giving no time on Sunday mornings to missions except for missions conference Sundays leans too far in the wrong direction. We are presently experimenting with an idea suggested by some other churches regarding commissioning and recognizing individuals or groups heading out in missions. For short-term (two weeks or less at this point) missions, we have begun to have the team stand up at the close of the service and recognize them as part of the closing prayer. Although it may not be a full-fledged commissioning service, it does highlight for them and the congregation at large that missions is alive and well.

Most supporters of missions agree that when it is possible to give visibility to missions in the corporate gathering of the church, it contributes positively to the cultivation of a healthy missions culture. But as the survey shows, giving attention to the development of discipleship among the members through faithful proclamation of the Scriptures week in and week out is fundamental to building a mind and heart for obedience to whatever the Lord leads us to do, missions not excepted. Pastors who want to grow a healthy missions culture would do well to continue to preach the whole counsel of God, to preach the Word in all its richness, and then missions will emerge as a prominent feature of a mature congregation. The vision for missions will be caught when the surrounding community of faithfulness demonstrates a willingness to stand up and speak up for all that God commends in His Word. Making room in the pulpit ministry and worship services for the message and heart of missions to be in view works very well toward that end.

In order for people to catch the missions vision, our survey indicates that churches would do well *to plan missions conferences* to educate, inspire, encourage, and provide a context for missions to be visible in a consistent manner *from the pulpit ministry* of the church.

Practice 4. Training and Experiencing—Missions Trips

The third and last of the best practices for making a way for people to catch the vision for missions is to plan regular missions trips with enough range and variety that people from many backgrounds and capacities can participate. Not everyone can afford, nor should everyone attempt, to take long, expensive missions trips. But with a little care, several options can be offered so that anyone with a heart to go can find a way to do so. Each year a passion is ignited in several of our people resulting in a long-term commitment to missions. Reading about what the Lord is doing in another part of the world cannot compare to seeing it for yourself, experiencing the culture and getting a taste of what the missionaries and national leaders go through in order to survive and make the gospel known in that demographic context.

Could there not be a better leveraging of the missions dollars involved in funding such ventures? Well, that depends on what end result you have in mind. Some object to the high cost of paying for what amounts to little actual ministry by the visiting missions team. Their objections have much to commend them if the intent is just to redirect the funds from the cost of the trip to the cost of specific projects on the field, or the support of people already there. Negative experiences with poorly planned, badly managed trips have soured some churches on the idea entirely. In fact, one pastor referred to the trips as "a horrendous waste of time and resources." Based on his experience, he observed that missions trips were nothing more than "vacationaries that drain billions from the missions field and furthermore do not inspire people to become missionaries as is typically thought."[1] If you are looking for financial support for your next trip, best not give that guy a call!

But even though I disagree with his conclusion, his argument needs to be factored in when we lay out our plans for what we hope to see accomplished by sending our members to the ends of the earth . . . or even across town for a mission of mercy. Good stewardship demands that we act strategically regarding missions trips and not just encourage anyone who can afford a ticket and accommodations to hop on board. For some, it becomes a substitute for obedience in some other area, or simply a church-sanctioned adventure trip—a chance to travel to exotic locations while fulfilling the notion that this satisfies all the requirements to qualify for your degree in the school of Christian discipleship.

Well, while the negative characteristics are prohibitive for some, the results of our survey indicate that fully 90 percent of the missions-minded churches responding indicated that they regularly conducted missions trips in order to make an impact on the world for Christ, support and encourage the work of their missionaries or of national Christian leaders, and to stir the hearts of their people toward a more active role in missions.

The primary factor for the majority of churches when planning short-term missions trips is the on-site presence of those with whom they already have an established relationship. It may be with missionaries sent from their own congregation, those who have become partners through their connections with missions conferences or with national leaders with whom a relationship has been cultivated. By coordinating the needs of those already in place with the resources of those coming, legitimate work can be accomplished, even in a short amount of time. Identifying meaningful projects for teams and seeing a project advanced by a large workforce can be a boost to the spirits of your missionaries. But that requires much sensitivity and care so that the trip does not force them to lay aside the work they are doing to accommodate a team that adds little of value and drains valuable time and energy from the reason they are there. Whether the contribution of the short-term team is manual labor and construction types of work (digging wells or training people in drip irrigation skills, building housing or church facilities), or evangelism projects that need many hands and voices to accomplish (like leading a sports camp or backyard Bible school for students or children), or providing medical and educational assistance, jobs training, training pastors and church leaders, or a host of other projects, the benefits can bring the work of the missionaries forward in significant ways when the right kinds of teams come. Seldom does a missions trip team have much success in cold contact evangelism without working in conjunction with those already invested in knowing and understanding the needs of the people in that culture. The logistics of putting that together with no missionaries or national partners already in place put severe restrictions on the effectiveness of such a project. Partnerships tend to offer the best possibilities for teams going on short-term trips.

Another purpose for the short-term team to go is to explore new relationship possibilities with national partners. Gaining a more realistic sense of what they are actually doing instead of having to take their word for it gives the work more credibility when presenting the case for supporting the partnership back home. Sometimes the result is positive and at other times the on-field observations run contrary to the pretrip expectations. In the course of a trip to one location, I was amazed by the breadth and depth of one partner's ministry and appalled by the severe limitations of another. Depending on the information about their work from someone else would never have given me the same degree of confidence that I gained from actually being there. Of course anyone can be misled, and none of us is immune to a great sales job—yes, even from people in ministry! But the likelihood of making good decisions about where to put our missions support is enhanced greatly by having the chance to have our people get their own impressions firsthand.

Other groups serve as advance teams for new works, church plants, and leading in the selection of an unreached people group to adopt by getting on-site information about them and learning as much about them as possible before, during, and after the trip. Several missions trips include a time for prayer walks around the cities or areas where a new effort is desired. The teams returning from such trips represent the needs far better because they have been there than would ever be possible from a mere academic research project about the people. Putting feet on the ground through missions trips pays dividends in prayer support that cannot be measured. As transportation and communication technologies continue to improve, I believe the churches with effective missions ministries will break new ground in what can be done with small teams taking trips to advance the extent to which the gospel reaches the nations.

Developing a Strategy for Missions Trips. Arbitrary choices and randomly picking places to go on trips is unwise. Most churches taking teams on trips understand the value of developing guidelines to determine where to go, how long they will engage in that area of the world, what the best use of teams for each area should be, how funding for trips will be provided, and so on. Other strategic questions have led many to establish policies for missions trips or, at the very least, guidelines to steer the process of knowing where to go, how often, how the teams will be selected, and a wide range of other questions that recur in the process of figuring out how to maximize the use of missions trips.

The strategies will vary according to the values and priorities of each church. For example, one church noted in the survey that they only took teams where they already had a missionary in place and when an invitation to come was issued. Others randomly select a place they want to go and then offer their services to bring a team to those with whom they have relationships. The relative strengths and weaknesses of building continuity by returning for at least five years to the same locale must be balanced against the appeal of getting involved in more places with more people and not going back to the same place until at least a couple of years go by—the latter valuing breadth of outreach and variety, the former valuing continuity and consistency.

Funding Approach for Missions Trips. The costs involved in funding missions trips can be astronomical. Every church sending teams on missions trips must come to some conclusions about how the trips will be paid for—who will pay, what part (if any) the church will cover, whether solicitation letters to the congregation will be allowed (per trip or some other approach), how staff involvement will be covered financially (missions budget, conference and convention expenses, personnel budget, etc.). Few churches can afford to foot the bill for anyone wanting to go on a trip. So some kind of guidelines have to be put in place to address the questions before they come up.

Missions for a congregation takes a major move forward when the people themselves take part in a direct way through special projects and trips that excite their passions, increase their understanding, and put feet on their praying and giving. It really is no wonder that taking missions trips stands out as one of the top ten practices followed by churches with an effective missions focus.

Of all the various ways people in your church can catch the vision for missions, these three stand out as the most effective among the churches we surveyed. By giving visibility to missions from the pulpit ministry of the church, presenting the case for missions during regular missions conferences and festivals, and inviting congregational participation on missions trips have proven to be extremely advantageous in the establishment and cultivation of a missions culture with the congregation. Catching the vision for missions enhances the support for missions in prayer, in giving and in going. When these three are added to the commitment to give ownership to someone within the church for the missions vision and implementation, the results bear witness to the importance and impact of emphasizing missions and elevating it to its proper place in the life of the church.

All of these practices contribute to building a vision for missions in your life and the life of your church. Defining who owns that vision, where the church is exposed to it so that they catch that vision, both work toward building a missions mind-set among the people you serve. Yet six "best practices" from the survey remain to be considered from these categories: adopting a strategy for missions, and sustaining support for missions.

---

1. Contrary to this assertion, nearly all of the missionaries who have been sent by our congregation were first introduced to missions via missions trips. Our prayer is that we will see at least a tithe of the number participating in missions trips making their way back to the field in some capacity. So far that has been realized much to our delight and God's glory. Whether the observation of the respondent is more typical than our experience, I am not prepared to address since that information lies beyond the scope of the survey.

CHAPTER 10 **THINKING AND ACTING STRATEGICALLY**

Once a church has succeeded in building a vision for missions within the congregation, containing the enthusiasm and excitement for reaching the nations with the gospel will be impossible. But who wants to contain it? The point of building a contagious vision shared throughout the church is to mobilize people to move out in pursuit of that vision. In order to do that effectively, two issues must be addressed—adopting a strategy for missions so that there is a consistent, logical method behind the effort, and then finding a way to sustain a missions culture to provide support for the vision for years to come.

The last six of the ten best missions practices fall into those two categories.

Category Two: Adopting a Strategy for Missions

Rather than embrace a noble vision and then attempt to pursue it in a haphazard manner, churches need a strategic approach to their efforts that takes into consideration not only the vision itself but also the purposes, principles, and values of the congregation as a whole. A strategy provides both a logic and a first level of detail for how a vision can be accomplished. If *your purpose* as a church tells you where you are going and why, *your principles* outline the fundamental, essential guidelines you follow in accomplishing your purpose and establishing your vision, and *your values* express what you consider to be of utmost importance among all that distinguishes your ministry, then *your strategy* is what provides a reasonable means of moving ahead. Two questions need to be answered as part of the strategy for missions: Who gets the support? Where do we focus our efforts?

Who Gets the Support?

Everyone wants a piece of the missions budget. Once the ball gets rolling and people catch the vision for giving and going, candidates will emerge who want a chance to present their case for financial support from your church for their missions calling. In the early years of our church, evidently word got out that we were motivated and shaped by our passion for missions. Soon we were swamped with requests from all kinds of people wanting to be included in our missions budget. Without a policy or guidelines already in place, we soon found that our support was far from strategic. Because several universities with strong campus ministries surrounded us, our missions budget tended heavily toward the funding of new college graduates going on staff with various campus ministries around the United States. We were grateful for them and blessed to have been a part of getting them started, but we soon realized that if we were going to reach the nations beyond our borders, we needed a strategic plan for how our dollars would be invested.

As we began to implement the strategy, we were not popular with those we had supported for years and now had to implement a reallocation of funding. Usually we set up a weaning process that gradually decreased the amount of our support over a three-year period for those who did not meet the criteria of our strategy. That way they had plenty of time to find alternate means of support as our funds were redirected elsewhere. Most of them understood our reasons, and soon we were on our way to becoming more prudent in whom we supported. Funding questions typically dominate discussions when church missions leaders meet because there is no easy answer with so many legitimate needs crying out for assistance. What we discovered in the survey reveals an interesting trend that showed up as something that was considered one of the best practices in over 85 percent of the larger missions-focused churches and around 70 percent among the smaller churches. That represents a widespread and significant emphasis!

Practice 5. Prioritize Partnerships with Indigenous, National Leaders

Partnerships with national Christian leaders, indigenous to their own country and culture, have become much more important with the rise in communication technology and the travel options available these days. Finding and developing relationships with those already engaged in gospel-centered ministry in a nation are much more likely to provide advantages and advances in the work of missions in that land. They already have knowledge of the culture in a natural way that would take many years to cultivate by someone from outside the culture.

Although this is not an exclusive plan for determining who gets the support, more and more churches are discovering the value of finding partners in the places they want to reach with the gospel. The need to maintain a portion of the missions allocations for those going from your own congregation is obvious. How discouraging would it be to lead someone through the process of listening and responding to the call of God to missions and then tell them that even though they are like family to you, because of your practice of supporting national leaders, you cannot support them!

Nearly every church recognizes the necessity of sending its own people to the locations of most strategic focus with the full support of their home church. That does not mean they receive all of their support from the home church but an amount that communicates genuinely the level of interest and concern present within their own congregation.

With the shift to the emphasis on support for nationals, there is great diversity in the way the respondents to the survey go about it and their reasons for doing it. Past patterns of missions strategy focused on transposing a Western model, even a United States style of church, into a vastly different cultural setting. Friends who served as missionaries in Central America told us that the village church they attended was an eclectic convergence of Latin and European/United States church forms and traditions. Two specific examples stand out in my mind. The vibrant, lively faith of the people did not survive the transition from daily life with Christ to the worship time on Sunday mornings. The worship singing was subdued and endured rather than enjoyed as English hymnals had simply been translated into Spanish, but the melodies were still as they always had been—clearly not in the musical tastes and styles of the Latin culture in which the church was located. At weddings and family gatherings, our friends noticed the excitement in the singing, the celebrative nature of the music, and the joy on the faces of the people. When they asked why that spirit never made it into the worship time at church, they were informed that they were merely reproducing what they were taught in church by the missionaries who started the church. National, indigenous leadership would have known that and corrected it, but the old patterns just superimposed the cultural preferences of the missionaries onto the people.

The second example is brief. Behind the pulpit was a choir loft, but during the time our friends attended the church, there had never been a choir. Behind the little wall separating the choir from the rest of the platform, the area served as a catchall, a storage area, with no real purpose. Again, when asked why they had built a place for a choir they never had, the reason was simple— American missionary teams had built the building, so of course they assumed it needed a place for a choir. Silly example perhaps, but symptomatic of old-school missions approaches that were often guilty of just such practices.

Support Goes to Nationals. With the rise in cultural awareness and the recognition that gospel distinctive and cultural distinctive are not always the same, there is a new day in partnering with those who are from the culture to be reached who can bridge the gap between the gospel and the people in ways that are not as culturally conditioned. These new developments suggest that more churches with a heart for missions are moving toward a better understanding of the gospel itself and a better recognition of the needs of the people groups they are trying to reach.

In order for the emphasis on partnerships with nationals to work well, several assumptions need to be addressed:

Assumption 1. To have a partnership with some indigenous national leader, the gospel must have been introduced to that people group for such a leader to exist.

Assumption 2. Pioneer work involving cold-contact, bridge-building works of evangelism cannot operate with this model. The Great Commission is to be understood as a directive to take the gospel to the nations and make disciples of those we find, not just search around to see if there are already disciples present and applaud them for believing. The assumption of the Scriptures is that wherever we find lost people, there is a need for someone to go and tell them of the saving power of Jesus Christ. This commission to make disciples of all nations cannot stop at the borders of the hard places where there are no indigenous Christians. Joel Rosenburg, in *Inside the Revolution*, stated that the gospel is for "all nations. . . . Not just the safe nations. Not just the democratic nations. Not just the free market nations. Jesus told His disciples to go make more disciples in *all* the nations. Even the difficult nations. Even the dangerous nations. Even the Radical nations."[1]

As churches find ways to engage in partnerships with national leaders, the strategic value of that practice is great—as long as we do not allow that approach to get in the way of our determination to reach all nations, even those where there is no gospel witness. We partner with nationals when we can but persist with the gospel because we must!

Assumption 3. Care must be taken not to develop unhealthy codependencies which would undermine the missions effort and keep it from developing appropriately. For this reason alone, some seasoned veterans among older missions leaders are not in favor of this method. A noted and respected leader of a missions agency with great influence for the gospel all over the world graciously warned me of the excesses he had witnessed in this regard over the years. Abuse of the relationship occurs often since there is little opportunity for the support base in the United States to monitor in a practical way how the support is being managed by national leaders. Furthermore, he explained that different value systems and assumptions set up potential misunderstandings in how the funds are applied. What may indicate wrongdoing in one culture may be viewed as perfectly legitimate in another. As one who has seen the sad consequences of such misunderstandings in the past, I appreciate the word of caution and pass it on.

However, just because there is the potential for problems does not necessarily mean that the practice should be avoided altogether. With careful planning and investigation before a partnership and regular communication between the partners is established, such issues may not be avoided entirely but can certainly be minimized. As global communications and travel improve and international economic practices become more standardized, some of the primary concerns related to the financial arrangements can be expected to diminish. Issues that arise related to faith and practice are another potential area of conflict, and that must be addressed as the next assumption points out.

Assumption 4. Unless you have a clear understanding of what the national leaders believe and teach, there is a danger that the gospel will be compromised and unequal partnerships will be formed that advocate some form of syncretistic religious experience instead of the biblical truth found in the gospel of Jesus Christ. When the Scriptures require that those serving in the role of either a deacon or an elder must not be a new convert, certainly no less scrutiny must be given to those with whom we would form partnerships that will serve to pass on the gospel. The apostle Paul felt passionately about the critical nature of this transmission of such a treasure when he wrote, "Dear friends, although I was eager to write you about our common salvation, I found it necessary to write and exhort you to contend for the faith that was delivered to the saints once for all" (Jude 1:3).

Surely we owe it to the integrity of the missions message to take care before we entrust ourselves to a partnership with any national leader who will be a spokesperson for the hope we have only in Jesus Christ.

Finding Partners. Finding those with whom to partner is no minor task. Many of them are discovered because of their relationships with missionaries with whom a church already has confidence. Others come by way of recommendations from agencies like Partnership International, which specializes in finding and funding national leaders, or Haggai Institute, which identifies and trains indigenous leaders and then sends them back home to build networks of others like themselves, or African Leadership, a training ministry which operates largely by identifying national leaders on that continent who can raise up others from within their own cultural contexts, usually within their own nation or people group. Working through your own denomination's missionaries who have observed firsthand the ministries of national leaders also provides a level of confidence because you know that you share with them the same vision and values in assessing the qualifications of those with whom you hope to partner. Many other organizations similar to these have a long history of service to and in the far corners of the globe and have established themselves as trustworthy "missions brokers" who serve to connect resources in the United States with needs abroad.

Once the leaders are identified and confidence starts to build, the partnership can begin in earnest. Before our missions team enters into a partnership with a new people group or in a new location, we make a commitment up front that our initial investment of time and people and funds will be for at least five years. During that time we will send regular teams and leaders from our church to spend time serving with folks from their team. Over the course of those years, we often find a kindred spirit that encourages us to dig in for the long haul so that many of our partnerships have now been in place for as long as twenty years or more.

Since its publication in 1990, Henry Blackaby's *Experiencing God* has made a lasting impression on those who have studied it.[2] Perhaps the most quoted idea from the book can be paraphrased in this way: "Find out where God is working and then join Him!" That seems to be the principle behind the move of so many churches to discover national, indigenous leaders who are doing a great work and then get behind them, partner with them, undergird their ministries with resources they do not have in order to have the kind of impact we as outsiders cannot have.

Support Becomes More Targeted. Of all the churches surveyed, large and small, the goal of spreading out our focus across the globe has found fewer advocates as churches favor going deeper in a few locations than maintaining a shallow breadth that covers many locations. At one time missions churches wanted to have a representative sampling of the globe in their missions support budget, but lately that has been reversed as over 78 percent of the surveyed churches are working toward a more targeted approach that focuses on depth rather than breadth. A pastor from Texas explained it this way, "Having come out of a tradition that supported a lot of independent missionaries with little amounts of money, we have moved our church and missions team to consider what we call 'Strategic Extravagance,' supporting and partnering with strategic missions partners with substantial support." How can you not love that phrase, "Strategic Extravagance"? While I am sure those who received the small amounts were grateful, getting some mileage out of more substantial investments in our missionaries must contribute greatly to their encouragement in the nature of the partnership and to the sense of connectedness on the part of the supporting church!

Partnerships Become More Personal. Whether the recipient of the support is a national indigenous leader, a member sent out from your own congregation, or a family you met through a third party, the beauty of partnerships is the development of personal relationships. Later in this section we will expand on this more fully in a separate consideration of that as one of the top ten best practices.

Strategic partnerships make a lot of sense. If you have not adopted a strategy for pursuing your missions vision that includes a way to engage national, indigenous leaders in ongoing relationships so that you can work together as a team, and if you have not made a priority to target your efforts instead of spreading your support out over too wide an area, perhaps it is time to reconsider why so many churches have done so with such good results. Making that transition may not be easy in light of your current approach; change is never easy or simple. But by doing so you will find that your efforts become more consistent and your connection to the work more dynamic.

Practice 6. Identify and Assess Candidates and Opportunities

What do you do to make an informed decision about the legitimacy of someone's appeal to you for support? How do you determine who is qualified and who may not be suited for the work to which they sense they have been called? After all, not everyone who thinks they have been called to be a missionary has been—or at least not in the way they perceive that calling. As a rule, people become uncomfortable when assessment and evaluation issues come up, whether they apply to them or they are expected to provide that for someone else. Annual evaluations for our church staff are necessary but hardly the most fun part of our ministry year. Interviewing job applicants and making a decision about who is most qualified to fill the position takes a toll because you know that all of the candidates but the one you hire are going to be disappointed.

Can we afford to be any less diligent in making good decisions about who we choose to support as missionaries or which national leaders we select? An astounding 93 percent of the larger churches we asked told us they use an assessment process before undertaking the support of any missionary or national leader. Even among the smaller churches 63 percent also made this an integral part of their process of deciding whom to support. This is encouraging! Because of the importance of making the most of our investment of the dollars available for missions, we cannot afford to spend them frivolously or carelessly on everyone who wants to be a missionary!

The practices we noted among all that were reported in the survey usually fell into two areas—initial assessment to determine suitability and fit with the strategic plans of the missions ministry and the regular evaluation of those who already receive support and who have once received that initial approval. Frankly, I learned quite a bit by reading how many great ways churches are using to accomplish these two tasks. Obviously, one cannot incorporate all of them, but certainly we can refine our processes according to the wealth of good ideas available. In discussing this practice, I will include many of the most consistent ideas we found in the survey and then post other ideas as resources for you to consider in Appendix C at the end of the book.

Initial Assessments. Before someone is sent out by your church with the endorsement of your people and the support of your budget, an assessment must be made to determine if this is the kind of person in whom you can have confidence, if the location to which they are called meets the criteria established to be within your targeted region or people group, and if they are needed and desired by those already serving in the area. If the missions vision takes hold in the church, there should be a stirring among the people as first one, then another, senses that perhaps the Lord is directing them to consider vocational missions. They need help in processing that sense of leading and will turn to the church's leadership, especially those carrying the banner for missions, to ask questions about what to do next. Then there will be others who have already been through that process, applied to various missions boards and sending agencies and are now looking to the church for approval, validation, encouragement, and support. Most of the churches we contacted have developed ways of handling those scenarios.

Assisting the Inquirer. After every missions conference you host, count on the fact that many will respond by making a commitment to be a missionary, but they honestly do not know the first thing about what to do next. In order not to leave them confused or frustrated, effective missions churches lead them through the maze of possibilities and help them ask the right questions, get the right training and experiences, contact the right people, and make a sound determination about the validity and direction of their calling. That might involve something as simple as giving them the address and phone number of the denominational missions headquarters or missions agency in which they have expressed an interest, or it may be as complicated as laying out a track of preparatory steps stretching over several years.

At our church we refer to those at this stage as those in the "missionary pipeline." For several years we have had no less than half a dozen and as many as twenty in that pipeline at various stages of assessment and preparation. Usually the preparation process involves not only missions education and information (such as taking the Perspectives course available through the US Center for World Missions, or joining a missions prayer team that gathers materials on missions needs—often nation by nation or people group by people group—so that their prayers are informed and specific); but in a broader way the process might also take them through a basic discipleship course to build into their lives the disciplines of a growing Christian life. In addition to that, they need to prepare theologically and doctrinally through formal and informal studies that introduce them to great writers and thinkers who will help them establish solid foundations upon which their faith will be built. Then, of course, the practical side of preparation will always engage them in direct ministry opportunities which demonstrate their humility and willingness to serve Christ and His body, to reach out and minister in the community, and to take advantage of service projects that train them in the realm of teamwork and submission to others. Sometimes many of those criteria have already been a part of their lives before they express their intent to pursue missions, and the length of the process is reduced. But in other cases the road of preparation may involve at least a couple of years of focused investment on their part.

On many occasions when faced with such an involved process, I have run into some resistance by those who want to just jump on the next plane and go somewhere. But it is important to point out to them that a call to go is also accompanied by a call to be equipped. Rather than seeing it as a waste of valuable time that only delays what they believe God wants them to do right away, a good process includes a well-designed rationale to explain the value of good training for those who really want to be effective where God leads them. Some churches have a defined, formalized process,[3] while others are more inclined to follow a custom design for each potential candidate which is informally administered by the missions leaders or pastors of the church. In any case, the goal is both to prepare the people responsibly and encourage them lovingly as they seek God's will regarding what He has in store for them.

Assessing the Candidate. Once the person has been properly trained and prepared, the next step usually is to apply formally for acceptance by a sending agency and to appeal to the church for its support. That is when you need to be ready with assessment tools and guidelines that move both the candidate and the church to reach a conclusion about whether support will be forthcoming and at what level.

Usually the first stage of assessment comes with an application submitted at the request of missions leaders. No candidates should expect a decision on support without providing extensive information about the nature of their conversion and calling, their qualifications and formal preparation/education, a brief description of their ministry history and service record, references who know them well enough to speak in depth about their character and ministry gifts, a thumbnail sketch of their theological perspective, and a statement of their understanding of the importance of being an engaged member of a local church[4] (with evidence of their personal commitment in support of that understanding).[5]

Beyond the basic application, a fair assessment of candidates extends the privilege of a personal interview, either with the person charged with that responsibility or with a committee/team chosen for that purpose. Among many of the churches, the interviews comprised a multilevel process, usually beginning with a preliminary conversation with a pastor or a designated church leader followed if warranted by an interview with a group of people whose task is to pose questions and ascertain through their general observations whether the candidate matches the criteria required to be appointed by and from their church.

Whenever possible, before your church gives serious consideration to a candidate for support, unless you yourself will serve as sending agency, it is best to expect that the entity that will be directly involved in overseeing their work as missionaries do their own assessment. Before putting their stamp of approval on a candidate, reputable missions agencies and boards submit every candidate to a battery of probing tests and interviews, run them through a rigorous series of training exercises, require extensive application forms be completed, and track down personal references with great vigilance. Not all boards or agencies use the same criteria for approval and appointment, so it is possible that a candidate may wash out of one process only to find the next agency ready to welcome them with open arms. On several occasions, candidates from our church have been devastated at being turned down by one group only to see the sovereign hand of God at work in keeping them available until they found an even better match with another group.

For those who are undecided about where to apply and whom they want to serve with, there are other unaffiliated groups offering general assessments for possible candidates. The Acts 29 Network and the ACMC (Association of Church Missions Committees) were mentioned in the survey responses as two groups providing capable and trustworthy assessment resources to assist local churches in their efforts to be diligent at such a pivotal moment in the life of the candidates and in the interest of faithfulness for the church being asked to make such a weighty decision.

Another useful resource in assessing a candidate for a particular field of service is to invite the scrutiny of those already on the ground in the place they want to go. On one occasion a short-term worker finished his term and applied to go back full-time to the same area to serve with the same team. Much to his dismay, the team was unanimous in its assessment that he was not a fit for their team, that he was, in fact, a disruptive factor and created many hardships that detracted from the work. Without that vital assessment from those on the ground, the missions team would have missed out on a critical piece of information in making their determination about the strong desire of the candidate to return. So the opinion of the existing team and the kind of additional staff they need for their work must be considered as part of the assessment process. It may take some creativity on your part to figure out how to get their input with the distance involved, but it will be well worth it in the end!

Whatever approach you develop to assess the suitability of those who come to you for your blessing, endorsement, and support, you can be encouraged with the knowledge that thousands of other churches are just as committed to getting this right as you are. As your people see the vigilance involved in the appointment and support process, their confidence will grow as they learn that they can trust both their funds, and possibly even their own missions calling, to a church that does this well.

Evaluating Missionaries. Although most of the initial insecurity comes at the front end of the process as new candidates are brought into the missions network of families supported by your church, the other part of the support puzzle includes a consistent plan to be informed about what is happening with those already on board. We heard over and over again in the survey the need to make sure the church is current regarding the status of their missionaries. The need can be summed up in one word—*communication!* Everyone supported by and connected to your church missions effort needs to understand that if they expect to maintain their good standing with you, they will have to submit to regular requests for information that will enable the folks back home to have a high degree of confidence that they are actually doing what they have been sent to do.

The access available through electronic media makes it inconceivable for churches and their missionaries to ever lose touch with one another. Granted, some missionaries serve in places with limited access to such things, but even they can usually find ways to connect with some regularly scheduled plan of communication. E-mail, Internet-based video and audio calls, cellular and satellite phones, as well as good old-fashioned mail through the postal service provide the means for nearly all missionaries and their churches to stay informed.

Some churches require quarterly reports from their missionaries to stay on top of recent developments in their lives and ministry. Others depend only on annual reports but expect regular, informal contact. Still others make it a matter of policy to have every missionary resubmit their application each year if they expect to be considered for continued support. In an ideal world with unlimited resources, having on-site visits with those you support is by far one of the best ways to do comprehensive evaluation of their life and work. Not many churches can afford to send someone on that many trips to that many places; but when you are considering the locations for missions trips, it is often a good idea to include many of the places you already have workers so that you can have direct reports from people from your own missions ministry who have been "on the ground" with those you support.

The results of the survey did not suggest that any methods of evaluation are obviously superior to others, so the field is rather wide open. The primary finding is that the old saying is true for missions: "Don't expect what you don't inspect!" If you want to stay current and confident about how your missionaries are doing, you have to ask and expect a response.

Three other notes are worth bringing up. First, when you decide on the means you will use to keep in touch for evaluative purposes, be aware that those same means will also serve you and the missionary well for encouragement purposes. When they hear from you regularly, it is not nearly as threatening to them to be asked to submit reports periodically since they are used to communicating anyway. Second, when the doors of communication are wide open, you can sense when you may be asking too much too often and impeding the progress of their work. Anyone in ministry can attest to the need for regular reports on the status of ministry but also to the danger of becoming so bogged down with administrative work that the ministry suffers from the time drain required to meet the demands of all the expectations back home. And since most missionaries receive support from many sources, what you require can be multiplied by the number of others like you expecting the same things. So pay attention when you are in touch to see if there is a sense of frustration, a sense that too much is being asked of them. Third, the communication path is a two-way street. Not only does it lead to your door with information and reports from them, but you can also make sure you are sending them resources that will encourage and build them up. Most churches have media resources—recordings of Sunday services, sermon series, online teaching resources, music and worship tools, and so on. While the communications are taking place, why would we not give them something back? Evaluation, as strategically important as it is, is not the only benefit to be gained from these interactions!

Assessment and evaluation play a major role in getting the right people to the right places around the globe and keeping them there. Effective missions churches seem to have latched onto this concept and are doing a good job worthy of imitation.

Where Do We Focus Our Efforts?

The world is a big place, and nearly seven billion people represent more need for the gospel than we can possibly grasp. So how do we go about deciding what to do and where to go in an attempt on our part to maximize our impact with the limited resources we have. Given that we serve a Sovereign God who has no such limitations brings great comfort, but we still must act wisely and strategically to leverage what we have for the greatest possible good in making the glory of God known in all the earth.

Two practices came to the surface in the course of our survey that help narrow down such a massive world into manageable target zones. As we have already noted, churches have now recognized the importance of a rifle approach instead of a shotgun approach, focusing on depth instead of breadth in where the church should focus its efforts in formulating our missions strategy.

Practice 7. Adopt a People Group or Region

By zeroing in on a specific people group, region, or nation, many churches have found that their focus in missions becomes sharper and their people are able to connect much better with more information about fewer places than they are with less information about more places. Although this practice has solid representation among larger churches (62 percent of the larger churches do this), it is less common among smaller churches (47 percent of them do). The survey revealed that some churches have this as a goal but have not yet implemented it as an integral part of their missions strategy.

When we first ventured into this area, I was not convinced that it would make much difference, especially since our missions team chose a rather obscure people group familiar to only a few unusually savvy missions supporters. But as we identified the people group to the congregation and invited them to start praying for them, several things happened—some immediately and some that are still unfolding to this day, nearly twenty years later! Information about the people started showing up on a missions bulletin board, and our members began to be inquisitive about them and the region in which they were located. Instead of trying to pray for an entire world each week, people could focus more personally on the people with whom they were becoming familiar through pictures and articles provided by the missions team.

Soon, instead of focusing exclusively on that one people group, the vision expanded to adopt not just them but the region around them that shared a common cultural and religious heritage as well as a common history of oppression and tribal hostilities. Teams preparing to take missions trips started looking for opportunities in the adopted region instead of the random approach normally used to determine where to go and what to do. Our church hosted a conference for other churches and individuals who shared an interest in the same region and with the same groups of people, and before long we started hearing reports of new missionaries being appointed to those nations who had been spurred on by things they had learned or confirmed in the direction they had been heading by the materials communicated through the weekend conference we hosted.

Missions trips started connecting our people with folks already on the field, vision started growing for the region, love started flowing for the people there, and in just a few years we have witnessed a flood of people relocating their families and their life together to various cities and villages throughout the adopted region. For security purposes I cannot disclose where they are, how many of our families have responded to God's call to the region, how many more are in the "pipeline" bound for the same part of the world, or many other amazing details of the ongoing story. What I can say is that we never could have anticipated what God has done. We had no strategic plan, made no direct appeals, shared no dramatic vision, endorsed no aggressive recruiting. All we did was adopt a people group, then a region of people groups with the same general background, started praying and learning about them, sending teams to help those who were already there; and now we have been blessed to see our folks planting churches where once there were none, pioneering into places where opposition to the name of Jesus Christ is fierce, and waiting on the Lord to show us what to do and where to go next.

Already there is a subtle movement to adopt other regions, and interest is rising among many of our people in other areas in desperate need of a gospel witness. Adopting is not really that difficult, but the benefits we have seen make it all the more likely that we will continue to encourage some form of adoption for years to come. Presently it is not so much a congregation-wide initiative as it is focused among people whose hearts have been impressed to start praying and learning about the next new wave of where God wants us to target our interests.

Among the churches in the survey, adopting regions or people groups or nations has resulted in one church working together on a goal to plant one hundred churches in a small Central American nation. Another church has adopted Peru and partnered with a national church there to "reach one hundred villages along a sixty-mile stretch of the main river" and have seen more than seventy-five of their own members participate personally on trips to Peru, and many more pray persistently and give sacrificially for the project. Another church has a five-year focus in the Dominican Republic that has resulted in scores from their singles ministry investing a couple of weeks each year in their adopted barrio. Now two young women have returned full-time for a two-year stint among the same people. Adopting a specific people and targeting the focus of your ministry has proven to be an effective way to inflame the passions of your people and excite them to pray more specifically and in a more informed way. It allows them to take action to go themselves (short-term and long-term) and increases the level of sacrificial giving among those who find themselves drawn to the place and people in a manner that broad missions appeals never did.

Among the ten best practices, adopting a people group, region, or nation may not seem like a big deal. But as many can attest, if you are willing to try it, get ready for God to show that He is able to make much of a little. Not every church that gets involved in doing this will see dramatic results or experience wholesale transformation of the people who buy into it, but the worst that can be said is that you united your hearts with the heart of the Father for yet another group of people in this world for whom Christ gave His life. On second thought, that actually is a big deal!

Practice 8. Plant International Churches

Terminology has changed quite a bit since our congregation began in 1978. In the initial days of our ministry, we were considered a mission, not a church. Early flyers and materials referred to us as Providence Baptist Mission, and only after we were properly constituted were we considered to be a church. So beginning a new congregation was called starting a mission church. Now all you hear is conversation about church planting. Everyone wants to plant a church these days. Over our thirty years, we have planted five local churches and have plans to do so every four or five years in our own area.

But what about church planting beyond the area? What happens when we get serious about planting churches around the nation and the world? A church in a neighboring city has announced that it plans to plant one thousand churches over the next forty years.[6] During the past decade, our congregation has witnessed an amazing period of sending folks away on purpose! Since 2000, we have planted two churches locally sending a total of nearly five hundred members to provide a strong starting foundation, while at the same time sending out nearly 125 missionaries, many of them committed to planting churches overseas. Perimeter Church in the metropolitan Atlanta area has planted thirty-nine churches in that area alone and more than double that internationally.[7]

According to the survey results, this phenomenon is being replicated by missions-minded churches all over. If the random sampling of the survey gives any encouragement, a little over 75 percent of the churches responding were involved *directly* in some way with planting churches internationally. The number would be higher if we included those who indicated that they were supporting such plants financially and through their denominational missions efforts; but when over three-fourths of the churches with a missions emphasis affirm that they are directly involved in planting churches, I cannot help but be encouraged!

As you might expect, with so many different churches going about this task, many distinctive ways of planting churches are being used. There are two main approaches to international church planting, each with unique characteristics of its own—working through providing resources for indigenous, national leaders and sending church planters from our own culture.

Working with Indigenous Leaders. When we identified the prevalence of the practice of support for national, indigenous leaders earlier, it should have been obvious that the natural connection would emerge with the church-planting process. By far this is the most common approach when planting churches in areas where the gospel has already been made known. Identifying the leaders, funding their efforts, training and equipping them, and then when possible offering on-the-ground assistance are the primary ways mentioned by those following this approach to church planting.

Low-key work sometimes produces the most lasting results. A church in California told of two couples who have spent their lives in church planting overseas without either one ever taking the role of pastor. Church planting among the Lauje tribe and the Satare tribe has been cultivated by two missionary families who understood their task to be one of reaching, teaching, and training indigenous leaders. Thirty years after coming to the Lauje tribe, and fifty years after coming to the Satare tribe, each of these people groups have somewhere around two thousand believers grouped in church families that look nothing like foreign imports because they have grown out of the leadership raised up from their own cultures.

Rather than sending missionaries who intend to plant the churches themselves, most of the churches have strategies that include some variation of sending workers in to introduce the gospel, take initial converts, and train them to reach others, and then serve as those who undergird the work of church planting with their support, encouragement, and training so that the work remains in the hands of nationals.

Pioneering into Unreached Areas. What if there are no known believers in the area to which God has called you to plant churches? In part that has been answered, as in the case of missionaries taking the gospel in but then leaving the planting to those who come to Christ out of the culture. But that begs the question: How do those first efforts to reach the unreached, unchurched unbelievers fit into the international church-planting emphasis?

That question has been on the minds of Great Commission Christians since the first missionary journeys of Paul! So I will not attempt to break any new ground in answering that question. However, one approach that is being field-tested these days is the idea of planting a church by being the church. Sending a team of believers into a city who are actually doing legitimate business in that city gives them the platform to be present as individuals.

But as many expatriots overseas do, they also meet together each week as a church. This model does not actually qualify as an international church plant, but the desire behind the strategy is to give a presence to the gospel in the community out of which proclamation will come.

Others have chosen a more pragmatic approach and provide services that give them platforms for the gospel. Through medical teams, agricultural workers, water and sanitation engineers, disaster relief, orphanages, sports camps and leagues—through a wide variety of creative venues—teams of people from churches like yours are assisting nationals in ways that generate new ways to introduce the gospel. In some locations drip-irrigation systems have opened doors previously slammed shut to Christians because drought had robbed entire regions of their means of survival. An answer to their need for survival opened their ears to the message of life from those who came to help. Camps and leagues have captured an international interest in a wide variety of sports, opening the door for athletes to give a reason for the hope they have within them.

By partnering with national Christian leaders in India, we were able to help them reach a small coastal village devastated by a tsunami a few years ago. Completely closed to any Christian presence prior to the disaster, village elders saw love and compassion from the hearts and hands of those who professed faith in Christ when no one from their own religious traditions did anything to help. New homes for seventy families were built, fishing boats were purchased to replace those destroyed by the tsunami, and livelihoods were restored in this tiny village. Now a community center built on the island serves as a church on weekends and a place of weekly children's Bible-teaching programs through the week. A national pastor serves the people of that village, and many are coming to know Christ because a storm blew away their reluctance to hear of the One who moved hearts and hands to help them. On a hot and humid afternoon two years ago, I sat on the floor in that center and watched as a room full of village children put on an hour-long program they had prepared just for us. They wanted to say thanks for loving them enough to help them in their time of extraordinary need but, more than that, to allow us to see these kids—mostly from Hindu families—singing Christian songs, acting out Bible stories, and quoting long portions of the Scriptures they had memorized! Frankly, not a large number of them had made any commitment to Christ, but God honors His promises and blesses His Word so I have no doubt that the pastor who is faithfully serving that small village will one day soon have planted a new church among those who have responded to the gospel.

As long as there are needs and interests and desires in any people group, there will be a way to make the gospel known among them. International church planting calls on us to partner with those present when possible; and to think outside the box when they are not, to make His glory known and invite people to embrace the treasure that resides in us, Jesus Christ the Savior of all who believe and Lord of all the earth!

A Word of Caution. Not everything that is called a church plant actually is one. Confusion arises when different definitions are used when declaring that a church has been planted. An underdeveloped understanding of biblical ecclesiology leads to some rather superficial labeling of what may not actually be a properly established church. Reports from one missions agency suggested that the number of church plants the previous year was not far from the number of actual conversions reported leading one to think that some clarification was going to be necessary before the reports could be viewed in the kind of favorable light in which they were presented. Standards will vary from denomination to denomination, but there must be some integrity in defining what it means to say that a church has been planted.

In one fairly rigorous definition used by one indigenous church-planting movement in a predominantly Muslim nation, a properly constituted church consists of at least thirty newly baptized converts from a previously unbelieving background. They adhere to this so strongly that seminary students are not granted their Master of Divinity degrees until they have planted a church on those terms. One student I met had completed his course work but had not yet succeeded in the church-planting requirement because he had not yet reached the minimum standard needed to reach that goal. Some may find that overly strenuous and arbitrarily punitive to those who had good intentions but had not yet enjoyed evangelistic effectiveness. Witnessing graduation ceremonies in that context can be somewhat overwhelming. In a recent year the number of graduates was reduced by two before the actual ceremony. Two student pastors who had fulfilled all the requirements had been martyred, killed in the line of duty because their labors for the gospel had not escaped the notice of those hostile to Christ in the villages where their new churches had been planted. With that as background, the impact is that each year as scores of graduates cross the platform to receive their degrees, the number of new converts and church plants represented, and the sacrifices made, humble the most aggressive church planter in the West!

At the other extreme would be the claim that a new church has been successfully planted when a "man of peace" has been discovered in a town or village who is willing to allow meetings in his home to discuss religious issues, including but not exclusive to the claims of Christ. Or a group has begun to meet to study the Bible together and is designated as a new church plant, even if no one has yet made any claim to have believed and become a follower of Christ. However, a church exists only when people gather together who actually know Christ as Savior. Then the claim can be made that a church has been planted.

Another example that falls between the two extremes is described by Leo Mooney, from Twin Oaks Presbyterian Church in Ballwin, Missouri, who considers a church to be composed of "a minimum of fourteen members (not just attendees) with at least one elder and one ordained preacher." They are committed to church planting with national leaders, supplementing their labors with missionaries from their own denomination.

> The two areas that our church is supporting are somewhat unique in that they are nationally driven with our denominational missionaries working in support roles. We love this model, and it is one we have been looking for. And the issue of enabling has been defused in that we still funnel finances used to help support nationals through our own denominational missionaries who know who they can trust and who truly is working to build the kingdom of God. Are there mistakes? Sure.
>
> However, with nationals leading their own to Christ, there seems to be much more stability than when we support works that were built around an American building a church in our image. We do send our pastors and other leaders who are apt to teach to places like India where they are used to help train the nationals in core seminary classes. It would take some time to spell out the whole structure, but we are excited in that trained national preachers and teachers, tested and approved by their own national presbyteries, are out there doing the work of church planting. It is working.
>
> Both our focus areas are in reality church-planting movements led by nationals. We are supporting six missionaries in India/Pakistan, four of which are nationals. We support four missionaries working in Northern Mexico; two are nationals. We are sending working teams and vision teams into these areas in support of the national effort. In India we have seen more than fifty churches planted this year by nationals.
>
> We believe there will be seventy church plants in India by the end of this year. This is truly a church-multiplication

movement. And the most exciting thing for me is that they are not building on just a John 3:16 mentality and then moving on; it is embedded into their church-planting DNA to teach the whole council of God and continue to provide the training necessary for nationals so they can do this.

Church plants in Northern Mexico are also nationally led. The group working out of Monterrey has their own Bible Institute for training potential pastors and church leaders. The movement is a little slower in this area of the world, but it is consistent, and it appears to be building on a foundation of permanency. We love this ministry.[8]

Obviously there is a marked difference between a rigorous and a superficial definition of what is rightly called a church plant. I am not as concerned about the former as I am about the latter because I see in that approach a serious minimizing of what it means to be a church. That is a genuine cause for concern for those who long to see legitimate, biblical, New Testament-style congregations begun with those who have been found and saved by the grace of Jesus Christ. We should applaud and encourage more of the multiplication model in India as described by Mooney and modeled by thousands of similar movements around the world. The success of the church-planting movement cannot depend on padded reports and exaggerated success stories. Yet we must keep introducing people to Christ and keep planting churches composed of new believers who are then given a place to grow and be equipped to do it all over again somewhere else.

As you think about how to get started to make international church planting a focus of your missions emphasis, think simple and small initially. Find someone you know and trust who is doing well in this area and ask if you can come alongside and help them do what they are doing while you are learning. Perhaps your denomination has already led the way for you and all that is needed is for you to plug in with a project they have underway. If you have already started meeting with and supporting national, indigenous leaders, they can become a great resource for you as you find creative ways to bring resources to the table to which they do not have access. However you do it, you will be blessed when you do!

I am thankful that international church planting ranks in the top ten of the best practices of effective missions churches because I love the church, the bride of Christ! What an honor to see the beauty of the bride enhanced by every new thread woven into her gown as people from every tongue and tribe are added to the garment of the one He has chosen to be His own!

---

1. Joel Rosenburg, *Inside the Revolution* (Carol Stream, IL: Tyndale House Publishing, 2009). See Appendix B, 219, for the complete quote.

2. Henry Blackaby, *Experiencing God* (Nashville: B&H, 2008).

3. In Appendix C, there is a brief summary of the process used by Bethlehem Baptist Church in Minneapolis, Minnesota, provided by their missions intern, Steven Lee.

4. Gary Coombs, Shadow Mountain Community Church and Southern California Seminary: "All our missionaries have a home church. Either our church or another. We believe the primary accountability to be to their home church." Whether everyone agrees with Dr. Coombs or not, if we intend to send missionaries to introduce people to Christ and plant churches made up of new converts, it seems contradictory to our purposes if those we send do not themselves place a high value on the importance of being an active, supportive member of a local congregation.

5. A sample application is provided in Appendix C, Assessment and Evaluation Ideas.

6. "At the Summit, we have a vision of planting a thousand churches in the next forty years. We expect God will accomplish this through our intentional focus on planting reproducing gospel-centered churches around the world." Curt Alan, pastor of church planting and community ministries, Summit Church, Durham, North Carolina.

7. Tom Mullis, pastor/director of global outreach, Perimeter Church, John's Creek, Georgia.

8. Leo Mooney, director of world missions, Twin Oaks Presbyterian Church (PCA), Ballwin, Missouri.

CHAPTER 11 MISSIONS WITH STAYING POWER

O nce you have made it this far, there is no reason to turn back! Building a biblical vision for missions among your people, then adopting a strategy to pursue that vision will have resulted in a favorable response in you and your church. But anything worth doing all that for is worth sustaining. How can you give missions the staying power it needs to bear fruit for generations to come? What do other effective missions churches do among their best practices to sustain their efforts?

Category Three: Sustaining the Support for Missions

Once you have developed and built a captivating vision for missions among your people, and have started to adopt a strategy that will show you the next level of detail in reaching that vision, it is essential that you find a way to sustain all of that so that missions will always be supported in a significant way wherever the Lord calls you to serve Him. Flash-in-the-pan passions are common in churches as people get excited by this new program and then another; but unless they are anchored in the culture of the congregation's life and values, sealed in principles and purpose, they will eventually fade away. Missions cannot be one of those passing fancies! It must become a sustainable, long-term, principled commitment of your ministry.

Practice 9. Personal Contact and Relationships

God calls people one by one and loves us enough to invite us into a personal, intimate, growing relationship with Him through His Son, Jesus Christ. His call to missions is intensely personal, just as is His call to any other way He has chosen for us to follow Him. In order to sustain the momentum for missions in the life of your church, the best thing you can do on the personal side of things is to keep up with relationships. Among effective missions churches, the amount of effort involved in doing this shows up in the way they continue to send more and more people as missionaries, and they sustain a healthy missionary support network among those who are already serving.

Keeping Up the Personal Contact. Loneliness leads to discouragement, despondency, depression, desperation, and a host of other unhealthy thought processes and emotions. Being alone is not the same thing as being lonely. One of the toughest battles missionaries have to face is the prospect of being lonely in a distant place with no recourse, no relief, and no remedy. Therefore, one of the most important ministries we can have on the home front is to maintain personal contact with those we send and keep up with the relationships that mean so much to all of us regardless of where we happen to live.

When the surveys started coming back in, a major point of emphasis for 95 percent of churches that do a great job in developing a missions focus is to maintain consistent, personal contact with their missionaries and with the national leaders they support. Loving the nations starts by practically loving Christ, who calls us to give ourselves fervently to love one another. No one who cares about others wants to share any responsibility in leaving people they love to become lonely. Therefore, it was a delight to see people reaching out in love to those God has placed strategically around the world. They are better able to show love to others when they consistently receive love from folks back home.

Having them come visit your church when possible does more to connect them to your church than you can imagine. But, going to visit them on their turf awakens your vision for what they are doing, assures them that yours in not some passive interest, and alerts your church to what they are doing because they see you taking a direct step toward personal involvement with those you support. One pastor even said that he personally writes a note twice a year to everyone his church supports. That totally intimidated me because I know what a massive undertaking that is given the number of people they support.

One congregation reported that their members regularly ask about national leaders they have met when they came for a visit. They make a concerted effort to keep in touch with individuals and families so they may know they are loved, missed, prayed for, and supported. Small groups and Sunday school classes adopt various missionaries and national leaders and send them packages periodically just to let them know that love connects them. We get the privilege of holding the rope for them while they do what God has called them to do.

Partnerships may take many forms, as our survey demonstrated, but the key to this wonderful trend is relationships. I am so thankful that missions is no longer just writing a check to the denominational headquarters for them to distribute as they see fit but that our own congregation gets the joy of knowing their own friends are answering God's call to missions, their new friends with odd last names and strange accents and unusual native garb are real people with life issues just like them. Partnerships are about people who love Christ, love lost people, love one another, and are connecting to make something happen in response to the call of God to make His glory known in all the earth.

The Relational Aspect of Calling People to Go. If people do not know you care, they will never care how much you know. Pastors can try to manipulate, bully, guilt, and in many other ways push people to become missionaries; but those things will never prove to be as effective (if they ever have been!) as simply loving people enough to help them discover the liberating power of living their lives for the glory of God.

Churches will never make a dent in the need for missionaries if our only interest is in maintenance of the existing workforce. We have to be committed to a continuous emphasis on helping those around us learn what it means to find God's will and follow it and to make sure missions is included among the options available to them. Most of the families and individuals we have sent out over the past twenty-five years discovered their missions passion through exposure to international ministries with someone they knew and cared about. Through relationships they learned that most of the people going out were not very different from them—in fact, very much like them in more ways than not.

Networking with people and getting involved in what they are doing generates interest like nothing else short of the direct intervention of the Holy Spirit. Making the congregation aware of the biblical mandate for missions is great and provides the necessary foundation for building a strong missions community in the church. But the key to effectiveness is found in the word *community*, as people find themselves surrounded by people they like, enjoy, and trust, who are seriously entertaining ideas about pulling up stakes and relocating their lives in another part of the world in order to do something tangible about the call of missions God has placed before them.

Pastors should never underestimate their own relational influence when it comes down to figuring out the significant factors involved in seeing people respond favorably to the leading of the Lord into a missions career. When you have loved them and walked through life with them, taught them and discipled them, they will probably be more surprised if you *don't ask* them to give their lives in a substantial way to serve Christ than they will be if you do ask. When you recognize someone within the sphere of your ministry with the gifts, temperament, and love for Christ who appears to be missionary material, you are not trading on your friendship in an inappropriate way to invite them to consider if they might be better suited for missions than for what they are doing right now. Because you know and love them, their relationship with you will prompt them to take the next steps with you to see if the Lord has something greater in mind.

Peer pressure gets a bad rap from parents of teenagers, but in a healthy community of Christ-centered people, watching as your peers pick up and go into missions can have a positive kind of pressure. Not the kind of pressure that pushes the wrong people to head off in the wrong direction, but I am referring to what happens when people love one another and see an opportunity to partner together in the pursuit of a vision with eternal value.

Personal contact with missionaries you already support plays a vital role in a healthy missions environment in your church. But just as important for sustaining the missions movement among your people is the relational side of their interactions with others who are giving missions a serious look. Many of the missionaries you talk to will tell you that they were influenced greatly toward their current place of ministry by someone they cared about and who cared about them—people loving people and leading them in a godly direction in their lives together.

The more you can do to foster a healthy, loving, relationally driven community of missions-minded folks in your church, the more likely you are to find a sustainable model for sending missionaries for generations to come.

Practice 10. Cultivating Generous Giving Communities

All of the preceding ideas and practices may be wonderful, but if no financial resources are provided to make them possible, they will never get off the ground. Therefore, the funding mentality of the church will make or break the best intentions regarding missions. People who have no direct interest in the overall work of the church often have a lot to say about how the money is spent. Although I have no documentation to back this up, I have heard it often enough and seen it in my own ministry, and I am convinced that some of the most vocal members on financial issues are frequently among the least generous with their tithes and offerings. In every church a percentage of people actually participate in the ministry but never contribute one penny, and our church is no exception. Teaching about biblical stewardship and modeling congregational generosity have no impact on what that select group does about their responsibility to be faithful givers to the work of the Lord. So when we enter into a discussion about what effective missions churches do to generate a culture of congregational generosity, we have no unrealistic expectation that any plan or practice will produce 100 percent participation!

However, as the church grasps biblical stewardship principles and practices them at both the individual and corporate level, the impact will be profound in the amount of resources that become available for missions and other ministries. The entry point into the Christian life, grace, introduces us to a God who loves us and gives life to us through no merit of our own. Gratitude for that grace then puts its stamp on all that we do as we seek Christ and walk by the Spirit, living by faith in the trustworthy provisions of the Lord. Giving generously arises from a clear comprehension of grace—that God has given generously in sending His Son—and reminds us throughout our lives that every good gift comes from above. When we get that, and understand that He owns all things and needs nothing from us, any appeal for us to give makes perfect sense to us. He owns everything and merely asks us to give regularly, generously, and sometimes sacrificially.

Churches with a clear and captivating vision, a good reputation for financial accountability and wise stewardship,[1] a trustworthy and mature leadership team, and the ability to communicate well the stories of life change that validate the way funds are being invested will do well in receiving the resources needed to do what the Lord has given them to do. But even if you are doing a great job overall yet withhold vital information, fail to give timely reports on where and how monies given are spent, make no connection between the gifts and the results, and offer no compelling vision or direction, people will be reluctant to buy in with either their feet or their finances. Make sure you are faithfully cultivating a climate of transparency and generosity in a context of visionary ministry that reaches beyond the walls of your own congregation if you want to see people become excited about giving.

When they do, most of the churches we surveyed received and distributed those funds toward missions needs in two primary ways—through a unified church budget that includes a portion for missions or through a separate fund designated specifically for missions. Both have merit, and as you would expect, both have strong voices advocating one approach over the other.

The Unified Budget. By including missions support through the operating budget of the church, the priority the church gives to missions shows up in a direct and measurable way without any special appeals, extra offerings, or division of effort. The basic idea behind the unified budget is that through the tithes and offerings of the congregation, all the work of the church should receive proportional support according to the priorities agreed on by either the leadership team or the congregation as a whole. Using this approach also proves the concept that as the water rises near the shore, all the boats in the harbor rise with it. In other words, as the operating budget increases each year, and the percentages remain constant, missions funds will also increase proportionally each year as well.

In a unified budget approach, the leaders must make sure that generous giving and faithful stewardship are modeled in how the allocations of that budget reflect the biblical pattern. A church will have a hard time convincing its members to tithe if the church does not do so. Asking individuals to give 10 percent according to the scriptural pattern when the operating budget of the church does not give away that much begs for charges of hypocrisy from the people. If you want the people to give both tithes and offerings, the church budget must reflect that in the way it gives to support ministries beyond its own. Missions is the normal place for those funds to go. Stated succinctly, if you want members to give away at least 10 percent of their income, the church needs to give away at least 10 percent of its income. The unified budget approach must reflect that priority.

Most churches using a unified budget also supplement the missions portion with special offerings during the year. Some people in the congregation will want to designate their gifts according to their own priorities and not those of the church. Special missions offerings give them an acceptable way to do that since those gifts are normally focused on a particular project or directed toward a unique area of need. At our annual missions conference, we have often presented a project toward which people could give over and above their normal tithes and offerings. When natural disasters hit, people want avenues for giving; and the church can provide that for them so they are assured their gifts will be directed through channels which have long since been tried and tested because of relationships already in place with those in the area of need. Last year an appeal for help came from our denomination's missions board. The annual Christmas offering was still several months away, and financial deficits were preventing missionaries from making it to their designated fields of service. So in August an opportunity was given for our people to make contributions that would help fill the gap until the major offering in December. But all these extra gifts only supplement what is well established in the annual operating budget, a unified budget that guarantees a percentage of all income will be directed to the support of missions.

A Separate Missions Budget. Lots of churches keep their missions giving in a separate fund and set it up so that the gifts going to missions are all funneled through designated offerings. Most of the churches we heard from use what is often called a Faith Promise plan to fund their separate missions budget. Annually, usually at a different time from the adoption of the general fund or operating budget, the congregation responds to a request from the church to make a Faith Promise, essentially a financial pledge over the course of one year. That Faith Promise provides the resources to fund the missions efforts over the coming year. Advocates of this approach virtually guarantee that more money becomes available for missions by following this process than by simply including missions in the unified budget. Whether that can be proven is the object of much debate between proponents of each, but what can be proven is that the track record for missions among churches using a Faith Promise approach (regardless of what they call it) speaks well of the generosity of their people in making and keeping their pledges to give to support the work of the Great Commission.

Special offerings at other times of the year are not excluded among churches using Faith Promise. Like those with unified budgets, these churches often respond to special projects and needs with other appeals during the course of the year. The primary difference is that multiple appeals are made in one context, and less direct appeals are made in the other.

The End User—Who Benefits from the Budgeted Funds?
As the money is collected—whether through a unified budget or a separate budget—where does it go? Who gets the support? Obviously the intent of gathering or designating money for missions is to send it where it can do the most good. Opinions about where that is can generate some lively discussions both within the congregation and among missions leaders from various churches.

In a surprising discovery, the survey indicated that approximately 56 percent of the churches who responded directed a portion of their missions giving through their denomination's channels. While that represents a majority, it also shows that 44 percent of them have chosen for various reasons not to go that way. Perhaps because of the problems with spending priorities at the denominational level as we noted back in chapter 1, many churches are looking for more efficient ways to leverage their giving so that they can be confident that the desires of the missions givers are honored in the best way possible. There are inherent benefits and downsides to either way you choose to do it, but making sure the funds get where they are most needed is one of the greatest challenges facing churches today. Without a strong commitment to missions, subtle drains on those funds can drastically impact the strategies and plans and people God is raising up to make Christ known among the nations.

Ideas for Gathering Resources. As you might expect, some passionate folks have come up with some creative ideas about how to increase the number of dollars available to support the work of missions. As we showed through the research of Christian Smith, Michael O. Emerson, and Patricia Snell, Christians in the United States are leaving approximately $46 billion on the table every year which could have been invested in ministry,[2] but instead went to support extravagant lifestyles and priorities that required them to drain the money out of God's account into their own. There is no nice way to say that Christians are embezzling from their Father to spend their money on themselves. But through a variety of ways, leaders like you are figuring out how to appropriate more for missions by coming up with ways to encourage reluctant people to give more and to show people how to be even more generous.

Without going into great detail, the ideas usually follow two main lines—simply giving people information about how to give and why the gift is important, and promoting fund-raising activities that engage even those who are not naturally moved by missions appeals but who see value in what is being offered. Garage sales, bake sales, service projects by youth groups, selling inventory produced by microbusinesses overseas that are underwritten by missions funding, auctions of services or goods provided by members (tax preparation services, autographed sports memorabilia, tickets to concerts, discount books for local businesses, etc.)—as many ideas as you can think of seem to have been used to raise money for missions.

Some churches, however, are philosophically opposed to the idea of raising funds by selling anything because they hold a conviction that God's people should give to support His work. They believe there should be no thought of getting anything in return other than the satisfaction of digging deep, sacrificing gladly, and making a generous donation. Making those opportunities available also stirs up some creative ways to generate interest in giving for missions. One church takes the entire morning offering on the first Sunday and designates it for missions to supplement their Faith Promise approach. Another produces videos of their missionaries and national leaders talking about and showing the congregation the results of their investment in missions. Another uses computer and Internet technology to include missionaries in their morning worship times, interviewing them and then allowing them to remain online to participate remotely in the corporate worship as a way of giving a personal face to the financial appeals. Still others publish prayer guides with photographs and biographical sketches of those who will receive support from the budgeted gifts.

When God's people catch His vision for missions, the results show that they are willing to go beyond the ordinary and give generously—if we will just do a good job of helping them see why it matters so much. If missions is merely an extraneous side issue for you and your church, you will have a hard time getting people to justify making any sacrificial efforts to give. But when missions defines much of what you are committed to become as a church, watch the excitement and the generosity grow.

The ten best practices of effective missions churches provide a working model for you to consider applying in your own context of ministry. For those who read through the first two sections, "Where We Are" and "Where We Want to Be," this section, "How to Get There" gives you some specific things you can do. And as the survey showed, large and small churches are following these practices with wonderful things to show for it. Regardless of where you are and what you are now doing, there is a way to move up, to improve, and to make more of a difference in leading your church to become the kind of congregation ready to step out in the power of the Spirit to spread the glory of Jesus' name to the ends of the earth.

Are Best Practices and Methods Enough?

Having conducted a survey and introduced you to the best practices we could find of churches making a significant impact in missions, the question has to be asked, "Is it enough just to imitate what others have done?" Telling the stories of success in other churches does not mean that by replicating their practices you will have the same experience. In other words, organizing and structuring our ministries so that we follow the best practices identified by the churches surveyed may in the final analysis turn out to be ineffective in seeing the desired result—a genuine, transforming commitment of our hearts to reach the nations with the gospel of Jesus Christ. Is it not possible that we could take a purely utilitarian approach and go through the mechanics of implementing every suggestion and still fail to find any real change in the hearts of our people regarding God's call to take the gospel to the nations? Before we conclude this section of the book, I don't want you to get the wrong impression. Numbering and explaining the best practices for building a strong missions culture in the church is not intended to be some kind of magic formula for success.

Organization or Transformation? In a day of rampant pragmatism in the church, a day when people are looking for short-cuts to success in their ministries, new methods and new structures may look attractive and promising. However, no organizational effort or redesign of ministry practices will produce life change. That is the work of the Holy Spirit.

One of the popular passages used in church leadership training contexts is Exodus 18:13–24, the account of Moses and his father-in-law, Jethro. The way I have taught it, and also heard it presented by others, portrays Jethro as the equivalent of a modern organizational consultant. Having observed the highly inefficient and ineffective way Moses was managing his role as the leader of Israel, Jethro laid out a logical, reasonable plan for the work to be divided and delegated. The simplicity of his plan and the obvious benefits to both leader and the ones led give it a natural appeal, especially to those overwhelmed with the monumental nature of their needs, assignments, and responsibilities.

But I missed something of vital importance in seeing this account as just a practical solution to manage a massive responsibility—to break it down into manageable parts, share the burden by organizing the effort and delegating the work to many people instead of a few (in Moses' case, just one). Like the idea of offering you ten suggestions of what you can do to cultivate an effective missions culture in your church, those best practices offer a practical solution as you look for ways to move in that direction. However, there is a principle involved that precedes action.

Earlier in this book I pointed out that the primary impetus for missions is not as an act of obedience to the Great Commission but as the overflow of joy and power from the indwelling Holy Spirit. The principle behind that observation must be noted again here.

Before Jethro gave Moses the organizational chart as a practical answer to the burden he was carrying alone, he charged him with four specific responsibilities of a spiritual nature. Trying to put into practice a utilitarian plan without a spiritual foundation would only increase frustration and ultimately prove to be futile. By adopting the suggestions of Jethro, Moses and the people did experience some level of relief because the burden was spread around and shared by many more responsible parties. However, the root problem remained—the unbelief and unwillingness of the Israelites that left their stubborn hearts unchanged. The system was great. The plan was sound. But the nature of the people was managed, not changed. Their basic character was not impacted by better organization because there had been no real heart transformation. So what counsel did Jethro give Moses before outlining the action points of his plan?

1. Intercede for the people. "You be the one to represent the people before God and bring their cases to Him" (Exod. 18:19).

2. Teach the people God's Word. Teach them how to live and what they are to do (v. 20).

3. Select leaders from the people. Break down the responsibilities into manageable groups (vv. 21–22).

4. Lead them to follow the plan. "You will be able to endure, and also all these people will be able to go home satisfied" (v. 23).

The lesson to be learned here is not complicated. Taking a practical approach to a major task may make sense logically and in fact produce some good results. But in order for there to be a transformation of the people and a change of heart regarding the issue facing them, no program or process or plan will make any lasting difference. Whether the issue is settling the disputes of a rebellious, self-centered people who refuse to walk with God (as was the case with Moses sitting all day every day making judgments between demanding people) or increasing the workforce of missionaries going out from our churches to a world without Christ and without hope, the solution cannot be man-made.

If Jethro Were Your Missions Consultant. What if Jethro came to you, observed what you were doing to lead the missions effort in your ministry and offered you his best counsel? As with Moses, I am fairly certain he would not begin with the nuts and bolts of an organizational plan, a series of practices you should put in place. First things must come first. Godly principles and spiritual transformation should precede the design of a system of actions. Before he offered the particulars of an organizational plan, Jethro laid out the spiritual priorities. Let's look at them again, this time in a slightly different format:

- **Prayer.** *Intercede for the people.*
- **Scripture.** *Teach the people God's Word.*
- **Discipleship.** *Select and train leaders.*
- **Model.** *Lead them to follow the plan.*

So the utilitarian nature of the specific plan was preceded by a spiritual understanding of what it means to lead by demonstrating spiritual leadership. Rather than depending on the mechanics of a structural solution, the key to effective obedience to God's plan is to speak to the heart as well as the mind, to appeal to transformation as more important than organization.

Therefore, following the pattern of Jethro's counsel to Moses, I could not recommend that you just take the ten best practices of effective missions churches and go to work implementing them.

No, it would be far more prudent and biblically sound to return to a different starting point. Jethro laid out four priorities for Moses that emphasized prayer, the Scriptures, personal discipleship, and modeling the character he wanted reflected in his people. Unless you can come up with better priorities than that, why not begin there? Neither the command in the Great Commission nor the best practices of great missions churches can overcome a heart that remains unchanged. Until the power of the Holy Spirit works in us and a transformation of our desires takes place, missions will remain an obligation to duty, not an opportunity for delight.

Now you know what you can do. The question remains: will you? As a pastor or Christian leader, will you be a *cork* or a *conduit* in the pipeline the Lord has put in place to get His people where they need to be to preach the gospel to the nations?

---

1. The survey shows that 84 percent of the churches responding follow a specific budgeting philosophy and plan for maintaining fiscal responsibility in missions, an overwhelming percentage that suggests they have learned that such care with the funds as they come in cultivates both trust and buy-in from those called on to give.

2. Christian Smith and Michael O. Emerson, with Patricia Snell, *Passing the Plate: Why American Christians Don't Give Away More Money* (Oxford: Oxford University Press, 2008), 13–18.

SECTION FOUR
CLOSING CONSIDERATIONS

CHAPTER 12 DO I WANT WHAT GOD WANTS?

Now that we know where we stand and have identified where we should want to be, and even offered several practical suggestions, how are we supposed to get there? Giving pastors and church leaders the benefit of the doubt, we will assume that once the first two issues are addressed, and truth of the biblical mandate is understood, the only reason not to move forward is a lack of knowing how. Then when the way forward has been outlined in the form of best practices from other leaders and churches showing the way, the remaining question we have to answer is whether we are willing to do what we know God wants.

The immediate response will not always reflect the reality. Of course we like to think we are willing to do anything we know He wants, but our fallback position is that we want to find a way to be absolutely certain of what He really wants before we start making extraordinary sacrifices. Since walking by faith precludes knowing by sight what is absolutely certain, I think it is fair to say that most of us choose the safe way. We like to perceive of ourselves as people of great faith, but, instead we frequently choose to walk by sight rather than by faith. So, are we really willing to do what God wants if it means stepping out into uncertain territory, going where the landscape is unfamiliar to us? That question must be resolved in our hearts and minds before we have any reason to figure out how to proceed. Until we know the intentions of our hearts, there is little value in pursuing what a pastor or a church can learn from what effective, missions-focused churches already are doing to develop and maintain a culture of missions that permeates their ministry.

A Personal Heart Check

The first step in a journey is a decision to go, but that step is nearly always preceded by several factors that contribute to our desire and willingness to make the trip. To become the kind of church that embraces its call to missions, a pastor with that commitment is needed. The journey to move in that direction must be preceded by an open heart and surrender of our will to Christ. Personal revival and self-surrender in the pastor and other church leaders must take place before anything of a lasting commitment to missions can take root in a church. Until the pastor is at least willing to go, he will not have much success rallying the church. Even if God does not call him personally to go, he needs to be willing to say without reservation, "Here am I, send me!"

No pastor can stand before his people and challenge them to consider a call to missions who has not dealt with that same consideration in a personal way. That is true for any subject we address from the pulpit, of course. An appeal for action as an obedient response to the leadership of the Lord must be preceded by some soul-searching of your own to see if the reason for the passion in your preaching and presentation may stem from the movement of the Spirit in your own heart. If you have ever been captivated by the prospects of seeing the nations come to Christ and if you have ever pondered what your role is to be in that venture, one of the possibilities you have had to factor into your thinking is that perhaps you are the primary target of the message. We have to ask, "God, what do you want *me* to do?"

What are some of the factors that should weigh into your consideration?

1. Do I Have a Willing Heart?

This elusive question might bring an immediate, affirmative response; but upon reflection, the answer may not be so obvious. No Christians in any kind of leadership capacity would like to think that they are not willing to do what God wants. As already noted, the first response to the question would likely be, "Of course!" What happens, then, if you ask the Lord to show you the true nature of your heart on this matter? Are you willing to submit to a thorough inquiry of the Spirit into the disposition of your will about actually going somewhere other than where you currently are if God called you?

I have been through that process personally and exposed my heart to careful investigation to see if there is any reluctance there. In all honesty, I did find some degree of reluctance to consider the possibility that God might want me to transfer my calling to another location and accept a different ministry than the place to which I have been serving for over thirty years. The sources of the reluctance vary. Age offers a good reason to stay put for my remaining years of active pastoral leadership. The value of longevity in ministry when compared to a series of sequential relationships with a number of churches or ministries could serve as a sound justification for not going anywhere else. The more sentimental and emotional attachments of family come into play—no longer concerned about the ages of my children since they are all grown up, married, and on their own, more recent objections arise from a desire to be near grandchildren (more for my sake than theirs but a cause for a gentle tug to stay near). Then there is the reason all of us face who have been brought up in this culture—the appeal of modern living in an affluent society with more creature comforts than we could name, until we are deprived of them. Could I live without the modern conveniences to which I have become so accustomed? Have I been swept up in the "American Dream" and developed a mentality of entitlement? So even though I might be able to say I am willing, I might do so knowing that I could come up with sufficient reasons to decline should a specific situation arise.

If I do not go, I must have a good, God-given reason to stay. Now it would be unfair to say that all such reasons are just excuses. Legitimate reasons for not going have kept me in the same church for just about my entire ministry. But it would have been wrong never to have asked honestly if God supported such a decision and was the Author of that special calling. After all, God does sometimes test the heart to determine our willingness to do what He requires. Abraham found out that God always provides when He sees the willing nature of our hearts. As he raised the knife to give his only son, Isaac, as a sacrifice, Abraham proved the willingness of his heart to go and do whatever God asked.

I have had to learn over the years what my role in missions is to be. To remain in the United States and pastor a people in such a way that they are equipped and ready to go, knowledgeable of the purposes and desires of God, introduced to the needs of a fallen world and given the opportunity to go and see them firsthand—this has been my privilege. Through a wide variety of confirmations, I know from the Lord that I have been called to stay and send instead of pull up roots and go. That may be the case for the rest of my life. But I hold that calling loosely knowing that the Lord has every right to change His direction for my life and ministry without getting my approval! So I have to live ready to go and to live ready to stay, but my will is not my own once I have committed all things to Christ.

Each year offers new opportunities to go and learn more as I continue to make trips overseas to serve Christ in circumstances that are foreign to me, among people who are different from me, and with challenges that stretch my faith by what I discover of the work of Christ all over the world. Short-term experiences are not the same as long-term career commitments, but they do afford an opportunity to invite the Lord to show me more, open my eyes, and answer my prayer, "Is this the time? Will this be the place you will direct me to go?" God's called-out people must be ready to pick up and go when the Lord indicates that is His will, but they also must be willing to stay, if He shows that to be His will. Do you have a willing heart, genuinely open to whatever, whenever, wherever the Lord may show you? Can you see that at the very least you are called to be an equipper and leader in the missions initiatives in your congregation?

2. Do I Trust God to Provide if I Conclude that I Am Supposed to Go?

Every follower of Christ knows the promises of Scripture that affirm unequivocally that God is able to provide for all we need. He never calls unless He also equips, we are fond of saying. If we are confident that is true, His call to relocate and resume our ministry in a new place should not concern us. His provision is not dependent on location but upon His liberal commitment to make all grace abound to us so that we may be certain we will have an abundance for every good work.

Intellectually that is well established—we understand at a certain cognitive level. But we have to admit that doubts do plague even the best and most faith—filled among us. Over the years I have heard them expressed in a variety of ways about a number of concerns: money, ability to learn a new language, concern for family members left behind, loneliness and the loss of a church community, health, threats of physical danger, and other such worries that can paralyze someone wanting to give honest consideration to God's call to go. Yes, we can *say* God is able, but deep inside we wonder if He is really willing to provide all that we will need. The needs we already know about are so far-reaching and the fear of the unknown so daunting that our uncertainty about His willingness to provide raises even more concern.

Although most pastors and others who are called into full-time vocational ministry make an implicit decision to relinquish the advantages of a career with a higher salary and standard of living, the harsh realities of living in an affluent culture force more explicit desires to be addressed. The idea of living sacrificially seldom survives the practical challenges of struggling to maintain a "normal lifestyle" when we are surrounded by others who have so much more. Believing that God will provide for our needs usually runs into a carefully calculated discussion of what a "need" actually is, given the neighborhoods in which we must live to serve the people to whom we must give ourselves in ministry. Consequently, as unlikely as it seems for people in a faith ministry to entertain such mundane concerns, how to make a reasonable living weighs heavily on the minds of ministry families. On the one hand, they do not want to appear to be greedy or preoccupied with salary, but on the other they must somehow figure out how they can make it financially in the costly realm that is the culture of wealth in the United States. So the ideal of believing that God will provide for all our needs suffers regular blows at the cruel hand of the economic realities around us.

God is trustworthy and faithful, we know. But will He only choose to bless us spiritually and leave us to scramble to make ends meet financially? Therein lies the crisis of our own faith—to believe God and trust Him to be sufficient or take the necessary steps to accept only those fields of ministry where the way is paved with guarantees of financial viability.

Now to that complicated scene we add the unknown character of considering a call from the Lord to serve Him outside the culture with which we are most familiar. What might happen in a foreign culture with an uncertain support base that promises to take care of our needs? Adding to that concern is the pragmatic issue of appealing to others for support. Unless you happen to be fully supported by a denominational mission agency or board, it is likely that you will face the onerous prospect of having to go out and plead your case for funding to a polite but reluctant list of friends, family, and church acquaintances who are not sure why they should have to give their resources when you tell them that God has called and will provide. Many people have faltered at the gate to missions when they realized that the cost of the venture would be paid for by funds that would need to be raised by them. Do they believe God will provide? In some ways, of course they do. But when the harsh realities of the bills come due, or the date for your departure to distant lands arrives, and funds are insufficient, what then? Is it just a matter of faith, or is a matter of failure in the church at large that we place the burden of gathering resources on the very ones who should be the beneficiaries of the generosity of those who are called to remain while others answer the call to go?

3. What Is the Primary Calling God Has Placed on My Life?

Plenty of answers to that question have been offered during the course of your life and ministry, of that I am certain—some by you and many by others who love to explain God's will for your life! But the freedom to run with abandon in our calling is to identify what we do best, how God uses that, and where we can use it to the full extent of its effectiveness. When we limit calling to vocational, pastoral ministry in a local church—or even more narrowly, limit it to the role of lead pastor in a local church—we eliminate many of the gifts present in the people of God. With our inability to define our own calling precisely, it does seem presumptuous for us to speak for anyone else on that point. To make everyone else who is called by God line up with a preconceived notion of what that should look like limits the creativity and unique gifts that God so gladly and freely grants to His servants. Vocational ministry, as it is often called, means far more than the traditional understanding usually intended by those who use the term. By elevating our definition to biblical standards of what spiritual gifts and ministries ought to include, we quickly realize that some who once thought their only alternative was to become senior pastor (or the preaching pastor, or the head pastor, or whatever terminology familiar to you), should realistically reassess their direction in the light of what they do best. Maybe they should pastor a local church within their own culture, but it is liberating to realize that the best use of their gifts may be in another vocation. When God calls you to serve Him, His creativity and imagination—which are evident in an extravagant way in creation and in the multiple experiences leading each of us to redemption—it would seem unwise to lock Him in and dictate the kinds of vocations to which He can call each of us. The freedom to respond to what God has prepared for us to do with our lives comes when we grasp what that calling is and what He is doing to equip us for it.

Whatever the nature of that vocational calling and gifting is, the truth is that there is usually a context in the sphere of missions for those gifts and callings to be fulfilled. I fear that far more have been called to missions than have responded in large part because they have not understood what can be available to them among the myriad of considerations. Somehow the future they envisioned when they sensed that God had set them apart for vocational ministry did not include the possibility that it could consist of anything other than local church ministry in the context of their own culture. Even if they are not particularly gifted in pastoral ministry and have never experienced much satisfaction or seen much affirmation in their years of pastoring,[1] it still does not occur to them that some other sort of ministry might be better suited to their gift mix. And that should open the door for them—or perhaps for some of you reading this—to reconsider where and how to invest the next chapter in your life of ministry.

Missions as a "backup plan" for those who wash out as pastors could not be farther from my mind. God's task in missions deserves that we send the best personnel we can find and provide for them the best resources we can give them.

What are your primary ministry gifts? Could they be best employed for the kingdom in a missions context? Or perhaps they could be equally effective in a missions context. Either way, if God has equipped you with the right tools and gifts for global missions, is it not important to give that at least as much consideration as the next church opportunity within your own culture? That leads up to the next question.

A Church and Ministry Priority Evaluation

Once you have submitted your own heart to the scrutiny of the Spirit, it follows that the next step would be to evaluate the place you have given missions in your ministry priorities as outlined in your vision for the church you have been called to serve. As we have observed previously in this book, far too many pastors and church leaders have neglected the biblical mandate for missions for so long that it does not occur to them that any reevaluation is necessary.

Hopefully, as the evidence of the absence of much missions fervor among the churches of the Western world has indicated, those undeniable symptoms of an unhealthy perspective and priority regarding missions will awaken many to the need for a well-applied cure. As one who has chosen to read about such things, perhaps you are just the one to take the initiative wherever you serve Christ and determine that you will take it upon yourself to lead those within the sphere of your influence to reconsider the proper place for missions in the overall call to discipleship for all believers.

1. Have I Submitted My Personal Ambitions to the Lord and Asked Him to Reveal Anything without a Kingdom Focus, Anything Selfish, or Anything Unworthy of a Servant of Christ? As with any other vocation, personal ambition can cloud the clarity of a godly vision. Without intending to do so and with the best possible motives, pastors and church leaders can want the right things for the wrong reasons. Seldom do I ever hear a pastor explain why he wants to keep the church small and limit its reach to just a few trusted families and friends. No, most speak of their vision to reach as many as possible and make as much of a difference in the city, region, or state in which their ministry is located. Usually that ambition is described in noble language—growing a strong church, building an effective ministry, reaching the multitude with the gospel—all of which are real and legitimate aspirations. But behind the words is often a secret ambition for personal success. After all, pastors are not immune to the appeal of the limelight that comes with leading an influential congregation.

As much as we would like to think we are above such things, I dare say that all of us have had to contend with the siren call of popularity. Recently I was forced to face this reality in my own life. Part of our evaluative process as a church is to identify the leading indicators of church health—budget giving, worship attendance, membership growth, Bible study attendance, and so on. From the perspective of spiritually minded people, none of those things can measure the spiritual maturity and vitality of the congregation. That is why they are called "indicators" and not true measures of the health of the church. But when I had to identify the indicator that had the greatest impact on how I felt about how the church is doing, I was forced to admit to myself that I have a tendency to look at worship attendance as a sign of congregational strength. Intellectually I can try to convince myself that if the people who are present are demonstrating genuine love for Christ and are growing in their love for Him and His Word, and are engaging with one another in meaningful fellowship and authentic caring relationships, then the church is doing well. However, if there is a decline in worship attendance, the intellectual and the objective often get trumped by the intuitive and subjective—my thinking gives way to my feelings. When that happens, I realize how easily I can give in to personal ambition and start trying to figure out how to overcome a downward trend in attendance, even if that means bailing out on what I know to be the biblical priorities of ministry. We all know of churches that have completely compromised themselves in order to cater to their drive for numerical successes.

A missions focus is often the victim of those subjective feelings. In an effort to shore up our personal sense of success and satisfy our drive to fulfill our personal ambitions, church leaders can lead the congregation to embrace lofty-sounding goals of reaching the lost around us and build a strategic emphasis around a ministry that does a great job of local church development. But as they do so, they push away any effort that dilutes their priorities locally. Big building programs and fund-raising projects, local outreach plans and internal improvement efforts make it virtually impossible for missions to emerge from the clutter created by all the ambitious labors to be the best local church around!

So it is necessary for all of us in pastoral and church leadership to take stock of our own ambitions on a regular basis. We cannot afford to think that if we have dealt with it at one time we are in the clear. Are you as ambitious for the glory of Jesus Christ to be made known among the nations as you are to increase attendance next weekend? Are you as excited when one of your friends and colleagues in ministry is sent out to a career in missions as you are to see the seats filled on Sunday morning? Are you protective of the missions budget to reach people among the nations when ideas start rolling out about how to enhance the church facilities and increase the staff so that you can reach and keep more people in your city?

Missions effectiveness and local church success are not mutually exclusive. When the Lord laid out His plan in His Word for the local church to reach out to the nations, He did not make it optional. God wants us to be as ambitious for the nations as we are for the city in which our congregations are located. Godly ambition calls us to be faithful in all things, not selectively choosing only those things which will build our egos and bolster our personal reputations. The nation is filled with megachurches with no vision for the nations because their eyes have been blinded by their own success locally. But for every megachurch pastor who is leading in that direction, many who pastor smaller churches in reality long to be just like him. Therefore, following his lead, they give just as little emphasis to missions hoping that by setting their sights on all that leads to increased attendance and local church growth, they too can experience the kind of success for which so many want to be noted.

Ambition can be a tricky thing to figure out. But until we pastors and leaders are wholeheartedly ambitious for the glory of God to be made known among the nations as we are in the local congregation, missions will take a backseat in our ministries!

2. Does the Congregation You Serve Care More for Its Own Comfort and Convenience than It Does for God's Call to Reach the Nations? Do you get the impression that your church family thinks more about feathering its own nest than about making the glory of God known in all the earth? Although it is impossible to know what others are thinking, or to understand what motivates them, a good indication of what occupies the highest place in their hearts can be discovered by where they are willing to spend their money, what they pray for,[2] what they discuss in their conversations with one another and with church leaders, and how they invest their time.

Churches with a passion for missions demonstrate it not only in the operating budget of the church but in the way they support missions over and above their regular tithes and offerings. It has been a delight for me to pastor a church that gives nearly as much outside the church budget to missions as it does through it, and that is just what we know about because it passes through our bookkeeping processes! Their generosity encourages me as I see that they are investing in missions themselves, not just relying on the church to do it for them.

When prayer groups with a heart for missions and people seeking information about missions, missionaries, and the nations, begin to show up throughout the church, you know that you have crossed an important line for the future of missions through the congregation. If all people are interested in praying for pertains to their own direct interests at home and within the church family, missions will have a hard time gaining much traction among them. The more you find people praying, the sooner you will find people giving and going. What can you do to encourage, educate, and equip your people to pray for missions?

What do the people talk about? Like every pastor, I have my share of conversations about church stuff. People are usually interested in expressing their opinions about what they like and don't like about worship, what they think of the latest facility changes, who and what they think is being neglected in the realm of ministry focus, what should be improved in what and how leaders communicate with the congregation, how leaders handled the most recent trauma or crisis within the church family—lots of talk about stuff that pertains to the in-house functions of the congregation on the local front. But what a shift in the wind occurs when people begin to get excited about the reports of the team that just returned from Ethiopia, the commissioning of the two young women to live and serve Christ in Central Asia, the news that congregational giving had exceeded the need for the new schools in the slums of Nairobi, the joy of sending long-term teams to launch church plants in two nations traditionally antagonistic to the gospel, the surge of interest in signing up for a seat at the next missions festival so that there is a waiting list weeks before the event! I am speaking of the level of enthusiastic conversations I have heard among our own people within our own congregation within the past year or so. When missions shapes the mission and passions of a church, the self-interests so common in the life of a congregation begin to fade into the background (although they still hold a place of prominence for plenty of folks, so don't build any naïve expectations that all of that will go away!). People talk about what they are excited about. Are they talking about missions in your church? As the song says, "Let's give them something to talk about!"[3] The more they hear it from you and see it emphasized in the life of the church, the more they will have to discuss.

Investing time and energy in missions comes from a core conviction that their contribution matters on a broad scale that will be measured only in terms of eternity. When people take their vacation time and their weekends to participate in missions projects and trips, you know that it is a work of the Holy Spirit in their hearts. People spend time on the things they value. So many churches try to come up with creative ideas to get a crowd together and end up contributing to the consumer mentality so rampant within the American church culture. If they can find the most entertaining program, a place which promises the greatest benefits or offers the widest range of choices, the sad state of affairs in our nation has shown that large numbers will line up to let the church cater to them. Contrast that with a church that values serving, giving, sacrificing, and going for the sake of Christ and the gospel. When people demand to be served, they show their true colors— not the colors of a disciple of Jesus Christ. But when you find a people who love serving and are willing to pour themselves and their time into it, then rejoice that you get to see a church where the heart of Christ is on display! A passion for the gospel will do that! In the neighborhood and on to the nations, people who delight in Him as their greatest treasure and see Him as the light and hope of the world will give themselves wholeheartedly to that which will last forever.

When you want what God wants, according to all that we have learned in His Word and from the history of His church on the move, you will want to be a major player in the missions movement making waves around the world this very moment. All the information available regarding the neglect of missions so common in churches and among pastors today will not be sufficient to move you to take action. All the statistics about how far we have fallen from God's intentions and how poorly we are casting vision for missions to be a top priority of our ministries will never be enough to get you moving. Neither will an intellectual understanding of the biblical mandate push you to do something, nor a list of specific actions/steps you can take to move missions back into its rightful place in your life and in the life of the church.

The only factor that matters in all of this is whether you have allowed your heart to line up with the heart of God so that you long for what He longs for. And when you do, then you will step out in faith, confident that only by the power of the Spirit will you be able to sustain what God calls you to do. If you are willing, then you need to be ready because you already know that He is able! "And God is able to make all grace abound to you, so that always having all sufficiency in everything, you may have an abundance for every good deed" (2 Cor. 9:8 NASB).

The time has come for pastors and church leaders to reclaim their calling as those who equip God's people to serve Him whenever He calls them and go wherever He sends them. The time has come for pastors to serve as conduits, not corks, to the magnificent ministry God intends for His people. The time has come for each of us to ask the Lord to show us His heart and how we are to reflect it in the way we embrace His passion for His glory to be made known in all the earth.

---

1. Caution is urged here because you may indeed be right where God has called you to be and yet not experience much outward affirmation or what could be construed as success in some circles. If you are called to pastor a local church in your own cultural setting, then do it with your whole heart and find joy in that choice service, but I believe many have never stopped to consider that their gifts might be better used for the kingdom in a different context than pastoring a local church.

2. "Prayer is the language of desire." Already quoted on page 93 of this book and cited in footnote 55. Gardiner Spring, *The Mercy Seat* (Morgan, PA: Soli Deo Gloria Publications, retypeset from the 1863 edition published in Glasgow, 2001), 2. Prayer serves as a window to the soul and displays in a practical way what the heart truly longs for. We pray for what we earnestly desire, and that tells a more accurate story than what we say we desire. We may *say* we desire God's glory to be made known among the nations, but until we *pray* that God's glory be made known among the nations, that desire is subordinate to what we do pray for.

3. "Let's Give Them Something to Talk About," written by Shirley Eikhard, copyrighted 1988 by EMI Blackwood Music and Canvee Music; Recorded by Bonnie Raitt, Capitol Records, 1990.

CHAPTER 13 SUMMARY AND CONCLUSION

On a beautiful January day several years ago, I enjoyed one of the highlights of all my years as a pastor. There have been many, but this day was the beginning of a week I will never forget. Nearly two hundred members from our church arrived at a location in Central Asia with a clear purpose—to assist and serve those on the front lines of missions by loving them, treating them to every conceivable good thing we could imagine, and getting them spiritually, emotionally, physically, and intellectually refreshed before they returned to the hard places in which they live as messengers of the grace of Jesus Christ. Physicians, computer specialists, salespeople, hairdressers, youth workers, musicians, teachers and preachers, counselors, educators, recreational specialists, a host of "worker bees," and a wild array of the kinds of people you find in any and every church—all took a week or more of vacation and paid their own way to take part in a missions project unlike any I have ever seen.

Before the workers arrived for their conference, we gathered our team together to answer last-minute questions, review assignments, and share the joy we were all experiencing of investing our lives in something we all could sense would be unforgettable. But we also shared a dream with them, a dream that at least a tithe of their number would return, not on a short-term missions trip but as missionaries themselves, returning to live and serve in that region.

The night before the entire workforce was due to arrive, those who came early gathered in the main meeting room for an evening of musical praise and worship. I frankly was not sure what to expect. Since the team of musicians we had brought with us were the cream of the crop from our church, I was personally filled with anticipation to have them lead us in worship all week. However, I was not sure how the workers would respond to a band of primarily contemporary musicians. Several hundred men, women, and children—workers in various Central Asia nations—whose sole worship experiences for months, sometimes years, had been with only a few other believers, or perhaps just their family, gathered in small rooms in places unfriendly to the idea of people worshipping Jesus Christ. Any misgivings I may have had about what worship would be like with this group evaporated in a moment as the first chords were struck and hands were lifted high, tears came streaming down, and voices exploded in one of the most moving worship times of my life. The tone for the week was set the night before the planned conference even began. At the end of nearly an hour of singing, the worship team closed in prayer. No one moved. Then a quiet voice was heard in the stillness: "More!" Hearts melted together that evening, and our dream has long since been realized as far more than a tithe of the number of our team have made their new home in that part of the world to make the name of Jesus known so that others may worship Him and cry out, "More!" whenever He is exalted.

I have loved missions for most of my life. That week in January opened the hearts of many others to that same love. What a thrill as a pastor to have that holy moment with such a representative sampling of the people I get to serve! Watching the Spirit ignite in them a holy passion for the nations created a memory in me I will treasure as long as I live. It is rekindled now each time we call our members up to the front of the congregation and pray over them and send them out. Missions has become a part of who we are as a kingdom-focused church. We have a local address but a global understanding of who we are and why we exist.

Missions can and should shape the mission of the local church. Not that it becomes the dominant emphasis but that it assumes its rightful place among the biblical priorities embraced and pursued by the church. As we have examined this premise throughout this book, the underlying assumption has been that we can do better! Pastors can exert greater influence, churches can engage with greater fervor, and missions can invigorate a passion among everyone to see the glory of God made known in every neighborhood and among all nations.

Where We Are

After reviewing the present status of missions in most churches, no one would deny that our condition is unacceptable. Rationalizing and trying to excuse where we find ourselves only compounds the problem. Rather than get frustrated and discouraged by the inaction of the majority, this book is intended to challenge the status quo and incite more of you to change columns from the majority who are neglecting missions for all practical purposes, to the minority who are stepping up to make the changes necessary to make a difference. Now that we have seen the current condition of missions in the church, responsible action has to be taken in order to be faithful to our calling. James described our responsibility vividly in his epistle when he wrote:

> But be doers of the word and not hearers only, deceiving yourselves. Because if anyone is a hearer of the word and not a doer, he is like a man looking at his own face in a mirror; for he looks at himself, goes away, and right away forgets what kind of man he was. But the one who looks intently into the perfect law of freedom and perseveres in it, and is not a forgetful hearer but a doer who acts—this person will be blessed in what he does. (James 1:22–25)

A new generation of churches and church leaders are emerging, and old loyalties and traditions are being questioned and often abandoned. Here is my plea to see the state of missions in the modern church as a symptom of an unhealthy body in need of a dramatic recovery. Making a lot of noise about all that is wrong with the body of Christ without a commitment to be a part of the solution to make things right shows an immaturity unworthy of those who aspire to lead the church back to its biblical glory. The church growth movement of the past twenty years will end up falling flat on its face if it does not do something to revitalize a comprehensive view of what the church is called to be—a view that must include missions as an essential and nonnegotiable element of the overall mission of the church.

Speaking again from my own denomination and tradition, is it possible to be satisfied with where we are when only .09 percent of the average attenders of Southern Baptist churches have responded to God's calling to career/vocational missions?[1] When only about 6 percent of the money received in local churches ever makes it out of those churches to support the missions efforts of the denomination? When just over a penny of every dollar given in local churches actually makes it to support international missions?

One of the conclusions we reached when a group of us started talking about the need for a book to push the church to become more proactive in missions was that the first hurdle that needed to be cleared was the appalling lack of interest among pastors. More than likely, unless you already have an interest in missions, you would not be inclined to pick up this book. So the question remains for us to figure out how to get this book, or the information in it, into the hands of those who serve as shepherds of the flocks, pastors of the churches which need an infusion of missions life. My heart still stings from the indictment of Dr. George Frederick Pentecost from the Missions Conference in New York City in 1900. It bears repeating in part at this point by way of reminder of what is at stake for pastors:

To the pastor belongs the privilege and the responsibility of solving the foreign missionary problem. Until the pastors of our churches wake up to the truth of this proposition, and the foreign work becomes a passion in their own hearts and consciences, our Boards may do what they can, by way of devising forward movements or organizing new methods for raising money from the churches, yet the chariot wheels of missions will drive heavily.

Every pastor holds his office under Christ's commission, and can only fulfill it when, as a missionary bishop, he counts the whole world his fold. The pastor of the smallest church has the power to make his influence felt around the world. No pastor is worthy of his office who does not put himself into sympathy with the magnificent breadth of the great commission, and draw inspiration and zeal from its worldwide sweep.

The pastor is not only the instructor, but the leader of his congregation. He must not only care for their souls, but direct their activities. If there are churches that do not give and do not pray for foreign missions, it is because they have pastors who are falling short of the command of Christ. I feel almost warranted in saying that, as no congregation can long resist the enthusiastic pastor, so, on the other hand, a congregation can hardly rise above cold indifference or lack of conviction regarding missions on the part of the pastor.[2]

I remember how I felt when I first read that and wanted to find every pastor I know and share it with them. To those who lead congregations, the calling and the privilege of upholding the missions banner is both overwhelming and frightening at the same time. Perhaps the reason you have read the book is not so much for what you gain from it and will do about it, but who you will give it to and how you will use it as a tool to help your colleagues return to this biblical mandate for the church.

One thing is certain—doing the same thing in the same old ways will never produce different results. If the churches will arise and embrace the call to missions, pastors must be at the front of the charge. Congregations with a heart for God's Word and will cannot continue to accept insipid leadership from pastors. When churches call a pastor, they need to ask before they call him if he is willing to teach and model a commitment to reach the nations with the gospel.

So where are we as leaders and churches regarding God's heart for the nations? The evidence makes clear that we need a grand overhaul, genuine repentance, and a biblical understanding of where we should be in order to line up with the heart of the Lord!

Where We Want to Be

Teaching and understanding what the Bible says about God's heart and plan for the nations to have opportunity to respond to His grace through Jesus Christ cannot be just an occasional tip of the hat to missions. It must be an integral part of the big picture of the biblical picture of the church. When the church approaches ministry from a principle-based perspective, the biblical principles lead to no other conclusion but that we have been blessed by the grace of Christ to be called His people. But that calling is never isolated from the eternal design of the Lord to reach all nations with the hope of new life in Christ. From the covenant with Abraham, one of the most basic principles upon which our identity as His people is founded is that we have been blessed in order that we may be a blessing: "I will make you into a great nation, I will bless you, I will make your name great, and you will be a blessing. I will bless those who bless you, I will curse those who treat you with contempt, and all the peoples on earth will be blessed through you" (Gen. 12:2–3).

In principle, nothing that God does for any one people is disconnected from His desire for His name to be known in all the earth. The church has an eternal purpose that must be reflected in our priorities. Principle-based ministry never loses sight of the comprehensive nature of that purpose. Therefore, we cultivate and sustain a sending mentality, a kingdom focus which refuses to give in to the modern idea that the church exists for the personal gratification of its members. So we send our best people, our best resources, and give our best attention to fulfill God's design.

If we are willing to aspire to greater days, our acquaintance with models from the past should inspire us so that we are not willing to settle for mediocrity but long for the best. Although there are many other characteristics of great missions movements than those we have noted, we can benefit significantly from understanding these nine:

- Power from on high as the Holy Spirit's work flowed freely
- A passion for Christ
- Prevailing prayer
- A rich soaking in the Scriptures and sound doctrine
- Unwavering faith that trusts God to be faithful in all things
- Holiness and purity of life (together with deep repentance and an abhorrence of sin)
- Eyes willing to see and have compassion on others
- A supportive, sacrificial, and generous sending community
- Persecution and opposition

Are these things apparent in your own ministry and the life of your church? If we are not interested enough to aspire to the pursuit of the kind of life and ministry that builds them into the fabric of our lives as His people, missions will always be a peripheral concern and not the longing of our hearts. From both a biblical and historical perspective, the Lord has shown us what it means to pursue the expansion of His kingdom through missions. It may be assuming too much to state that we want what God wants, but let there be no mistake about what God's desires are. Missions has always been central to His plan for His glory to be made known. How can we say we long for the heart of God if we are not ready to embody the characteristics of effective missions movements of the past and live out the principles for missions from His Word?

How to Get There

If we are ready to keep the priority of missions intact, the proportional emphasis on missions in balance, and the purpose of mission in perspective, the means are available. No one can say that what the Lord requires of us He will not provide through us. His resources for accomplishing His will abound toward us in Christ by the power of the Spirit.

The starting point for becoming the kind of missions-focused church that reflects the mandate of the Great Commission and the might of Pentecost is to learn how to walk by the Spirit. For each follower of Jesus Christ, everything we do is to be done for His glory; and nothing will be for His glory that is not consistent with His Word, preceded by prayer, and clothed with power from on high. Therefore, the spiritual state of the church must be healthy before the missions emphasis can be effective in sending out godly witnesses who understand what the gospel is, how to live in the power of Christ, and why the world needs to know Him. If the church is anemic spiritually and knows little of the dynamic of spiritual living, why would we want to export that? But when a church is sound in teaching and godly in character, when worship is vibrant and love is abundant, when Christ is central and the Spirit moves freely, that is the starting point for a new day in missions.

Once the people have learned to walk by the Spirit, you can count on it, the Lord will show them where to go and how to get there! Lead the people to walk by the Spirit by walking with Him yourself, and then appeal to them to follow you into a full-fledged commitment to put into practice what you have seen and heard about the great ideas of other churches. Until you are ready to get to the place God wants you to be, why ask how to get there? But once you want to go, you will then want to know how and hopefully what we have discovered from scores of effective missions churches will steer you in the right direction.

Will You Allow Missions to Shape the Mission of Your Church?

In some ways the title of this book is an overstatement. Missions should not shape everything about the nature and focus of our entire ministry. But when God is at work stirring His people with a passion to live for His glory in such a way that the nations want to cry out for the brightness of the shining of His splendor to come their way, that beauty will become visible in other things we do.

Worship becomes richer when we treasure Christ so much that we cannot help talking to Him and about Him. *Biblical instruction* becomes more exciting when we see that the wonder of Christ can be viewed in each successive text. *Prayer* becomes more specific and strategic, more passionate and intimate, when we know that God stands ready to answer whatever we ask Him in Jesus' name. *Acts of mercy* at home become a prelude to what can be done around the world. *Giving* becomes a delight when we see the fruit born from even the smallest gifts of those least capable of giving and long to make genuine sacrifices for the sake of the gospel. *Evangelism* comes alive at home once we have tasted the sweetness of it in other contexts.

The shape of our ministry in the local church cannot help but be impacted favorably when missions assumes its rightful place at the table with the rest of our priorities for the church. If we neglect it or shortchange it, how can the Lord be expected to bless a church demonstrating only a partial obedience? Jesus said that we are blessed when we do what we know (John 13:17), so how can we hope to be blessed when we know missions is the heartbeat of God and we do not give it our best?

So now you know.

What will you do?

Far from being an exhaustive treatment of missions and the church, and far from being bold enough to think that it offers just the right answers for how to make your church the kind that can reach the entire world, this book is simply intended to be a useful tool in your hands to spur you on to be a missions-focused congregation led by a missions-minded pastor looking to honor a missions-hearted Savior.

Remember what Jesus said, "But an hour is coming, and is now here, when the true worshipers will worship the Father in spirit and truth. Yes, the Father wants such people to worship Him. God is spirit, and those who worship Him must worship in spirit and truth" (John 4:23–24). When I think of those words, the importance of missions excited me once again. John Piper said it well, "Missions exists because worship doesn't."[3] In order for Christ-honoring worship to happen, the kind of worship He is seeking from His people, the kind that satisfies the Father's heart, they must hear the gospel and learn of the transforming power of Jesus Christ and the glorious truth that it is theirs by grace through faith.

You know that.

Now, will you and your church choose to be among those blessed with the privilege of telling them? If the answer is yes, then I promise you that missions will shape the mission of your church in such a way that you will watch in amazement as it conforms to the image of Jesus Christ. After all, missions is His passion; it must become ours!

---

1. Refer back to pages 17–20 to refresh your memory with more details.

2. Andrew Murray, *Key to the Missionary Problem* (Fort Washington, PA: Christian Literature Crusade, 1979), 11–12, quoting Dr. G. F. Pentecost.

3. John Piper, *Let the Nations Be Glad* (Grand Rapids, MI: Baker Books, 1993), 11.

APPENDIX A **ELMBROOK CHURCH GLOBAL AND LOCAL MISSION VISION**

Mike Murphy, Elmbrook Church, Waukesha, Wisconsin

Mike and his team set a high bar for how a local church can outline an exciting vision for the congregation to embrace the biblical mandate for missions.

Elmbrook Church Global and Local Mission Vision . . . giving witness to Christ—in word and deed, in our community and world—while embracing the global dimensions of God's kingdom.

Guiding Values

1. We engage in this missional witness by listening to, learning from, and serving with our brothers and sisters in cultures both near and far to expand God's kingdom. We lead with relationship.
2. Elmbrook's engagement in the community and world is missional.

Strategic Focus and Priorities

1. Leadership and church-planting resourcing, training and development
2. Least-churched contexts—post-Christian contexts, those most resistant to the gospel, unreached people groups
3. Those suffering under injustice and oppression—those marginalized in our world who are oppressed, disenfranchised, and living in economic, social, and spiritual poverty
4. Ministry to greater metro Milwaukee area—creating partnerships and bridges with ministries, agencies, and churches so that Elmbrook people can engage and serve those who are living in spiritual, economic, and social poverty in Milwaukee and Waukesha county

Guiding Criteria

As we evaluate initiatives or potential missionaries in any of the above areas, we will use the following criteria to guide our thinking and decision.

1. We will invest in initiatives that have strong, growing relational connections to EBC as a whole and to our international partners, missionaries, or pastoral staff of EBC. (Relational)

   > [Note: We need to keep in mind that the funding source for the faith promise is the EBC congregation; therefore we need to encourage the development of relational connections with groups and ministries in the Elmbrook laity.]

2. Initiatives that can be undertaken in the context of a "partnership paradigm." (Partnership)
3. Initiatives that engage in educational processes that are transformational (as opposed to merely transmissional) and that go beyond traditional schooling models. (Transformational)

4. Ministries or initiatives where EBC missionaries serve or have served that can be LEVERAGED to resource and partner with other new EBC initiatives (or partners) in strategic ways. (Leverage) In other words, we will seek to multiply the effort and investment of prior works either of missionaries or global partners.

5. Initiatives that can be assessed and evaluated using criteria mutually agreed upon by all partners. (Assessable)

> [Note: We need to ensure that any initiative or project is assignable within the HRT structure for purposes of accountability and evaluation.]

6. Initiatives or ministries that are trying to address issues of contextual sustainability. (Sustainability)

7. The value of breakthrough: We will give priority to funding "breakthrough projects"—those projects and/or initiatives that will move a ministry to the next level, either in terms of inside efficiency or outside effectiveness. (Breakthrough)

Unpacking the Vision: What Might This Look Like in 2012?

A. General: As Elmbrook Church, we are all growing in our love for God and our missional engagement in His world. This is evidenced in our praying, learning, giving, and serving.

B. Specific: Some indicators of what this would look like in the life of Elmbrook Church in five years.

1. Missional lifestyle. Every person at Elmbrook Church can not only tell you where and how but also who they are engaged with in their community or world.

2. Sending church. Elmbrook grows in sending some of its members into intercultural ministries around our community and world.

3. Vision casting and story communication of the stories and the impact of the Faith Promise is constant, wide, easy to access, and compelling throughout the year.
4. Faith Promise. The Faith Promise grows significantly in the next five years in terms of number of participants and dollars.
5. Connection and support. All missionaries, global initiatives, and partner ministries are CONNECTED to Elmbrook in ways that are wide, ongoing and growing.
6. Prayer. More people are praying for the church, the world, and the concerns and ministries that flow in and out of Elmbrook.
7. Next generation. There is growing involvement and leadership on the part of young adults in Elmbrook's global and local mission endeavors.
8. Mutuality in the global church. The worldwide church continues to speak into and impact Elmbrook Church that she might glorify Christ more fully and obediently.
9. Accountability. Ministry initiatives, partnerships, and missionaries are evaluated prayerfully, regularly, and systematically.

APPENDIX B
DISCIPLES FROM ALL NATIONS

Joel C. Rosenberg, Inside the Revolution, 2009

Regarding the call to reach all nations with the gospel:

People in the epicenter are coming to Christ in record numbers. Millions in Iran. Millions in Sudan. Millions in Pakistan. Millions in Egypt.

He is the King of kings and Lord of lords. When He gives His disciples an order, it must be followed. And that order, they note, is to preach the gospel to the whole world and make disciples—not just Christians but truly dedicated and devoted Christ followers—of all the nations.

Not just the safe nations.

Not just the democratic nations.

Not just the free-market nations.

Jesus told His disciples to go and make more disciples in *all* the nations.

Even the difficult nations.

Even the dangerous nations.

Even the radical nations.

APPENDIX C
ASSESSMENT AND EVALUATION IDEAS

Laura Lange, Calvary Memorial Church, Oak Park, Illinois

We use a sort of grid system which reflects our values and priorities. They are namely:

1. Going to unreached people groups
2. Direct involvement in evangelization and church planting
3. Strong relationship to our church

Each missionary candidate is evaluated across these three categories. Our missions policy is that no candidate (or any missionary on our roster) is to be supported at more than 40 percent of their need. This is to inhibit putting all of one's eggs in one basket.

We take this possible 40 percent and divide it across the three categories as follows:

1. For unreached people groups, a maximum of 20 percent of the total missionary need
2. For direct work in evangelization and church planting, a maximum of 10 percent
3. For relationship ties to our church, a maximum of 10 percent

This grid was established several years ago (I inherited it), obviously by someone (or a group) who is rather analytic. But it has really saved us in group decisions because it takes the subjectivity and hand-wringing out of the financial decision-making process. It is always viewed as a GUIDE, not an unbending structure. We allow a little subjectivity to creep in; that's OK. Each missionary/ missionary family is unique and has their own set of stories and circumstances which must be considered.

Also, when a missionary is first going out, we might start them slightly lower than their possible "points," to allow room for increases in support over the next few years.

I should also note here: although we publish this grid for all candidates—or even any church member—to see, we no longer publish individual monthly support amounts for our missionaries, as we wish to avoid comparisons which can lead to misunderstandings. However any congregant is allowed to request the numbers and receive the list, and then a missions committee member can offer to review the figures with the congregant.

Steven Lee, Bethlehem Baptist Church, Minneapolis, Minnesota

We have a missions pastor that interviews all individuals at various times in their process. We have a Global Outreach Team that also interviews individuals by asking difficult questions and reading their references and application. Our GO Team is made of former missionaries, MKs, professors of missiology, laypeople, longtime members, and others passionate about missions at the church.

Also, we have an official missionary training program, called the Nurture Program, that takes two years to complete which prepares all of our missionaries theologically and spiritually and trains them for ministry. It has multiple components of reading, attending seminars, taking classes, learning to study the Bible, getting a theological foundation, building a support team, getting accountability partners, joining a small group, taking Perspectives, as well as engaging in cross-cultural ministry in the Twin Cities.

APPENDIX C, CON'T
ASSESSMENT AND EVALUATION IDEAS

Sample: Missions Application Form—Providence Baptist Church, Raleigh, North Carolina

Thank you for your interest in becoming a Providence Baptist Church missionary. The selection criteria are described in the church's Mission Policy approved August 5, 1993. The information you provide on this form will help us determine your eligibility. Eligible career and short-term (4+ months service) applicants will receive a second form requesting detailed information on their Christian beliefs and preparation for service. Upon receipt of this completed form, they will be invited for an interview to be conducted before the Missions Ministry Team makes the final decision. Financial support requests may only be submitted and approved for persons who have been approved as Providence missionaries. Please complete the following questions by typing or printing the answers on the lines or spaces.

Name, Address, and Phone

1. Name _____
          (Last)   (First)   (Middle)

2. Present Mailing Address _____

3. City _____ State _____ Zip _____ Country _____

4. Home Phone _____ Daytime or Work Phone _____

   E-mail: _____

5. Birth City, State, & Country _____ Date (M/D/Y) _____

6. Spouse _____ Birth City, State, & Country _____

   Date (M/D/Y) _____

7. Children

Name(s)	Place of Birth	Date (M/D/Y)

Church Considered as Your "Home Church"

1. Name _____

2. Street Address _____

3. City _____ State _____ Zip _____

4. Pastor's Name _____ Phone Number _____

5. How long have you been a member? _____

Relationship to Providence

1. *Circle* your status:

   a. CURRENT member   b. PAST member
   c. REGULAR attendee   d. OCCASIONAL attendee
   e. NONE

2. If a member, when did you join the church? (M/Y) _____
   How long did you attend before joining? _____

3. If past member, when did you join? (M/Y) _____ How long
   were you a member? _____ months

4. If regular attendee, how long have you been coming to
   Providence? _____ months

5. If you have never been a member or regular attendee, please
   describe your relationship with Providence.

Current or Proposed Missionary Service

1. What is your current or proposed job description? *(What are/
   will be your main responsibilities or activities?)*

2. Are you now serving as a missionary? Yes / No
   If yes, how long have you been serving? _____

3. Is this a career, short-term (4+ months), or seasonal (less than
   4 months) missionary position? _____ Please list the dates of
   proposed service (from m/d/y to m/d/y): _____

4. Where is/will be the geographic location of your ministry
   (town or city name, state, country, region)? _____

5. Describe the *target* group of people you are/will be serving
   in terms of ethnicity, religion(s), language(s), socioeconomic
   conditions, literacy, education, etc. *(Please be as specific as*

possible, e.g., "mothers of young children," "Muslim students from Algiers," "T'boli tribal people living on XYZ island," etc. Also, if there is more than one target group, please estimate the percent of time you are or will spend with each group).

6. What is the estimated population of the target group(s) of people in this location that your ministry is most likely to affect? _____
Are they mostly living in a rural or an urban area? _____

7. Please estimate the evangelization status of these people in the area you are/will work. *(If you are unsure, contact your mission agency.)*

   • What percentage has *never* heard the gospel? _____

   • What percentage is *professing* Christians (nominal and nonchurch attendees)? _____

   • What percentage of this group is Evangelical or *born-again* Christians?_____

   • How many indigenous/local churches or missionaries (Evangelical and nonevangelical) are working with or among your target people group(s)? _____

8. What were your main reasons for selecting these people, this location, and this ministry?

9. If English is not the language of your target people, please describe your proficiency in it on a scale of 0 to 10. What are your plans to become proficient? How will you be able to communicate with them?

10. Please estimate the average percentage of time you anticipate spending each month (or seasonal experience) on the following activities.

____ % Administration/ Management	____ Church Planting	____ % Medical/Public Health

___ % Linguistics/Bible Translation	___ % Discipleship/ Leader Training	___ % Development/ Relief Work
___ % Christian Education	___ % Evangelism	___ % Social Action
___ % Church Nurturing	___ % Literacy Training	___ % Other (explain)

Mission Agency, Board, or Sending Organization

1. Name _____ Address _____

2. City _____ State _____ Zip _____

3. Name of Agency Organization Contact _____

4. Work Phone _____ Fax _____

5. Why did you choose this board, agency, or organization?

_____

References

Please list the names, addresses, and phone numbers of three people who know you well and are willing to provide information about your potential service as a missionary. Do not include family members.

Information	Reference 1	Reference 2	Reference 3
Name			
Mail Address			
City/State/Zip			
Daytime Phone			
Relationship			

Please give any other information you think might be helpful in the evaluation of your application:

_____   _____
Signature   Date

Please mail this completed form to:

Providence Baptist Church
Attn: Missions Ministry
6339 Glenwood Avenue
Raleigh, NC 27612–2638

Missionary Application: Sharing of Christian Beliefs

Name _____
            (Last)   (First)   (Middle)

Address _____
            (Number and Street)   (City and State)   (Zip)

Daytime Phone _____ Evening Phone _____

We shall appreciate your sharing candidly in these areas. There are no specific words for which we are looking. Please type or print the answers within the space allowed and sign the form.

1. Describe briefly your Christian salvation and baptism experience. How have these experiences continued to affect your life?

_____

_____

_____

2. Describe your beliefs regarding the Bible. How do you use it in your personal life?

_____

_____

_____

3. How are you involved in witnessing to lost people? What training have you had? Briefly relate a recent experience of sharing your faith with someone who was not a Christian.

_____

_____

_____

4. Give a brief statement of the basic Christian message that you hope to proclaim or share with persons with where you plan to go.

_____

_____

_____

5. List some gifts you possess and how you intend to use them in missionary service.

_____

_____

_____

6. Please add any other statement concerning your beliefs that would help us know you and what you consider to be of major importance.

_____

_____

_____

_____   _____
_____   _____
            Signature   Date

(At this point in the document, we include our Statement of Faith for them to sign)

Please read and sign that you agree with our Statement of Faith. If you disagree, please provide an explanation on a separate sheet of paper.

_____   _____
            Signature   Date

Missionary Financial Support Needs

Date (m/d/y) _____

Name _____
          (Last)   (First)   (Middle)

Address _____
        (Number and Street)   (City and State)   (Zip) (Country)

Daytime Phone _____ Evening Phone _____

Mission Agency/Board

The mission policy of Providence Baptist Church requires annual evaluations of all missionaries and the monthly support approved by their agency or board. Unfortunately, the budget categories and definitions usually differ among the various agencies and boards. Therefore, the following support categories are more generic and may require some separation now included in your budget. Your help in answering the following questions and budget categories is most appreciated.

Agency-Approved Support Budget

Monthly Support	Amount	One-time Special	Amount
Personal Living Costs		• Travel to Field	_____
• Salary or Living Allowance	_____	• Shipment of Goods	_____
• Housing Allowance	_____	• Agency Admin Fee	_____
• Special Allowances (explain)	_____	• Training, Conference, Etc.	_____
• Transportation	_____	• Taxes	_____
• Other[1] (explain)	_____	• Other (explain)	_____
• Taxes	_____	• Other (explain)	_____
• Federal & SECA	_____		
• State & Local	_____	**TOTAL ONE-TIME COSTS**	
• Agency Administration Fee	_____		
• Benefits	_____		
• Medical Insurance	_____	**EXPLANATIONS & COMMENTS**	
• Medical Expense & Deductions	_____		
• Retirement/Annuity	_____		
TOTAL PERSONAL COSTS			
Ministry Expenses			
• Work Budget	_____		
• Support Raising & Maintenance	_____		

• Ongoing Training	_____		
• Designated Projects *(explain)*	_____		
TOTAL WORK COSTS			
Other Expenses			
• Support Attrition Allowance	_____		
• Cost of Living/and $ Devalue Allowance	_____		
TOTAL MONTHLY COSTS			

APPENDIX D **MISSIONS SURVEY RESPONDENTS**

State	City	Church	Pastor
AL	Auburn	Lakeview Baptist Church	Al Jackson
AL	Birmingham	Briarwood Presbyterian	Harry Reeder
AL	Hoover	Hunter Street Baptist Church	Buddy Gray
AR	Fayetteville	First Baptist Church	Douglas Falknor
AZ	Peoria	Church of the Cross	Brent Thomas
AZ	Paradise Valley	Camelback Bible Church	Timothy Savage
AZ	Tempe	Missio Dei Communities	Chris Gonzalez
BC (CAN)	Agassiz	Mountainview Community Church	James Flom
CA	El Cajon	Shadow Mountain Community Church	David Jeremiah
CA	Escondido	Emmanuel Faith Community Church	Dennis Keating
CA	Fullerton	First Evangelical Free Church	Dale Burke
CA	Irvine	Voyagers Bible Church	Gary Stubblefield
CA	Los Angeles	Shoreline Community Church	Scott Mehl
CA	Los Angeles	The Hollywood Church	Chris Barksdale

CA	North Hollywood	Tribe Church	Mike Brown
CA	Novato	Trinity Presbyterian Church	Reid Hankins
CA	Pasadena	Lake Avenue Church	Greg Waybright
CA	Rocklin	Origin Community Church	Mark South
CA	Rolling Hills Estates	Rolling Hills Covenant Church	Byron MacDonald
CA	San Jose	Mercy Hill Church	Steve Fuller
CO	Denver	L2 Church	Russ McKendry
CO	Denver	Park Church	Brian Brown
CO	Highlands Ranch	Cherry Hills Community Church	Jim Dixon
CT	Avon	Valley Community Baptist Church	Jay Abramson
FL	Tampa	Covenant Life Church	Justin Perry
FL	West Palm Beach	First Baptist Church	Jimmy Scroggins
GA	Albany	Sherwood Baptist Church	Michael Catt
GA	Alpharetta	North Point Community Church	Andy Stanley
GA	Atlanta	First Baptist Church	Charles Stanley
GA	Duluth	Cross Pointe Church	James Merritt
GA	Johns Creek	Perimeter Church	Randy Pope
GA	Macon	New City Church	Keith Watson
GA	Roswell	Fellowship Bible Church	Crawford Loritts
IL	Oak Park	Calvary Memorial Church	Todd Wilson
IN	Evansville	Bethel Temple Community Church	Stephen Schwambach and Bret Nicholson
IN	Indianapolis	College Park Church	Mark Vroegop
KS	Leawood	Christ Community Church	Tom Nelson
KS	Wichita	First Evangelical Free Church	Mike Andrus
LA	Baton Rouge	First Presbyterian Church	Gerrit Dawson
MA	Boston	Boston Chinese Evangelical Church	Steven Chin
MD	Annapolis	Bay Area Community Church	Greg St. Cyr

MD	Temple Hills	Reformation Alive Baptist Church	Eric Redmond
MI	Grand Rapids	Calvary Church	Jim Samra
MI	Northville	Ward Evangelical Presbyterian Church	Scott McKee
MI	Southfield	Highland Park Baptist Church	Brent Slater
MN	Eden Prairie	Wooddale Church	Leith Anderson
MN	Elk River	Glory of Christ Fellowship	Charlie Handren
MN	Minneapolis	Bethlehem Baptist Church	John Piper
MO	Ballwin	Twin Oaks Presbyterian Church	Ronald Steel
MS	Byram	Grace Presbyterian Church	Roger Collins
MS	Hattiesburg	First Presbyterian Church	Sean Michael Lucas
MS	Jackson	First Presbyterian Church	Ligon Duncan
MS	Jackson	Trinity Presbyterian Church	Kenneth A. Pierce
MS	Ocean Springs	Mosaic Church	Dustin Boles
NC	Andrews	Andrews Presbyterian Church	Gary Litchfield
NC	Asheville	Biltmore Baptist Church	Bruce Frank
NC	Asheville	Missio Dei Church	Bryan Robbins
NC	Burlington	Glen Hope Baptist Church	Larry Redding
NC	Charlotte	Calvary Church	John Munro
NC	Charlotte	CrossWay Community Church	Mickey Connolly
NC	Durham	Summit Church	J. D. Greear
NC	Greensboro	Westover Church	Don Miller
NC	Matthews	Carmel Baptist Church	Wayne Poplin
NC	Raleigh	Christ The King Presbyterian Church	(Open at time of publication)
NC	Raleigh	Treasuring Christ Church	Sean Cordell
NC	Raleigh	Vintage21 Church	Tyler Jones
NC	Rocky Mount	Englewood Baptist Church	Michael Cloer

NC	Statesville	Front Street Baptist Church	Tim Stutts
NC	Wake Forest	North Wake Baptist Church	Larry Trotter
NC	Wendell	Central Baptist Church	Ed Rose
NC	Winston-Salem	1.21 Church	Stephen Wagoner
NC	Winston-Salem	Calvary Baptist Church	Al Gilbert
NC	Winston-Salem	Old Town Baptist Church	Rick Speas
NH	Concord	The River of Grace Church	David Pinckney
NY	New York	Grace	David Whitehead
NY	Snyder	Restoration Church	Dan Trippie
NY	Troy	Terra Nova Church	Ed Marcelle
OH	Akron	The Chapel	Paul Sartarelli
OH	Chagrin Falls	Parkside Church	Alistair Begg
OH	Dayton	Christ the King Anglican Church	Wayne McNamara
OH	Grove City	Grove City Church of the Nazarene	Mark Fuller
OH	Lebanon	Urbancrest Baptist Church	Tom Pendergrass
ON (CAN)	Toronto	The Peoples Church	Charles Price
PA	Hershey	Evangelical Free Church of Hershey	George Davis
PA	Philadelphia	Tenth Presbyterian Church	(Open at time of publication)
SC	Greenville	Second Presbyterian Church	Richard D. Phillips
SC	Mount Pleasant	East Cooper Baptist Church	Conrad "Buster" Brown
SC	Spartanburg	First Baptist Church North Spartanburg	Mike Hamlet
TN	Chattanooga	First Presbyterian Church	Tim Tinsley
TN	Chattanooga	North Shore Fellowship	Gary Purdy
TN	Elizabethton	Memorial Presbyterian Church	Dwight Basham

TN	Knoxville	Cornerstone Church of Knoxville	Bill Kittrell
TN	Knoxville	First Baptist Church Concord	Doug Sager
TN	Memphis	Independent Presbyterian Church	Richie Sessions
TN	Nashville	Christ Presbyterian Church	Wilson Benton
TX	Allen	Grace Evangelical Free Church	SP Joel Walters
TX	Austin	High Pointe Baptist Church	Juan Sanchez
TX	Cypress	Cypress Bible Church	Dave Gibson
TX	Houston	Bethel Church	Michael Boys
TX	Plano	Prestonwood Baptist Church	Jack Graham
TX	Wake Village	First Baptist Church	Scott Neathery
VA	Falls Church	The Falls Church	John Yates
VA	Leesburg	Potomac Hills Presbyterian Church	David V. Silvernail, Jr.
WA	Marysville	Damascus Road Church	Sam Ford
WA	Spokane	Grace Christian Fellowship	Bill Farley
WI	Bristol	CrossWay Community Church	Mike Bullmore
WI	Brookfield	Elmbrook Church	(Open at time of publication)